RESURRECTING NAGASAKI

T0385767

Studies of the Weatherhead East Asian Institute, Columbia University

The Studies of the Weatherhead East Asian Institute of Columbia University were inaugurated in 1962 to bring to a wider public the results of significant new research on modern and contemporary East Asia.

RESURRECTING NAGASAKI

Reconstruction and the Formation
of Atomic Narratives

Chad R. Diehl

CORNELL UNIVERSITY PRESS   ITHACA AND LONDON

Cornell University Press gratefully acknowledges receipt of a grant from the Center for the Humanities, Loyola University Maryland, which aided in the publication of this book.

First published 2018 by Cornell University Press

Library of Congress Cataloging-in-Publication Data

Name: Diehl, Chad, author.
Title: Resurrecting Nagasaki : reconstruction and the formation of atomic
    narratives / Chad R. Diehl.
Description: Ithaca : Cornell University Press, 2017. | Includes
    bibliographical references and index.
Identifiers: LCCN 2017023943 (print) | LCCN 2017025760 (ebook) | ISBN
    9781501709432 (pdf) | ISBN 9781501712074 (ret) | ISBN 9781501714962 |
    ISBN 9781501714962 (cloth)
Subjects: LCSH: Reconstruction (1939–1951)—Japan—Nagasaki-shi. |
    Nagasaki-shi (Japan)—History—Bombardment, 1945—Influence. | Atomic bomb
    Victims—Japan—Nagasaki-shi. | Collective memory—Japan—Nagasaki-shi. |
    City planning—Japan—Nagasaki-shi—History—20th century.
Classification: LCC DS897.N2957 (ebook) | LCC DS897.N2957 D54 2018 (print) |
    DDC 952/.244044—dc23
LC record available at https://lccn.loc.gov/2017023943

For my family

So we beat on, boats against the current, borne back ceaselessly into the past.
—F. Scott Fitzgerald, *The Great Gatsby*, 1925

I still cannot even comprehend what the devil is meant by the First International Cultural City.
—Naruse Kaoru, Nagasaki City Construction Office Chief, 1950

Contents

List of Illustrations

Preface

The research for this book began, in a way, in spring 2001 while I was studying abroad as a foreign exchange student at Kumamoto Gakuen University. Nagasaki is only a few hours away from Kumamoto by bus, and so, when my brother came to visit me that February, I thought it was important that we make the effort to visit. At the Atomic Bombing Museum, I encountered an exhibit that, in retrospect, changed my life. A display dedicated to Nagai Takashi and the Catholic community of Nagasaki caught my eye: I found out for the first time that the United States had dropped an atomic bomb on the most Christian city in all of Japan. On our way out of the museum I purchased one of Nagai's works, *Kono ko o nokoshite* (Leaving these children behind, 1948), from the bookstore in order to learn about the postatomic experience of the Urakami Catholic community. I had also hoped that reading the book would help me practice my Japanese.

Upon returning to Montana State University, I began reading Nagai's book. When I made it to a chapter entitled "Providence," I read Nagai's interpretation of the bombing in which he described it as a gift from God, declaring that the Catholics should offer gratitude to God for having chosen them as a sacrificial lamb to end the war. My first thought was that my Japanese reading ability was terrible: How could a person and a community possibly view such extreme devastation in such a light? I must have been misreading something, right? After reading it several more times and writing my senior thesis comparing Nagai to writers in Hiroshima, I began to realize that I had encountered one atomic narrative among many that were based on the regional and historical contexts of each city.

I wanted to continue exploring the perspective(s) of Nagasaki survivors, especially, and so I applied for and received a Fulbright Graduating Senior Fellowship to live and research in Nagasaki for one year after graduating from MSU in 2003. I studied under Takahashi Shinji at Nagasaki University, during which time I was fortunate enough to meet many survivors, including some who appear in the pages that follow. Taniguchi Sumiteru is one such survivor; another is Nagai Kayano, who was one of Nagai's two children whom he spoke of leaving behind in his book that first caught my eye in 2001. I also met former mayor Motoshima Hitoshi, who also appears in the present book, and the mayor at the time, Itō Iccho.

After one year in Nagasaki, I continued my research into the postatomic history of Nagasaki while in graduate school at Columbia University beginning in 2004. From 2007 to 2009, I made several research trips back to the city, spending weeks collecting materials in archives at the Nagasaki Prefectural Library, the Nagai Takashi Memorial Museum, and the Nagasaki Catholic Center in Urakami. Archives in Nagasaki contain an abundance of fascinating materials; in fact, in the process of writing this book I have managed to employ only a small percentage of the materials I collected. These research trips to the city also allowed me to become acquainted with other atomic-bombing survivors, such as the photographer Takahara Itaru, who makes an appearance in the book as well, along with many of his photographs. Among the survivors whom I knew well but who do not appear in this book is Yamaguchi Tsutomu. Yamaguchi was one of a small group of people who survived both of the atomic bombings. I met Yamaguchi first in 2006 after translating a documentary on the double-atomic-bombing survivors (*nijū hibakusha* in Japanese), but I was lucky enough to live with him in Nagasaki in summer 2009 in order to translate his tanka poetry into English. After he died in 2010, I self-published the English translations.

While many of the people I met in Nagasaki remain close to my heart, the survivors whom I met, both those still living and those now gone, remain dearest to me. They each were wonderful people—patient, kind, and accepting of me. I never conducted formal interviews with them because, for one, many published oral histories already exist, but, more important, I simply wanted to get to know each of them on a human level. Of course, our conversations included discussions of their experience of the atomic bombings, but they never demanded that I become some sort of mouthpiece for their peace activism. Even though the present book in some way reflects my time spent living and learning in Nagasaki, I have always envisioned the book as first and foremost a work of historical writing that seeks to answer a fundamental research question: What can the story of postatomic Nagasaki teach us about the relationship between destruction, reconstruction, and the politics of narrative formation, especially in contrast to and in dialogue with the case of Hiroshima? I hope that I have offered at least some semblance of an answer to this question in the pages that follow. Moreover, I understand that lenses of historical inquiry can sometimes be slow to shift, but I hope that at the very least the present book stimulates the academic conversation on the atomic experience of Nagasaki, both the city and its survivors.

Acknowledgments

This book would never have existed without the mentorship, assistance, and friendship of many people. Carol Gluck believed in the book from the beginning, even before I had typed a single word. She has always shown extraordinary grace and patience, and I am grateful for her mentorship, encouragement, and support throughout my professional career. I could not have asked for a better professional role model. I am also grateful to Kim Brandt, Marianne Hirsch, Marilyn Ivy, and Laura Neitzel for their guidance when the book was in its earliest form. Their suggestions helped me reimagine my research as a book. Others at Columbia, such as David Lurie and Gregory Pflugfelder, provided their guidance and mentorship in different capacities.

In Nagasaki, Nagai Tokusaburō, Takahashi Shinji, and Tasaki Noboru made tremendous contributions to my research. I would like to thank Nagai, especially, for allowing me access to abundant archives and the use of a photograph. Yamasaki Toshiko and her family always made me feel welcome in their home. I thank the many atomic-bombing survivors who have graciously shared their stories with me over the years, some of whom I included in the following pages, but there were too many that I could not. I thank Takahara Itaru for allowing me the use of many of his photographs. In Tokyo, Inazuka Hidetaka and Iwasaki Minoru were indispensable for completing my research. The members of the Kōdōgakusha judo dormitory, whom I considered like family, made my stay in Tokyo from 2007 to 2008 one of my most cherished memories to date. In New York, Nakamura Hideo was always a source of good advice and friendship. At Montana State University, Brett L. Walker, who first introduced me to Japanese history, has consistently supported my research, for which I am grateful. I thank Yuka Hara for introducing me to the Japanese language, encouraging me to study abroad, and remaining a close friend long after my first language class with her.

Many institutions have provided support. Portions of my research benefited from a Fulbright Graduating Senior Fellowship to Nagasaki University from 2003 to 2004. I am also indebted to the Japan Society for the Promotion of Science for a generous research grant to Tokyo from 2007 to 2008, as well as a writing grant from the Whiting Foundation from 2010 to 2011. I am grateful to the Terasaki Center for Japanese Studies at the University of California, Los Angeles, for a postdoctoral fellowship from 2011 to 2012, during which time I began reformulating the book. I also received assistance from Emmanuel College to present versions of two chapters at conferences in 2013 and 2014. During that time, EC student Patrick Carland also helped with some research at the Boston Public Library. A version of chapter one appeared in *Urban History* 41, no. 3 (August 2014): 497–516. Assistance from Loyola University Maryland has given me both the opportunity to present at conferences and the time to work on the manuscript, including in the form of a summer grant in 2015. The Center for the Humanities at LUM also provided a generous subvention to help bring the book to publication. I am indebted, further, to the intellectual support provided by my wonderful colleagues in the History Department.

I could not have completed the manuscript without the many librarians and archivists who helped me gain access to the materials included in this book. I would like to extend my sincerest gratitude to the staff at the Loyola–Notre Dame Library, especially Gail Breyer, Christy Dentler, Zach Gahs-Buccheri, Nick Triggs, and Pat Turkos. Kara Newcomer and Alisa Whitley of the U.S. Marine Corps History Division were helpful in locating photographs used in the book. A special thanks to Yukako Tatsumi at the University of Maryland Libraries for guiding me through the materials of the Gordon W. Prange Collection and for general encouragement and support along the way. Anne Hancock at Emmanuel College accompanied me to library workshops on Japanese Studies. When I was at UCLA, Toshie Marra provided support in various ways, including working with me on a small exhibit about Nagasaki. At Columbia University, Ken Harlin, Rich Jandovitz, Ria Koopmans-de Bruijn, and Sachie Noguchi made sure that my time spent in the C.V. Starr East Asian Library was always fruitful.

I am deeply grateful to Roger Haydon at Cornell University Press for believing in the book and giving it a home. He also showed extreme patience with me during the final stages of revisions. Meagan Dermody and Sara Ferguson at CUP were also crucial to preparing the book for publication. I would like to thank Kristen Bettcher and Patricia Cattani, both of Westchester Publishing Services, for their meticulous attention to detail and extensive work on the manuscript. I am indebted to Ross Yelsey of the Weatherhead East Asian Institute at Columbia University for his guidance through the publication process, as well as for his unwavering encouragement and faith in the book. I also thank the two anonymous readers whose comments and suggestions helped to greatly improve the manuscript.

Emotional support has come from many people in many places. My cohort while in graduate school at Columbia offered friendship that kept me sane. I am grateful to Adam Bronson, Reto Hofmann, D. Colin Jaundrill, S. E. Kile, Yumi Kim, Aleksandra Kobiljski, Peiting Li, Lee Pennington, John Phan, Mi-Ryong Shim, and Tim Yang. My band mates in Boston, Shawn Fitzpatrick, Nick Richards, and Todd Williams, reminded me that life is always better, and work is always easier, with music. Clare Mehta and Adam Silver, too, offered stability and friendship. Franziska Seraphim occasionally checked in on me to make sure I felt supported during my time in Boston, and she provided helpful feedback on an early version of chapter six of the book. In the Washington, D.C. area, Michele Mason and Jordan Sand both provided friendship and intellectual support at various stages. In Baltimore, I am indebted to Dr. Timothy Witham, primarily for putting me back together and renewing my life, but also for making it physically possible to finally finish the book.

My family in Montana always sends love and encouragement to me wherever I am. My mother and father, Gay and Joe Diehl, are a constant source of support and comfort, as are my siblings, Erin, Korie, and Matt; my nephew, Keegan; my sister-in-law, Makiko; and my brother-in-law, Pete. Anri Yasuda has been a steadfast source of inspiration and love since our days in New York. Without you I would be lost. Thank you for your compassion, good company, and sense of humor, not to mention your brilliance. Stanley, too, has kept me smiling every day.

I am indebted to everyone mentioned here and to many more not listed. Even so, the faults of the book are no one's but my own.

RESURRECTING
NAGASAKI

VALLEY OF VISIONS

When Nagasaki and Hiroshima set out to rebuild after the atomic bombings of August 1945, the cities took strikingly different paths. Hiroshima made commemoration of the bombing the focus of its urban identity, abandoning its past as a military city and quickly rising as the center of antinuclear activism and peace symbolism in Japan. Nagasaki, too, processed the atomic experience in reconstruction, but the distinctive history of the region and the particular actors who led the response produced diverse and conflicting narratives of the bombing that contested for space in the city's urban identity. The centuries-old history of Nagasaki as a center of trade and cultural exchange constituted the bedrock on which officials and citizens planned to rebuild as an "international cultural city," a vision which set the parameters of discussions surrounding the bombing's significance and place in the historical memory of the city. This book tells the story of how the diverse narratives of postatomic Nagasaki emerged out of the discordant visions and processes of reconstruction during the first two decades after the bombing. It also explores the ramifications of the particular ways the narratives unfolded in Nagasaki.

Many groups worked for the reconstruction of Nagasaki, but few shared exactly the same vision. Differing views of politics, religion, history, and memory informed the kinetic enterprise of reconstruction, and the groups who held these views constituted what must be called a social cartography of reconstruction. Mayors, council members, and other municipal officials developed a vision for reconstruction that recalled the Nagasaki of days of old, when the city had maintained economic ties to China and the Netherlands for more than three hundred years. From the seventeenth to the nineteenth century, when Japan was closed off from relations with Europe, Nagasaki remained the sole window to the West, both in trade and intellectual exchange. Because the bombing did not erase this historical legacy, officials called for the reconstruction of Nagasaki to revive and boast again of that history, an approach that became official in 1949 when the Nagasaki International Cultural City Construction Law passed unanimously in the National Diet in Tokyo. By comparison, the Hiroshima Peace Commemoration City Construction Law, which was passed by the same Diet, solidified Hiroshima's past, present, and future as an atomic-bombed city. Nagasaki officials created their own memorials, museums, and committees to commemorate the tragedy, too, but the removal of symbolic physical remains of the bombing against vocal opposition of survivors, other residents, and activist groups demonstrated their unwillingness to compromise their central vision of building an international cultural city. The story of the atomic bombing appeared as part of the city's long history, not as its primary characteristic. Unlike Hiroshima, addressing the human destruction and suffering caused by the bomb was never a top priority for politicians in Nagasaki.

Other groups supported the official narrative and vision for reconstruction, linking the destruction to peace and a mission to rebuild the city in light of its past. In the eyes of the Allied occupation forces, the Catholic community, and even Emperor Hirohito, the bomb brought the end of the war, or as a common saying put it, the bomb was a "harbinger of peace." As the logic went, Nagasaki was the second and the last atomic bombing in the war, and so city officials used the saying "Peace starts from Nagasaki" to rally city residents to embrace their vision. In doing so, officials set the city's catastrophe in the broader context of the end of the war, surrender, and the new postwar beginning. In the early years of reconstruction, city politicians, leaders of the Allied occupation in Nagasaki, and the emperor all encouraged Nagasaki residents to "turn tragedy into happiness" by rebuilding their international cultural city.[1]

The Catholic community of Urakami figured largely in discussions of international culture. Nagasaki has historically been home to the largest population of Catholics in Japan, the majority of whom have resided in the northern valley district of Urakami. The Urakami valley was ground zero of the bombing, requiring the most physical reconstruction, and so the Catholic presence shaped narratives of the bombing and visions of reconstruction in significant ways. For their part, the Urakami Catholics viewed the significance of the bombing through a religious lens, interpreting it as the martyrdom of their community for a greater good. In November 1945, the leader of the Catholic parishioners, Nagai Takashi, declared the tragedy an act of Providence, claiming that God chose the land of Urakami—home of generations of Catholics—as a sacrificial lamb on his altar to expiate the sins of humankind for the sake of ending the war. For Nagai, the bomb became a so-called harbinger of peace with the martyrdom of the Catholics, which he considered the only worthy sacrifice to bring the war to a close. For reasons discussed later, Nagai emerged as the public voice of Nagasaki's atomic experience and a key figure in the city's physical, social, and spiritual reconstruction. His influence, especially on discourse surrounding the bombing, linked the tragedy to the Urakami region and Christianity in popular memory for decades.

The Urakami Catholics supported discussions of restoring the international nature of the city, not only for the purposes of promoting trade, culture, and tourism but also because it suited their identity as part of an international community of Catholics. The presence of American occupation forces, many of whom were Christian, helped to empower the Catholics. For Nagasaki Catholics, reconstruction became a vision of the complete renewal of the Urakami Valley, even if that meant demolishing the ruins of their cathedral, which by the late 1940s had become the symbol of Nagasaki's destruction, often compared to the ruin of Hiroshima's Atomic Dome. Catholics advocated removal of all atomic-bombing relics in Urakami that reminded them of the tragedy and threatened their total recovery. They promoted remembrance of the bomb but also encouraged moving past it, an approach shared by city officials intent on promoting the international culture of the city.

For the atomic-bombing survivors who were neither Catholic nor members of the city council, the bomb only meant personal trauma and human loss, and so they wanted the city to emphasize the atomic-bombing experience in the reconstruction process, just as Hiroshima City was doing. In their eyes the bomb brought not peace, but destruction, the death of loved ones, and physical and mental scars, as well as lifelong debilitating illness caused by exposure to radiation. In the first decade after the bomb, however, most of the survivors had almost no political voice, which meant no influence in the plans for reconstruction and no respite from their physical and psychological pain. From the late 1950s, their activism began meeting with some success in asserting demands for municipal and national assistance for medical treatment and living costs. And after political infighting fractured the unity of the antinuclear peace movement in the early 1960s, their suffering became a central and symbolic component of social, peace, and memory activism.

In both Nagasaki and Hiroshima, many of the key players in reconstruction were survivors of the bombing. The conventional term used to refer to an atomic-bombing survivor, hibakusha, became widely used only in the late 1950s, and it was used largely as a legal definition for the purposes of allocating national medical relief to sufferers. The word has taken on other meanings, also referring to those who died as a result of the bombings, and, when written with a different character for *baku*, it can mean a person generally exposed to a flash of radiation. I use the term here primarily to refer to the groups of survivors who worked as peace and memory activists, regardless of legal status, as well as the voiceless survivors for whom they spoke. My usage of the word hibakusha to refer to the survivor-activist groups of the late 1940s and early 1950s is somewhat anachronistic, but it provides a useful way to discuss these survivors in contrast with other groups. Carol Gluck's term "memory activists" provides a useful way to describe the hibakusha groups active in postwar Nagasaki because they, like memory activists elsewhere, were "dedicated to preserving the memory of their own particular experience and seeking a place for that experience within the larger field of public memory."[2] Many of the foundational members of the postwar Catholic community and the municipal leaders of the immediate postwar years were also hibakusha in the literal and legal senses of the word, but commemoration of the bombing never emerged as a central theme in their visions of reconstruction. The hibakusha memory activists, on the other hand, gave priority to the commemoration of the bombing and sought to write the human experience into the official narrative. To sum up, the main historical actors in my analysis are the city officials and politicians, the American occupation personnel, the Catholic community, and the hibakusha, as defined here.

If visions of reconstruction took many forms, they all shared the same vocabulary. Many words emerged for "reconstruction." The conventional word *saiken* was used in postwar discourse, but not nearly as often as the word *fukkō*, meaning revival. *Saiken*, literally reconstruction, usually referred to physical rebuilding, whereas *fukkō* implied a general revival of physical, social, and psychological well-being. Residents all agreed on the first stage of *fukkō* as rebuilding the destroyed physical landscape of Nagasaki, but after that the definition fragmented. At times, *fukkō* meant the building of houses and repair of roads; at other times, it meant the revival of the spirit of the citizens, which in large part relied on the success of physical construction. At times, *fukkō* meant restoring international trade, removing the ruins of the cathedral to restore Urakami and the Catholic community, overcoming psychological trauma, and winning national compensation and medical relief for survivors. Other words, such as *fukkatsu* (rebirth), *kaifuku* (recovery), and even *fukko*, which more directly implied the restoration of the past, appeared in the vernacular of reconstruction.

Still other words pointed to the tension among competing narratives. The term *gisei* (sacrifice) served the purposes of all parties to refer to those who died in the war and the atomic bombings. The word also informed political and religious rhetoric. Politicians directed the citizenry regarding what they must do to overcome the hardships of the postwar years and tirelessly make sacrifices to revive the nation. The hibakusha used the word primarily about those who died in the bombing, but also in reference to their own individual trauma and collective plight. Catholics, of course, used the word with the connotation that identified the destruction of their community with the death of Christ. The word *inoru* (pray) was ubiquitous in postwar Japan, often in the phrase "pray for peace," but it had an additional connotation in Nagasaki because of the city's historical relationship with Christianity. In the late 1940s and the 1950s, both Nagasaki and Hiroshima prayed for peace and reconstruction, as even a cursory glance at local newspapers reveals. *Inoru* gradually came to imply a passivity that was linked to Nagasaki's Catholic history, a popular view best captured in the mid-1950s saying "Hiroshima Rages, Nagasaki Prays" (*Ikari no Hiroshima, Inori no Nagasaki*).[3] The phrase suggested that Nagasaki's peace activism lagged behind that of Hiroshima, in that Nagasaki continued to passively pray about its atomic experience rather than exerting active efforts to commemorate it and work for world peace. In short, some thought that Nagasaki peace activism had not evolved with the times, remaining stuck in the late 1940s when incantations of "pray for peace" were a common tactic of the emerging peace movement.

From the 1940s to the 1980s, the word "memory" did not appear much in Nagasaki or at least it was not identified as public memory (*kioku*), a term that only became prominent in the 1990s. Instead, a number of memories developed in and about Nagasaki, which were informed and shaped by the events discussed here. When those who envisioned the revival of Nagasaki related their memory and interpretation of the bombing to their view of reconstruction, they fashioned narratives of the atomic experience that have left clear traces even today. At least three prominent narratives emerged. First, for municipal officials, city history provided the primary source for the official narrative because it was something to be revived and evoked, not created or affected by the atomic bomb. The bomb was part of the identity of the city, but not its central motif. Second, Catholics took a complex and at times contradictory approach to discussing the bomb. The martyrdom, as they saw it, continued the history of Christian martyrdom in Nagasaki, which had preceded the bombing by hundreds of years. Although they thought that the tragedy should not be forgotten, the physical traces that connected them to "a tragic past," as the Nagasaki bishop once put it in the 1950s, also prevented the full recovery of Urakami.[4] This view encouraged, as it were, both remembering and forgetting in a single breath.

Third, the hibakusha saw the story of the bombing and especially the human tragedy of it, however painful, as something to be protected from threats coming from many directions. The national government, by not accepting responsibility for the livelihood of survivors, did not acknowledge their experience, which for the hibakusha was tantamount to neglecting the memory of their trauma. The municipal government removed symbolic relics of the bombs, supplanting them with what the hibakusha considered *kyozō* (empty symbols) that failed to convey the reality of the bombing and cost vast amounts of money, while survivors suffered without relief. The Urakami Catholics, especially Nagai Takashi, presented an interpretation of the bomb that took root during the occupation and dominated the discourse of the bomb for decades, overshadowing the efforts of Nagasaki hibakusha in the peace movement and inhibiting the recognition of their experience. Perhaps the greatest threat to Nagasaki hibakusha memory, though, came from Hiroshima, whose experience has dominated popular memory and scholarship, and where officials at times sought to exclude Nagasaki from their narrative of atomic destruction. Hiroshima has become the "metonymy of all 'Hiroshimas,' past and future," as John Treat puts it.[5] Hiroshima has also become a standard of measurement for any nuclear or radioactive event, but especially for the history of the atomic bombings of 1945. Of course, Nagasaki officials, city planners, and the hibakusha never intended to forget the bombing. Indeed, they considered it an important responsibility to convey their experience to the world to ensure that such a catastrophe never happened again. But still, while the plea of "No More Hiroshimas!" can still be heard today, the "No More Nagasakis!" of the 1940s and 1950s have been muffled by the decades of Hiroshima dominance.

It is tempting to attribute Hiroshima's dominance to its bombing having occurred first. Perhaps it is true to say that Hiroshima is historically significant as the site of the first atomic bomb ever used in war, but that alone does not explain why that city's experience has overshadowed Nagasaki's. By the same logic, Nagasaki would be the dominant city in popular memory had it been bombed first. Such an approach to understanding history discounts the postwar trajectory of the two cities, which did not depend on the chronological order of the bombings. This is not to say that Hiroshima's precedence did not factor into that city's identity as an atomic-bombed city and leader of the antinuclear peace movement; indeed, that fact helped municipal officials bolster their reconstruction plans as a "peace commemoration city" because, as they argued in front of the National Diet in 1949, as the first city to be destroyed by an atomic bomb they had a responsibility to become a "peace city." Hiroshima as a world event—the site of the first atomic weapon used in war and the dawn of the nuclear age—is no doubt significant. And yet that significance does not alone explain Nagasaki's place in popular memory. The dominance of Hiroshima as *the* representative atomic-bombed city was never predetermined, but instead grew out of the politics of reconstruction and narrative formation. Nagasaki scholar Takahashi Shinji agrees that Nagasaki's experience has been neglected in popular history and memory, but he blames the narrow-mindedness of "the world" for being unable to see past "Euro-shima" simply because it was the first atomic bombing.[6] Takahashi rightly points out that people often cannot see past the fact that Hiroshima was the first bombing, but the answer to how Hiroshima has come to dominate popular and scholarly discussions of the bombings can only be found in the history of the reconstruction of the cities.

The circumstances and events of the first two postwar decades discussed in this book laid a foundation that has led scholars, politicians, activist groups, and popular media to favor Hiroshima for more than seven decades. Nagasaki's municipal vision of reconstruction, which was intent on restoring the international history of the city, diluted the focus on the bomb for decades. This approach to reconstruction immediately set the city apart from Hiroshima, which made the bomb the center of its postwar identity. The prominence of Nagai Takashi and discussions of the Urakami region in representations of Nagasaki's atomic experience further drew attention away from the fact that most hibakusha, like their Hiroshima counterparts, raged against the inhumanity of the bomb and the postwar threat of nuclear weapons. Numbers also played a role. Estimates of the population in the two cities on the day of the bombing have fluctuated, but it is generally agreed that there were around 350,000 people in Hiroshima and 270,000 in Nagasaki. The number of affected persons rose in the following weeks as tens of thousands of people entered the highly radioactive areas to help in the relief efforts. Nagasaki is a smaller city surrounded by mountains, which buffered the destruction of the bomb when it exploded in the northern valley, preventing much of the destructive power from reaching the central part of the city. As a result, the human damage was greater in Hiroshima, with about 120,000 dead by the end of 1945, and about 74,000 in Nagasaki. In 1950, a national census based on data from the U.S.-led Atomic Bomb Casualty Commission (ABCC) counted 158,597 hibakusha in Hiroshima and 124,901 in Nagasaki. In the same year, the death toll had risen to 200,000 and 140,000, respectively.[7] The larger population of hibakusha in Hiroshima depicted their collective experience as a complement to the image of a peace commemoration city, an atomic-bombed city with a mission of peace activism. In other words, the atomic narrative of the hibakusha in Hiroshima fit perfectly into the official narrative of the city.

The Nagasaki hibakusha's lag behind Hiroshima, as commentators often phrased it from the 1940s through the 1970s (and into the present), can be attributed in large part to the challenges they fought to overcome from the early postwar years. They found themselves in constant competition with Hiroshima for a place in popular media as well as in scholarship on the bombs. The hibakusha of Hiroshima had a larger presence than their Nagasaki counterparts in the peace movement and produced more atomic-bomb literature, resulting in a larger collective voice shaping popular discourse on the bombings. In order to strengthen their own collective voice, though perhaps too late, Nagasaki survivors began a literary movement in the mid-1950s, which increased in effort and production from the late 1960s. In light of Nagasaki's "delayed" peace activism in comparison to Hiroshima's, some critics have referred to Nagasaki as an "inferior atomic-bombed city" (*rettō hibaku toshi*).[8] In media portrayals of the bombing, Nagasaki remained an international cultural city first and only then an atomic-bombed city. National publications removed Nagasaki from discussions of the bombings from as early as the late 1940s. The journal *Shūkan asahi* published a special issue on August 7, 1949, entitled "Nō moa Hiroshimazu" (No More Hiroshimas), which highlighted the city's "prayers for peace," before praying for peace became associated with passivity. Written primarily by editorial staff in Tokyo (one article was by a contributor in Hiroshima), the publication detailed the aftermath of the bombing and the works of hibakusha authors such as Hara Tamiki and Ōda Yōko. It also included "reflections on the 'ethics' of the atomic bomb" and placed Hiroshima in the context of the world peace movement.[9] Nagasaki was mentioned only once in passing, and a separate issue for the city was never published.

Many groups outside of Nagasaki presented challenges to the Nagasaki hibakusha's place in popular discussions of the bombings. Activists in Hiroshima, for their part, were sometimes condescending to activists in Nagasaki, pointing out how they could not match the quality of both Hiroshima's activism and its urban reconstruction. In May 1950, the Hiroshima-shi seinen rengō kai (Hiroshima City Youth Association) visited Nagasaki for a conference with youth groups that had visited Hiroshima for a similar event in 1949. After the conference, which spanned several days, Iwada Yukio, president of the Hiroshima youth group, noted how his "brothers and sisters" of the Nagasaki groups had improved over the past year and exhibited the passion of youth, but they still needed work. Before he returned to Hiroshima, Iwada gave three points of advice as "words of parting," claiming they needed to establish themselves as a politically savvy group that demonstrated to people outside of Nagasaki "what it was they were doing." Having a clear and meaningful purpose, Iwada argued, constituted "the essence of us youth groups."[10] More than the condition of the youth groups in Nagasaki, Iwada thought that the reconstruction of Nagasaki in general "lagged a step" behind that of Hiroshima. Speaking as the "representative of Hiroshima," he was "surprised at the filthy streets and that there were houses built in the middle of traffic routes." He said that if Nagasaki were ever to become a so-called international cultural city, then it needed to reevaluate its city construction plans to address such destitute conditions.[11] In his appraisal of Nagasaki conditions, Iwada, as well as other such commentators, bolstered the claim of the superiority of Hiroshima as an atomic-bombed city.

Meanwhile, groups within and outside of Nagasaki viewed the bombing as a tragedy that befell the Urakami Catholics, creating a Christian image of ground zero that persisted for decades. The Catholics and even some non-Christian residents argued that the bombing was primarily a regional catastrophe centered in the Urakami Valley and only secondly a Nagasaki citywide one. More specifically, some claimed that the "atomic bomb fell on Urakami, not Nagasaki."[12] Some residents in southern Nagasaki City thought that the annual commemoration in August was "only for the people in Urakami. We do not go," as one person explained to writer Hotta Yoshie.[13] Other southern residents claimed that the bombing was divine punishment for the non-Shinto residents of Urakami.[14] Furthermore, the demolished Urakami Cathedral served as the popular symbol of the bombing from 1945 until 1958, when the cathedral ruins were replaced with a brand new church. Photographs of the cathedral ruins often accompanied articles about the bombing in local and national media, linking the atomic catastrophe to Urakami and Christianity when narratives about the bombings were taking shape. The first months of newspaper coverage of the bombing played a major role in localizing the tragedy of the bombing to Urakami. On September 15, 1945, two reporters for the *Yomiuri hōchi shinbun* called for the preservation of the ruins of the cathedral as a symbol of the catastrophe. They speculated that the Catholic "sacrifice" was perhaps 30 percent of the total number of casualties.[15] Another mid-September 1945 article in the *Nagasaki shinbun* argued that while the "dark silence of the pain of war devastation and the sadness of defeat continues," residents should find comfort in the fact that "Nagasaki escaped total destruction" because the bomb had exploded in the northern Urakami district; the article neglected to mention that Urakami lay smoldering in a flattened landscape of rubble and ash.[16] Local and national media depictions of the Nagasaki bombing continued to localize it as an Urakami tragedy for decades.

Prefectural and municipal officials, as well as the American occupiers, linked the bombing to the city's historic relationship to Christianity. Prefectural Governor Sugiyama Sōjirō announced in August 1947 that the "land of Nagasaki is a land of Christian martyrdom," and because of that, the reconstruction of the city as a "cultural city" was "all the more significant."[17] Later, in 1949, Mayor Ōhashi Hiroshi introduced a publication of twenty-one testimonial accounts of the bomb by framing the destruction in terms of "peace" and a "revelation of heaven."[18] Other municipal officials promoted the singularity of the Urakami district, perhaps most notably Motoshima Hitoshi, who was mayor of Nagasaki from 1979 to 1995, as well as an avid scholar, peace activist, and fervent Catholic. Motoshima related the atomic destruction to other "destructions" (*kuzure*) of the Urakami Catholic community in the form of religious persecution that occurred in the region's history.[19]

The perception of Nagasaki lagging behind Hiroshima in peace activism in the mid-1950s, vocalized in popular phrases such as "Hiroshima Rages, Nagasaki

FIGURE 0.1.   Family gathered where their home once stood in the Urakami Valley. Notice the ruins of the Urakami Cathedral in the background to the right. Photo taken by Ed Rogers, a member of the U.S. Marine Corps stationed in Nagasaki during the first year of occupation. His original caption reads: "NAGA-SAKI Oct. 1945–Mar. 1946: A Family survived the A-Bomb blast but their house was destroyed. On the left, in a bowl, the bones of their relatives which they found in their destroyed house."

Source: Ed Rogers, "Nagasaki, 1945–46 (10th Marines)," box 2, A Bomb Area folder, print no. 64, Reference Branch, U.S. Marine Corps History Division, Quantico, VA. Used with permission from the Edward A. Rogers Trust.

Prays," emerged in part because of the perceived Catholic image of the city's atomic experience. This phrase, especially, illuminates the popular understanding of Nagasaki's bombing as an Urakami tragedy, implying that the appropriate response from survivors of such a trauma (i.e., the Catholics) would be to pray, not to rage. Implied in such a view, also, was a critique of the historical uniqueness or non-Japanese-ness of Nagasaki, which for centuries had a popular image of an international melting pot. The saying "Nagasaki Prays" was a manifestation of the narrative of the bombing as a Catholic tragedy that invited criticism of the city's peace activism, especially after 1954 when simply praying no longer sufficed as appropriate peace activism. Seen another way, the phrase also highlights the disparate urban identities of Hiroshima and Nagasaki, which, despite both having been destroyed by an atomic bomb, had taken starkly different paths in their reconstruction: Hiroshima as a raging activist for peace, and Nagasaki as a site of international culture, of which Christianity was a part.

. . .

I use "resurrecting" in the title to signify the subject and purpose of the book in three ways. First, "resurrecting" refers to the process of reconstruction, both the project of reviving a physical landscape and the emergence of social and cultural meanings of an event that stem from the involvement of disparate groups. Rarely does a single group determine the reconstruction of a city, and many groups demonstrated varying degrees of influence throughout the process of Nagasaki's recovery, thus shaping discussions of its bombing. Karl D. Qualls describes reconstruction as an "urban identification project," one that grows out of a conversation among "competing visions for restoration."[20] Many visions for restoration emerged in Nagasaki, but there was little competition, as municipal officials controlled the conversation, even as the presence of the other visions and interest groups helped shape the landscape. The reconstruction process shaped both the urban identity of the city and the atomic narratives on regional, national, and international levels. Second, "resurrecting" points to one of the defining characteristics of Nagasaki's postatomic experience: the historical presence of Christians in the city, which in part helped shape the official local and national narratives of the bombing. The Catholics had a strong voice during the first decade and a half after the atomic bombing, although the effect of their voice on reconstruction depended on how the Christian appearance fit into municipal plans.

Third, this book seeks to "resurrect" Nagasaki in the scholarly literature on the aftermath of the atomic bombings. In comparison to Hiroshima, which has been so much studied, the story of Nagasaki provides a contrasting opportunity to explore the relationship between mass destruction, reconstruction, and narrative formation. And yet there is not a single scholarly monograph on Nagasaki in English.[21] Canonical works on the bombs in a variety of fields look overwhelmingly—and sometimes exclusively—at Hiroshima.[22] Popular writers and artists, too, have shown a preference for Hiroshima when seeking to understand the atomic bombings and their aftermath.[23] But, in doing so, these intellectuals and artists have become, unintentionally to be sure, activists working to convey Hiroshima's official narrative while limiting the presence of Nagasaki in popular memory. The focus on Hiroshima in scholarship in particular has been deleterious to our understanding of the atomic bombings from an analytical and historical perspective because it has siphoned away attention from an equally important case study of atomic destruction and aftermath. The focus on Hiroshima deemphasizes the fact that the United States dropped atomic bombs on two cities and only three days apart; it reduces two significant events and their aftermaths to a single historical event, Hiroshima; and it perpetuates a false assumption that the only instructive case in regards to atomic experience is Hiroshima's or, worse, that it is the only one that matters. The present book contributes to our understanding of the historiography on the bombings by revealing how postatomic reconstruction and the formation of atomic narratives over subsequent decades have shaped that historiography, just as historical writing everywhere is shaped by the time and contexts in which it is produced.

To understand the atomic bombings, we must also look at Nagasaki. The story of that city's reconstruction shows the relationship between destruction, politics, religion, and memory that so often exists in societies recovering from traumatic events. In this sense, the case of Nagasaki is not unique. But the various groups who resurrected Nagasaki worked from a historical context and generated atomic narratives that were indeed unique to Nagasaki. This book sets out to see what happens when we shift the focus to Nagasaki, because it is surely time to write Nagasaki into the history of the atomic bombings and their aftermath.

ENVISIONING NAGASAKI

The Rise of the Municipal Vision of Reconstruction

On May 3, 1949, representatives from Nagasaki and Hiroshima met in Tokyo to discuss the title of Nagasaki's reconstruction law. Hiroshima had already submitted a proposal to the National Diet to reconstruct as a "peace commemoration city" (heiwa kinen toshi), and Nagasaki officials, too, sought a reconstruction law that recognized the "special nature" of their city's destruction. The main problem for Hiroshima officials was that Nagasaki wanted to include the word "peace" in their law's title. The meeting "saw the confrontation of fiery opinions" from both sides, but the "attitude of Hiroshima," as Nagasaki representative Tsubouchi Hachirō saw it, was already set. Hiroshima officials claimed a monopoly on the word "peace," asserting that there could be only one "peace city." They argued, as Tsubouchi explained in an op-ed in the *Nagasaki minyū* on May 11, that the existence of two peace cities in Japan would "undoubtedly blur the focal point" and dilute the essence of a "peace city" altogether. Whether the concern over a blurred "focal point" refers to "peace" or "Hiroshima" was not clear. In fact, Hiroshima officials went as far as requesting the Diet refuse Nagasaki's proposal for a special reconstruction law entirely. In the end, Hiroshima's unwillingness to share the designation of a "peace city" determined the fate of the two cities. Nagasaki's law passed, but the city was now destined to become the "international cultural city" (kokusai bunka toshi). As Tsubouchi titled his op-ed piece in the *Nagasaki minyū*, Nagasaki had lost to Hiroshima.[1]

The competition between Nagasaki and Hiroshima grew out of the postwar need for national reconstruction funds. In the early months after the war, Nagasaki and Hiroshima were among all the other cities razed by Allied bombs. Little was known about the two cities except that they were destroyed by a new type of bomb that was atomic, the significance of which only gradually came to be understood. In all of the bombed-out cities, the initial reaction was to rebuild what had been destroyed, but resources were scarce. The national government developed a plan in November 1945 to aid in the reconstruction of 115 war-torn cities, including Nagasaki and Hiroshima.[2] Before the 1949 special reconstruction laws for the two cities, among forty-one cities slated to receive national reconstruction funds, Hiroshima placed sixth on the list, but Nagasaki trailed far behind at thirty-first. As the dust began to settle and the significance of the atomic bombings gradually gained recognition, city officials from Nagasaki and Hiroshima thought that the special nature of their destruction entitled them to national funds. They began appealing to Tokyo from 1946 but found themselves in competition with one another for national funds, culminating in the 1949 reconstruction law debates. The laws solidified Hiroshima's place as an atomic-bombed city over Nagasaki, but it also placed both cities at the top of the list for national funds.[3]

Nagasaki's struggle in Tokyo for recognition of its atomic experience in the face of a powerful Hiroshima lobby illustrates one of the first moments when Hiroshima memory activists, in this case municipal representatives, sought to establish an atomic narrative that placed their city at the center. But it also reflected the disparate paths of reconstruction taken by the two cities. Nagasaki officials had been developing a reconstruction plan based on the goal of reviving and cultivating an urban identity in keeping with its historic past as an international city. As a former military city, Hiroshima had no such usable past, and so officials there, led by Mayor Hamai Shinzō, the "atomic-bombing mayor," drew on their immediate, tragic past to cultivate an urban identity that gave special significance to the postwar catchword of "peace." That is, they thought that through an emphasis on their identity as the world's first atomic-bombed city, they could make Hiroshima a symbol to represent the importance of peace; in that scenario, however, there could be only one symbol. Nagasaki did not have a place in Hiroshima's narrative. By mid-1949, when officials from the two cities met to discuss issues related to commemoration of the bombings, representatives from Hiroshima thought they had a claim to "peace" as their privilege because they had dedicated reconstruction efforts to commemorating the atomic bombing, while Nagasaki had not.

The path of reconstruction, in both cities, was not predetermined but rather grew out of the many visions for reconstruction that emerged during the first several years after the bombing. A combination of economists and other scholars, the American occupiers, and Christians envisioned the revival of Nagasaki in similar ways to municipal officials, creating what I call the municipal vision of reconstruction. The vision gained the most traction early on and persisted above the rest. It sought to link the city's international past to its atomic present instead of defining Nagasaki's place in history solely in terms of the bombing. Even before the Americans arrived, city officials had hoped to restore the "old Nagasaki" (*mukashi no Nagasaki*) that had existed before the bombing. For a city that was once known as the "Kyoto of Kyushu" and even the "Naples of Japan," it was natural to wish to rebuild the city in those terms rather than associate it with an atomic wasteland.[4] Unlike in Hiroshima, it made little sense to officials in Nagasaki to draw on the immediate past—war and atomic destruction—for a model to define the city's urban identity going forward when the distant past shone brightly in their eyes. The American occupiers, too, saw a revival of Nagasaki's past as a "gateway to the Orient" as the key to building a bright future.[5] As a result, from the first years of restoration planning, the memory of the atomic bombing figured relatively little in the discourse of reconstruction. To realize their vision, officials emphasized in media representations the historic characteristics of the city, not least of which was the history of Christianity, and they focused on rebuilding, refurbishing, and maintaining historic sites. Discussions of the bombing that centered on the Catholic region of Urakami served a dual purpose for officials who sought to boast of the Christian history while locating the bombing in the northern part of the city, far removed from central Nagasaki, thus distancing the dark, recent memory from the bright past.

The Destruction

The atomic bomb exploded over Nagasaki at 11:02 a.m. on August 9, 1945. The blast leveled all buildings made of lighter materials like wood and left few others standing. Of the approximately fifty-one thousand buildings in Nagasaki before the bombing, 36.1 percent were completely destroyed or damaged. By comparison, the number in Hiroshima was 91.9 percent, even though the plutonium bomb in Nagasaki had more destructive power. Because the bomb exploded in the narrow Urakami valley, much of the power of the plutonium bomb, including the blast and heat rays, was buffered by the surrounding mountains.[6] Mount Konpira protected most of the central part of the city in the south and southeast—which was the intended target—from the worst part of the explosion, heat, and radiation blast. The physical destruction extended south about 4 kilometers, but broken windows were reported as far away as 19 kilometers. Wholesale destruction by the bomb reached up to 2.5 kilometers from the hypocenter, 0.5 kilometer farther than the reach of the Hiroshima bomb. Shortly after the blast in Nagasaki, various locations throughout the city spontaneously combusted, ignited by the intense heat rays, and conflagrations quickly spread across the landscape, raging through the streets and into the buildings still standing. At around noon, fires ignited in areas several kilometers from ground zero and spread over what remained of the city.[7] At 2.4 kilometers away, Nagasaki train station was rocked by the initial blast and subsequently burned in the fires. Many government buildings within 4 kilometers of the blast in the southern part of the city, while ravaged, remained structurally intact. The solid stone structures of City Hall and the Prefecture Office stood standing, but fires destroyed their interiors. The conflagration flattened all the buildings surrounding the Prefecture Office, but the fires stopped short of the southernmost part of the city.[8] The Urakami valley was virtually erased, save for the skeletons of larger buildings such as the Nagasaki Medical University Hospital, which stood 750 meters from the hypocenter, and the reinforced steel frames of some of the Mitsubishi factories. The damage inflicted on human bodies varied depending on their location and proximity to the blast as well as their amount of exposure to the radiation, including in the weeks following. In general, immediate injuries have been categorized as thermal, blast, and radiation injuries. Thermal injuries resulted in keloid scarring on one's body, and radiation-related injuries often plagued a survivor throughout their life by producing illnesses such as various types of cancers.[9]

The greatest aftereffect of the atomic bomb, indeed, that which distinguished it from conventional bombs used during the war, was radiation. Although Mount Konpira prevented the blast from reaching parts of the city, it could not save the city from radioactive fallout and residual radiation. People who seemed unharmed after the blast or who entered the blast radius after the bombing became sick with radiation poisoning and died in days, weeks, months, or years after the bomb. On August 23, the *Mainichi shinbun* printed the theory that the bombed areas of Nagasaki and Hiroshima would remain biologically sterile for at least seventy years. The *Asahi shinbun* and the *Yomiuri hōchi shinbun* ran the same story the next day.[10] The Manhattan Project scientists knew of the radioactive element of the bomb, and Japanese scientists suspected it. But no one knew exactly what would happen from radiation; everything was speculation. Even some American Marines stationed in Nagasaki did not understand why their hair was falling out or why they had bloody diarrhea. For weeks and months, tens of thousands of people, including U.S. military personnel, moved around the irradiated part of Nagasaki, mostly unaware of the danger.

The radiation in Nagasaki, which was much greater than in Hiroshima, continued to affect residents for months and years after the bombing. Residue from the bomb, sometimes called "ashes of death" in Japan, and which included radioisotopes, became a component of the fallout and harmed anyone exposed to it. The black rain that fell from the mushroom cloud in Nagasaki about twenty minutes after the explosion contained massive amounts of radioactive matter, which rained over the aid workers, local survivors, and other "early entrants" into the city who were searching for family members or who were engaged in such tasks as corpse disposal. Scientists have measured the maximum value of overall exposure dose from fallout, strongest at around 15 centimeters above ground, to range from 4 to 40 rads (radiation absorbed dose) in Hiroshima and from 48 to 149 rads in the Nishiyama District of Nagasaki. In early October 1945, the Japan–United States Joint Commission measured the gamma-ray dose at one meter above ground about 3 kilometers to the west of ground zero in Hiroshima (where black rain had carried much of the fallout) to be 0.045 milliroentgen per hour, and in Nishiyama, Nagasaki, the number was 1 milliroentgen per hour, or more than twenty-two times the dose in Hiroshima.[11] The black rain had transported radioactive fallout over Mount Konpira to the Nishiyama reservoir east of the hypocenter, which was one of four main water supplies of the city even after the bombing. Additionally, unfissioned plutonium-239, which has a half-life of twenty-four thousand years and is highly radioactive, was detected in Nishiyama in 1969, and has been persistent in the soil in the form of plutonium oxide.[12] In the early 1980s, the soil surrounding the reservoir was again shown to be "highly contaminated with the plutonium due to Nagasaki Atomic Bomb."[13] The radioactive fallout in this way created countless "secondary A-bomb victims," including American military personnel during the occupation.[14]

The population of Nagasaki in 1945 (prebombing) was around 270,000, but the exact number of people in the city at the time of the bombing is unknown. Some residents had moved, evacuated, or been mobilized to work in industrial factories, and military troop movements around the city were not recorded.[15] Tens of thousands of people died in a matter of seconds, others more slowly. By the end of 1945, approximately seventy-four thousand people had died in the explosion and fires, or from the immediate release of gamma radiation and the radioactive fallout, another seventy-five thousand were injured. An estimated sixty to eighty Allied prisoners of war (POWs), including American soldiers, died in the bombing, and around two hundred others were injured. Since 1943, Allied POWs had been sent to Fukuoka POW Camp No. 14—a prison in Nagasaki 1.65 kilometers away from the hypocenter, which was completely destroyed. Various factors, such as radiation, made it difficult for scientists to calculate precise numbers of atomic-bombing dead and wounded in both Nagasaki and Hiroshima, which led to varying estimates.[16]

After the bombing, Nagasaki residents immediately set out on the long road to physical reconstruction.[17] As survivors emerged from the rubble, clearing debris and corpses took months, and for a long time residents lived in destitution in trenches and improvised huts. Air-raid trenches provided a place to sleep and after most of the fires had faded days later, residents began constructing makeshift

FIGURE 1.1. Urakami Valley, looking south, October 1945. Notice the train traveling south, as well as the people traveling on the road. Ground zero in the photograph is just above the center and slightly to the left. Photograph taken by F. Clay Nixon, a member of the USMC occupation of Nagasaki.

Source: F. Clay Nixon Collection, COLL/888, Archives Branch, U.S. Marine Corps History Division, Quantico, VA.

homes in the trenches out of surrounding debris, such as burned wood and broken tiles. Police forces began removing corpses a few days after the bomb, but until then the trenches were filled with the "corpses of people who had escaped to the air-raid shelters." A survivor who lived in a trench for a week said years later how "even now I cannot forget the putrid smell of the corpses in the trenches."[18] The trench-huts (dugout houses, or *gōsha*) lasted for about a month.

Over the course of the first few years after the bombing, the residents of Urakami slowly began to see a semblance of normalcy through the various stages of physical reconstruction. The trench-huts days were the first of what Nagai Takashi, a survivor and parishioner leader of the city Catholics, identified as the four stages of house reconstruction in the atomic wasteland (*genshino*) of Urakami. The trench-hut days were also the stage of the refugees. The second was the stage of the makeshift huts; the third, provisional construction; and the fourth, proper construction. The makeshift huts, built as communal spaces approximately six meters square from burned poles and sheet iron, lasted for a few months until winter forced the residents to build more stable and warmer structures. The resulting provisional constructions did not provide a luxurious living, having "a rough coat of plaster, and there were no ceilings—only a roof of straw." Nagai noted in 1949, "They were places where one could live in comfort," relatively speaking. He also pointed out that around the time of the provisional construction, in late 1945 and early 1946, residents tried to resume normal life: "They began to get married; and weddings were celebrated at the rate of more than ten a week." Nagai declared that such activities marked this phase as the stage of rehabilitation. Even so, when Nagai wrote these descriptions in 1949, the fourth stage of "proper construction," or "luxury," had yet to come.[19]

Recovery was gradual, yet steady. Electric light was restored two days after the bombing in central Nagasaki, but did not reach the Urakami valley until October 20. Of course, there was no electricity in the trench-huts, and an "eerie darkness" blanketed the bombed-out area, which was dimly lit with torches.[20] Combined with the makeshift huts and provisional structures, Nagai thought that Urakami probably looked to passersby like a hopeless pile of roof tiles and ash, and the revival of it doubtful. "It may not be visible to the eye," he declared in 1949, "but the atomic wasteland is being restored little by little."[21] But early on, something invisible to the naked eye proved a major obstacle to reconstruction in the bombed-out area: fear.

The fear that the bombed-out area of Nagasaki was poisoned with radiation and would not be habitable for seventy years haunted the residents of Urakami for months. Rumors spread in the press and among scientists and townspeople. In September 1945, a letter from prefectural officials addressed to Nagasaki neighborhood association heads stated, "All living things have been annihilated by the atomic bomb that was dropped on Urakami District. Because vegetation will not grow in the Urakami area for the next seventy years, there is a danger to the lives of the residents. It is recommended that residents seek out appropriate land and relocate." Officials echoed the belief of many scientists that the radiation from the atomic bomb had sterilized the area surrounding ground zero, making it uninhabitable. The seventy-year sterility theory (*nanajūnen fumō setsu*), as it came to be known in Japan, stemmed from a statement made by Columbia University professor Harold Jacobson, a Manhattan Project scientist. He declared, "In the atomic-bombed-out area of Japan, there is a risk of dying for anyone who enters the area

FIGURE 1.2.   Man harvesting vegetables at ground zero, which is marked by the pole, in 1946.

Source: Victor E. Delnore Photograph Album, 1949, Victor E. Delnore Papers, Gordon W. Prange Collection, University of Maryland Libraries.

over the next seventy years."[22] In other words, the Urakami valley was considered not just sterile; it was toxic. On September 9, 1945, the *Asahi shinbun* ran an article, in part to allay the fear of Nagasaki's infection from the atomic bomb's radiation, and pointed out, simply, that plants had rebounded in the bombed area.[23]

The radiation in the Urakami valley may have presented a danger for residents, but they did not let the rumors keep them from staying or impede their reconstruction of the area, perhaps because most of them had nowhere else to go. Nagai Takashi took it on himself to quell the fear of radiation. As a resident of Urakami, a neighborhood association head, and a role model of the valley's Catholic community, Nagai attempted to prove false the seventy-year sterility theory. After making observations similar to the *Asahi shinbun* article that plant and animal life had once again begun to thrive in the bombed-out area, Nagai built a one-room shack near the hypocenter and lived in it with his two children, Makoto (age nine) and Kayano (age four), from October 1945. In January 1946, they moved into a makeshift hut near the same area, and later in 1948, some Catholic community members built him a provisional structure on the same spot.[24] Nagai's decision to live in the bombed-out area was intended to inspire hope in his fellow residents that their land had not been converted into an eternal landscape of death and that they could indeed rebuild their city and community.

Early Development of the Municipal Vision of Reconstruction

Over the next several years, the government housing authority and numerous individuals and volunteers built provisional structures throughout Nagasaki and laid a physical foundation on which the city created a long-term reconstruction plan.[25] Before the arrival of American occupation troops, when Nagasaki residents still lived in trench-huts, ideas about reconstruction were already caroming among officials and intellectuals. On August 28, only nineteen days after the bombing, members of the Nagasaki Prefectural Association of Commerce, Industry, and Economy (Shōkō keizai kai) met with the mayor of Nagasaki, Okada Jukichi, to discuss plans to "revive the Great Nagasaki City of yesteryear bathed in its brilliant light (kyakkō)." Two days later, the group submitted its official recommendation, the Great Nagasaki Revival Plan (Dai Nagasaki-shi fukkō keikaku), which outlined the path the city should take in its reconstruction. Nagasaki, the economists declared, should draw on its history and become an international center of trade and tourism. It should "be the gateway of western Japan" and serve as the base of trade with China and Taiwan, in the end becoming a "free trade port." In addition, historic areas of Nagasaki should be "beautified" to develop the city as a sightseeing center.[26]

The ideas in the petition gained immediate traction. Economist Itō Hisa'aki pointed out in mid-September that Mitsubishi Heavy Industries, especially its shipbuilding factories, had dominated industrial Nagasaki (before and) during the war, but the conglomerate "suffered a fatal blow" with defeat. Therefore, he argued, the city "has no choice but to continue its economic existence as a traditional port of trade." Nagasaki, he added, should also take the opportunity to rebuild in such a way as to attract tourists. Once the rubble had been cleared, and the "scattered dung of horses and cows" removed from the streets in the manner of a "civilized country," then the city could erect "modern hotels and recreational facilities," as well as "wide streets, greenbelts, and flower gardens." Then, the "sightseeing city of Nagasaki" would surely attract "high-class people of culture" to its various historical sites and museums that celebrated the city's rich past as an international port city.[27]

Nagasaki culture, it was noted, had not been destroyed in the bombing. Itō admitted that the ruins of the "exotic cathedral" on a hill in Urakami aroused sentimental thoughts in everyone who looked on it, and it would indeed become "a historical memento of Japanese Christians," but he declared that the tragic scene should not dishearten the city. The destruction of Nagasaki's Christian community and its cathedral by the atomic bomb dropped by "Christian America," Itō pointed out, was a "regrettable event for cultural Nagasaki," but "historical traditions cannot be destroyed by mere violence."[28] Itō concluded, "In this aerial bombing, the cultural Nagasaki of history sustained no fatal wound," and "the modern cultural city of Nagasaki" should continue to have deep contact with the "new China."[29] Itō's message was clear: Nagasaki could overcome its tragic fate and rise from the ashes by embracing and reconstructing its past as an international trading port.

Mayor Okada agreed. The reconstruction of Nagasaki would require exorbitant amounts of money—over the next ten years, the mayor predicted that recovery (*fukkyū*) costs might exceed ¥100 million—and the national government could not be counted on to supply the money. Nagasaki was not the only city in Japan that lay in ruins, and the national government needed to spread its resources over the entire country. The mayor also pointed out that Nagasaki could not count on the industrial profits of Mitsubishi and other destroyed companies as a source for reconstruction funds. The decrease (*gen*) in numbers of residents in Nagasaki due to the atomic bombing made taxes an unreliable source of funds. Nagasaki's only recourse, the mayor thought, resided in the city's future as a hub of trade, which he hoped would soon resume with China, and as a city of tourism. The mayor's discussion of the urban reconstruction of Nagasaki as *fukkyū*, too, revealed that he and the municipal officials had set their mind on "recovering the past." The term implies "a return to the old state of things," and city planners often used the same *kyū* character in the term, "old Nagasaki," evoking the Nagasaki of the past.[30] And so it was that less than one month after the bombing Nagasaki had been put on the path of reconstructing in light of its past.

Private-sector organizations also had a hand in conceptualizing—and realizing—the direction of Nagasaki's future as a city of trade and tourism. The young businessmen of the Nagasaki Prefectural Association of Commerce, Industry, and Economy, who had initially submitted the dual-themed reconstruction proposal to the government, formed the Nagasaki Revival Company (Nagasaki fukkō kaisha) and immediately joined governmental efforts to reconstruct "Great Nagasaki." Even though torrential rains impeded construction through September, the first stage of construction was completed by October, which brought residents out of the dugout air-raid trenches and into makeshift huts. As one commentator put it, "a breath of new life flows strongly in Nagasaki City."[31]

In early October, the City Planning Division of the Prefectural Public Works Department released an official plan for the city. Considering the wishes of the "people of old Nagasaki" as well as the "people of new Nagasaki," the city planners proposed the reconstruction of Great Nagasaki as a "city of free trade" and a "city of tourism" (*kankō*). An elaborate system of trains and trolleys would cover the city, so that residents would not have to walk more than two- or three-hundred meters to ride public transportation. Streets would be wider than before and public parks would abound.[32]

Reconstruction projects also sought to create an atmosphere of modern culture in the city. In 1946, the Nagasaki Cultural Association (Nagasaki bunka konwa kai) emerged to propose a name for the reconstruction of the city, and the intellectual elite who made up the group organized an informal meeting in August to discuss with planning officials the merits of their suggestion to envision Nagasaki as a so-called cultural city. Several city planners attended the Cultural City Construction Colloquium (Bunka toshi kensetsu kondankai), including the head of the Prefectural City Planning Division as well as the chief of the City Facilities Department, Naruse Kaoru, who later became head of the City Construction Office. The group discussed concrete ways to construct modernized streets, shopping areas, improved harbors, an airport, parks, sports grounds, and other facilities to enliven the city, or as one member called them, "good policies for prosperity." They discussed creating a Nagasaki City of tourism by building hotels and such and also the possibility of setting aside two or three areas for the construction of pleasure quarters (or, red-light districts: *kanrakugai*).[33]

The rhetoric of the "cultural city"—and indeed "cultural" everything—was standard postwar language, but in Nagasaki the word held a specific significance that drew on the city's history. Making Nagasaki a city of culture relied on its past, but as city planners quickly realized, reconstruction in the wake of war and the atomic bombs also required the promotion of another popular postwar term: peace. Public discourse focused on the peace that many Americans and Japanese argued the bombing had brought. Thus those who survived the devastation of Nagasaki endured the first years of defeat and occupation by viewing the atomic tragedy through a discourse of peace.

The discourse of peace pervaded Japan. Prime Minister Higashikuni Naruhiko declared in September 1945 the general hope of Japan to "construct a nation of peace not inferior to the United States." "We will build a completely new, peaceful Japan," he said, "and it will become a cultural nation (*bunkakoku*) of high morality."[34] John Dower writes that the "two most familiar slogans of the early postwar period—'Construct a Nation of Peace' (*Heiwa Kokka Kensetsu*) and 'Construct a Nation of Culture' (*Bunka Kokka Kensetsu*)—resurrected two key themes of wartime propaganda, construction and culture, and turned them into rallying cries for the creation of a nation resting on democratic, antimilitaristic principles." In the immediate postwar, "Catchphrases were like valises," Dower notes, "waiting to be emptied of their old contents and filled with something new."[35] The word "peace" found its way into every corner of society and culture, from festivals to reconstruction laws to the Peace Constitution of 1946, written by the Americans. The constitution's Article 9 forever renounced war, underlining Japan's resolve to maintain peace. The ideas of peace and culture became intertwined as the country sought to rebuild as a demilitarized and democratic nation.

Although Higashikuni did not last long as prime minister, the concept of building a nation of peace quickly took root and persisted. The first year of reconstruction in Nagasaki, as a local newspaper put it, represented the city's "first step toward the historic construction of peace." "Among the ruins of atomic-town Nagasaki (*genshi no machi Nagasaki*)," the *Nagasaki shinbun* wrote on August 4, 1946, "a town of modest houses has emerged," and the "city-plan of Nagasaki City, which was established in the 'atomic town' of ruins and dust, embodies a beautiful dream aimed at the reconstruction of a port city of bright and virtuous peace." Nagasaki was "making a comeback" as it slowly rebuilt its prestige as an international port, "conveying its spirit of new life" as far as "the mountains that surround the port."[36] One year after the atomic bombing, city planners and townspeople did not dwell on the event. To be sure, it was lamented and remembered, but not to the point of impeding the "beautiful dream" of reviving the old Nagasaki that had welcomed foreign ships and served as gateway to the wider world. For years afterward, the "atomic citizens" (*atomu shimin*) of Nagasaki City, as the *Nishi Nippon* newspaper put it, worked to fulfill their hope of reconstructing the city as a center of trade and tourism.[37]

The word "peace" pervaded discourse in Nagasaki from late 1945, but from 1948, it became ubiquitous. By 1948, the idea of Nagasaki culture effectively blended the two images of the city as a promoter of peace and an international city. In 1949, after years of cultivating the image of Nagasaki as a center of trade and culture and recognizing Hiroshima's competitive spirit to be *the* atomic-bombed city, Nagasaki officials sought to emphasize their atomic bombing as a part of the reconstruction plan and increased concrete efforts to that end. As in Hiroshima, Nagasaki's approach to promoting peace took shape through the preservation of ruins, the implementation of reconstruction projects and policies that included the term "peace," and the organization of annual ceremonies. Each city implored people to remember the tragedy. Nagasaki worked for "everlasting world peace" and "No More Nagasakis" while Hiroshima called for "No More Hiroshimas"; each city was concerned primarily with its own reconstruction.

Officials and townspeople understood the importance of preserving the ruins as reminders of the horrors of war, even if the municipal vision for reconstruction did not give priority to the memory of the bombing. Indeed, preservation of atomic ruins offered one way to fulfill the mission of building a nation of peace, at least for the time being. More importantly for those who had lost loved ones in the bombing, preservation work and peace activism provided an opportunity to give meaning to their deaths. Dealing with the trauma in this way promised to build a path forward for the city's revival as a whole. At a city council meeting on October 6, 1945, Councilman Kunitomo, who had lost his wife in the atomic bombing, declared that rallying cries for the revival of the city were not enough. As an atomic-bombed city, Nagasaki had a responsibility to do more. He argued that the city should retain the ruins of the atomic bomb that "snatched away the existence of tens of thousands of our countrymen." By preserving the physical traces of the bombing, he claimed, "we must provide to the world research material on the menacing atomic bomb of science that laid the foundation for world peace." "We have a human obligation," Kunitomo continued, "to fully record the aftermath of the destruction, and preserve all important research material, such as factory ruins, scorched trees, and the crumbled Urakami Cathedral." These ruins, he believed, would long interest historians, much like the ruins of Pompeii. Kunitomo asserted that it was "the duty of a cultured nation" to conduct the necessary preservation work.[38]

The preservation of ruins presented an additional advantage in Kunitomo's mind. He pointed out that a Western scholar claimed that even though Japan was a "civilized nation," it was not a "cultured nation." For Kunitomo, postatomic reconstruction was Nagasaki's chance to help the country rise in the eyes of the world through the "sacrifice" of his wife and tens of thousands of others. Preservation of the ruins would demonstrate to the world that Nagasaki and the Japanese people truly regretted their part in the war, and that the "noble sacrifice of tens of thousands of Nagasaki City residents has rid the world of war forever."[39] Atomic ruins also promised to contribute to Nagasaki as a city of culture and tourism. The pinnacle of modern, scientific culture had devastated the city, leaving ruins, such as the Urakami Cathedral, to stand as reminders both of modernity and of the folly of war. Humans had conquered the power of nature by splitting the atom, and Nagasaki testified to that tragic achievement even as the Roman Catholic cathedral was evidence of historic and international Nagasaki culture. The ruins of the cathedral became the central site of atomic-bombing tourism until 1958. In fact, city planners played up all of the historic Christian spots in the city, including the hill of the Twenty-Six Martyrs near Nagasaki Station, which, from early on, they considered an ideal tourist spot that supported their plan to rebuild as a city of trade and tourism.[40] As the planning progressed, the path of the city looked bright as it overcame its atomic devastation to rebuild its past as a modern city in control of its future.

Cultivating the Vision and Overwriting Memory, 1946–1949

Once city officials had decided the path for reconstruction, they set out to cultivate their vision and to ensure that it took root. First, they needed to acquire funds. In August 1946, months after Japan had begun laying out national city-reconstruction plans, delegates from Nagasaki and Hiroshima traveled to Tokyo to discuss their cities' plans with officials from the Ministry of Home Affairs. Nagasaki officials acknowledged that the benefits of international trade and tourism had yet to produce revenues to support the reconstruction efforts, so they were caught in a kind of chicken-and-egg dilemma. The national government, as Mayor Okada had pointed out, could not be counted on for reconstruction funds in 1945, but by fall 1946, Nagasaki had no choice but to ask for help.

Throughout 1946, officials from both cities, inspired and supported by local public opinion, worked together to request special funds from the national treasury for their cities, which they argued required more aid than the "general war-damaged city."[41] The August 1946 meeting in Tokyo, as Deputy Mayor Kan'no reported on his return to Nagasaki, had gone smoothly. The delegates from the atomic-bombed cities and ministry officials had agreed that Japan should promote the reconstruction of Nagasaki and Hiroshima over the other war-damaged cities of Japan. The meeting took into consideration the fact that the two cities were destroyed by atomic bombs, which national officials agreed made them different and declared that the reconstruction of the two cities was also special.[42] Here was official recognition that the two cities were indeed different from the other bombed-out cities of Japan. At a plenary meeting of parliament on August 23, 1946, Nagasaki representative Honda Eisaku and Hiroshima representative Kuroda Yoshi submitted an official petition. Parliament adopted the proposal without delay, and on negotiating a "concrete figure" from the Treasury Office, Nagasaki prepared to "launch full-blown city reconstruction."[43]

With funding partially secured, municipal officials set out to implement their vision. August 1947 presented an especially key moment for officials to make their mark on the conceptual landscape of reconstruction. The month of the two-year anniversary of the bombing was primetime, as it were, and eyes from all around Japan and the world would be on Nagasaki (and Hiroshima). Moreover, mid-August's association with the atomic destruction and the end of the war made it the perfect moment for city officials to define (or redefine) the month in a way that suited their vision of reconstruction. They attempted to encode that month with their vision over commemoration of the bombing, which helped shape early formation of an official atomic narrative in and of the city.

The first, and perhaps most important, event was the two-year commemoration of the bombing. City officials sought to distract from and downplay as best as possible the commemorative atmosphere of the anniversary, which residents wanted to use to publicly remember their friends and family lost in the bombing or later to its radiation. By this time, Nagasaki and Hiroshima no longer seemed to be working together but rather taking different paths, exemplified in the municipal approaches to the 1947 anniversary. Hiroshima held a massive commemoration ceremony for the second anniversary of the bombing on August 6, for which it received a special message from General Douglas MacArthur. This was the first peace festival held in Hiroshima, and it attracted more than ten thousand people. Nagasaki officials, for their part, instead organized a city-sponsored, weeklong Foreign Trade Revival Festival (Bōeki fukkō sai) rather than a commemoration of their atomic bombing on August 9.[44] Organizers of the festival intended it to "celebrate the shining rebirth (*kadode*) of the promotion of foreign trade and the reconstruction of the economy" of the city, but it revealed not only the disparity in municipal approaches to atomic memory in the two cities but also a rift between municipal officials and city residents in Nagasaki.[45]

The Nagasaki minyū newspaper company, after receiving letters from residents expressing jealousy over the situation in Hiroshima, decided to investigate. City officials seemed to have been so consumed by their goal to make Nagasaki a city of trade and tourism that they neglected to commemorate the atomic bombing, a point made on August 8 by a reporter named Sakamoto in an interview with Mayor Ōhashi. The mayor, failing to see it as a major problem or setback, placed the blame on the national government.[46] "Hiroshima is holding a massive peace festival," Sakamoto stated, "and [residents here] feel lonely (*sabishii*) since Nagasaki is not. We have received many letters expressing their envy of Hiroshima, which received a message from General MacArthur." Mayor Ōhashi responded, "We thought a good deal about holding an August ninth commemoration, but we were unable to hold any memorial service (*ireisai*) or commemoration (*tsuitōkai*) that would be sponsored by the city, prefecture, or public group." "What do you mean public groups couldn't sponsor it?" inquired Sakamoto. Ōhashi explained, "We received a notice from the government." "What do you mean 'from the government'?" asked an unsatisfied Sakamoto. Ōhashi answered vaguely, "I forget if it was from the Ministry of Home Affairs or the Ministry of Health and Welfare, but it came from one of the ministries in charge." So the city decided instead "to hold an event with a special purpose. Of course, if the war-damage federations, religious groups, or youth groups hold [commemorative events], we will not hinder them."[47] The mayor held firm: "Hiroshima is holding a special peace festival. Here we will be holding a peace trade festival (*heiwa bōeki sai*) from the ninth through the fifteenth. On the fifteenth we plan to pray for peace by sounding sirens and praying for the eternal repose (*meifuku*) of those who died in the war."[48] Sakamoto persevered, "But the atomic bomb fell on August ninth. For the people of the world to understand, it's meaningless if it doesn't take place on the ninth."[49] In reply to Sakamoto's query about a message from General MacArthur, the mayor replied that a letter had been sent via a prefectural representative. But Hiroshima had sent a personal delegate directly to Tokyo, countered Sakamoto, and considering that the representative had not yet answered by today, which was August 8, "there's no way it will make it in time, is there?"[50]

Many in Nagasaki (and Hiroshima) could not understand the official decision not to commemorate the bombing in 1947. Perhaps there existed no notice from the government at all in regard to a public ceremony. It hardly seems likely that Hiroshima could hold a massive peace event and Nagasaki could not. Now that they were receiving extra funds from the national government, to divert from the course of reconstruction would make little political sense, and further, it would not distinguish the city from Hiroshima. In addition, officials in Nagasaki had been speaking of the bombing in somewhat positive terms, similar to the Americans, as having brought peace. Mayor Ōhashi told residents in August 1947 that the Nagasaki bombing ended the war and "saved countless lives" that might have been lost in the continuation of the war, and he called on Nagasaki residents to "turn misfortune into happiness" by reconstructing Nagasaki as a "cultural city."[51] At the same time, Governor Sugiyama portrayed the destiny of Nagasaki not as a reminder of "misfortune" but rather as a beacon of hope for "the ideals and morality of mankind" based on prosperous international trade.[52] Nagasaki officials were seeking to use the significance of August, to the extent possible, to overwrite the memory of the bombing by encoding that special time with a celebration of the city's past and its goals for the future. In other words, they downplayed the bombing and emphasized the city's international history in August in order to promote the municipal vision of reconstruction.

National media also bolstered the municipal vision in August 1947. Nihon nyūsu released a newsreel that month, *Nagasaki monogatari* (Nagasaki Story), intended for national audiences, which reported on the state of reconstruction in Nagasaki (it was joined by a similar clip about Kagoshima). The newsreel features Nagasaki's shipbuilding and maritime-based economy and the presence of the Catholic community, celebrating these two features as central to the revival of the city and the preservation of its historical identity. The film suggests that the recovery of both symbols after the atomic bombing demonstrates the recovery of the city as a whole. The first part of the film features the area of atomic destruction in the city, discussing the Urakami district's recovery from the bomb with a

soundtrack of pipe organs as if in a church; focusing on the leader of the Catholics, Nagai Takashi; and commending him for his research on the effects of radiation on the human body. The latter part of the film, accompanied by triumphant
music, stressed the importance of Nagasaki Bay to international trade and shipbuilding, displaying scenes of the harbor and workers building massive ships.
The newsreel reflected the image of the city as promoted by municipal officials
because it deemphasized the memory of the atomic bombing as a major factor
in the reconstruction process. The newsreel depicted the bombing as a trauma
endured by the Urakami Catholics located in the northern valley, not by the city
as a whole, a trope in popular media that began as early as September 1945. In
other words, the film presented the official, municipal narrative of the bombing
and reconstruction. The events of August 1947—the trade festival and the
newsreel—marked the beginning of a national perception of Nagasaki, and
especially in Hiroshima, of a city not willing to step up, as it were, to sufficiently
commemorate the bombings and work for peace.

One year later, discussions of the bombing figured more prominently in
commemorative rhetoric surrounding the anniversary, but officials persisted
in constructing an atomic narrative within the context of their vision of reconstruction. The third-year anniversary saw the first of what would become standard commemoration activities, with citywide public ceremonies and pledges to
"never repeat the tragedy of Atomic Nagasaki (atomu-Nagasaki)" blended with
the official insistence on building a "city of trade and tourism." The 1948 city-
sponsored ceremony was called a culture festival (bunka sai), as well as a reconstruction festival (fukkō sai), but not an atomic-bombing commemoration or
the like. However, what would later become Peace Park was called Atom Park.[53]
Colonel Victor E. Delnore, commander of the Nagasaki Military Government
Team of the American occupation, and other American officials attended the official ceremony. When Mayor Ōhashi spoke, he stated that "the sacrifice we paid
was enormous, but the result has been even grander. Nagasaki is not just a city of
Japan," he continued, declaring that Nagasaki was a city of the world with a mission
to rebuild as such. In order to "repay the noble sacrifice, [we] commit ourselves to
the realization of the cultural Nagasaki that the world expects, to conquer all
obstacles and to exert great effort and diligence" in the reconstruction.[54] Here, the
mayor successfully subsumed the memory of the bombing within the historical
narrative and urban identity of the city, making it simply a part of the municipal
plan to rebuild the city. In other words, officials argued that in order to properly
commemorate the tragedy of the bombing, the city had a responsibility to rebuild
as cultural world city.

Other attempts in 1948 to cultivate the municipal vision of reconstruction dis-
torted local history. Local historian and city planner Shimauchi Hachirō linked

the historic mansion of British Merchant Thomas Glover to the opera *Madame Butterfly* despite, historically speaking, there not actually existing a link between the building and the opera. Shimauchi understood this when he said to a reporter in 1948, "Nagasaki means Madame Butterfly, and Madame Butterfly means Nagasaki," but he declared that there needed to be a monument to recognize the opera's place in the city's history. The mansion seemed like the "best choice," Shimauchi thought, and, later, the building was briefly referred to as "Madame Butterfly House." The link between the mansion and the opera seemed to be intended to appeal to the American occupiers in Nagasaki and Tokyo, as well as to other foreigners. The American occupation government was fascinated with the opera for ideological reasons, supporting Tokyo performances of *Madame Butterfly* and *The Mikado* because both presented the ideal postwar relationship between Japan and the United States in which the former was submissive to the latter. The first step taken to officially promote the link between the mansion and the opera came in August 1948 when a news article appeared in both the English and the Japanese versions of the *Mainichi shinbun* declaring the "discovery" of the remains of Madame Butterfly's house at Glover's mansion. The Japanese version appeared on August 10, beside an article about the commemoration of the bombing the day earlier.[55]

Of course, the drive to promote historical sites such as Glover's mansion stemmed from the need to revive the economy of the city through such means as tourism, but the timing of the article points to additional motives. The article and accompanying photograph of an American occupation official's wife on the mansion grounds had been prepared three months earlier, despite the reporter's declaration that the discovery was made "on the eve of the cultural festival commemorating the third anniversary of the atom bombing of this city." The delay suggests that both municipal and American occupation officials sought to build on a narrative of postwar Nagasaki in which memory of the atomic bombing did not dominate local consciousness or national perceptions of the city. In other words, just as city officials had done in 1947, the international past was being used to overwrite—or at least dilute—the memory of the bombing, but this time by celebrating a false history.[56]

By 1948, Nagasaki and Hiroshima had settled into their individual paths of reconstruction, each professing the greater significance of their city's atomic destruction and peace work. The first ever Peace Declaration (heiwa sengen) in 1948, which would become a staple of the anniversary ceremony of Nagasaki (as in Hiroshima), made no mention of Hiroshima. "Peace Starts from Nagasaki" and "No More Nagasakis" became the phrases that defined Nagasaki's perception of itself and its role in establishing everlasting peace by virtue of its "world status."[57] Furthermore, officials in each city considered their own tragedy as the

FIGURE 1.3. Colonel Delnore with municipal and prefectural officials, including Mayor Ōhashi and Governor Sugiyama, at a cocktail party in the afternoon on December 30, 1948.

Source: Victor E. Delnore Photograph Album, 1949, Victor E. Delnore Papers, Gordon W. Prange Collection, University of Maryland Libraries.

cornerstone of world peace, but the term held different meaning for each. Hiroshima officials viewed their city as different from and, in terms of the emergence of the nuclear age, more significant than Nagasaki, because it was the first city in history to experience the destruction of an atomic bomb. Nagasaki officials, however, considered their atomic bombing as more significant precisely because it was the second and last atomic bombing, which meant that their atomic tragedy had ended the war. But the approach of Nagasaki officials and city planners to rebuild the city as a center of international trade, tourism, and culture made them appear less eager than Hiroshima to stress the horror of an atomic bomb and the necessity to work for world peace.

In early 1949, Hiroshima officials took steps to lay official claim to the status of representative atomic-bombed city. In late April, delegates from Hiroshima traveled to Tokyo for the May 10 National Diet meeting to propose the ratification of the Hiroshima Peace Commemoration City Construction Law (Hiroshima heiwa kinen toshi kensetsu hō). The mayor of Hiroshima, Hamai Shinzō (the "atomic-bombing mayor"), spearheaded the move. He was, from early on, instrumental in cultivating the peace identity and ensuring the rise of Hiroshima in popular and official discourse on the bombings. The law that he and the other Hiroshima representatives proposed to the Diet reflected the direction the city had been taking since its bombing, as well as the image that officials wanted to project into the future. As the first atomic-bombed city, Hiroshima must stand as the preeminent symbol of the horror of war and the importance of peace.

Officials in Nagasaki received no notification from Hiroshima of its plan to propose the legislation to the Diet, catching them off guard and unprepared. Nagasaki officials felt betrayed because they claimed there had existed a promise between the cities to work in harmony to protect the special character of the two atomic-bombed cities among the rest of the bombed-out cities of Japan. That it had come to Hiroshima's need for individual recognition ahead of Nagasaki as a special atomic-bombed city, Nagasaki officials thought, was regrettable.[58] Mayor Ōhashi and a few other officials from Nagasaki rushed to Tokyo in time for the National Diet meeting, working through the night to cobble together a proposal for their own city-reconstruction legislation. The Nagasaki representative in the Diet, Kadoya Seiichi, attributed his city's "slow start" (tachiokureta) to the self-serving attitude of Hiroshima, considering that Nagasaki officials had to "stop an already departed train, jump on with a lot of luggage, and stand shoulder-to-shoulder to ride together" with Hiroshima.[59] City council members who stayed behind in Nagasaki organized an ad hoc meeting on the night of May 9, the day before the Diet meeting. Some members thought that Nagasaki, too, should be a "peace city." Indeed, Hiroshima did not hold a monopoly on the word, but the designation of Nagasaki as a "cultural city" had already gained traction.[60] Either way, Hiroshima was not willing to share its unique designation as the "city of peace."

Hiroshima officials sought to exclude Nagasaki altogether. At an earlier meeting of the Liberal People's Party (Minjitō), Hiroshima supporters objected to the inclusion of the word "peace" in Nagasaki's official title. The word, they argued, defined the reconstruction of Hiroshima because the city could not draw on its past and revive its history as a major military headquarters for the Imperial Army. One Hiroshima representative at the Minjitō meeting pleaded that only Hiroshima's law be passed because its purpose, he explained, was to rid the city of its military traces, specifically former "land for military use." Nagasaki had none to speak of, he pointed out, saying, "I ask that you approve only Hiroshima's law." Nagasaki's representatives did not attend that meeting, but later they joined Hiroshima representatives for another meeting with the Minjitō, where it became clear after intense debate characterized by "heroic hometown love" that Hiroshima's law could not pass the Diet without a similar law for Nagasaki. Only the content of the law needed to be decided, including a title for the city to define its path of reconstruction.[61]

The resulting laws reflected each city's municipal vision of reconstruction. On May 10, the National Diet unanimously passed the Hiroshima Peace Commemoration City Construction Law and the Nagasaki International Cultural City Construction Law (Nagasaki kokusai bunka toshi kensetsu hō). Hiroshima, as planned, became the peace city of Japan, while Nagasaki joined a clique of international cultural cities that included Kyoto, Nara, Beppu, Itō, and others. Despite the ubiquity of "culture" and "peace" in postwar Japan, the former dominated in the titles of city reconstruction laws. Nagasaki hoped to emphasize not only its history of international culture that had defined it for centuries but also the contemporary international culture that included peace activism. Beppu put emphasis on its "international tourism and hot spring culture," using the term "international" quite loosely, but Kyoto came close to resembling Nagasaki with its Kyoto International Cultural Tourism City Construction Law (Kyōto kokusai bunka kankō toshi kensetsu hō). Nara's law was nearly identical to Kyoto's. Like Nagasaki's law, each city aimed at the "achievement of the ideal of everlasting world peace," a phrase that appeared, identically, in the opening clause of the laws.[62] In the end, among the bombed-out cities in Japan, Hiroshima managed to preserve its image as the sole peace city. Nagasaki, on the other hand, found itself placed among the rest.

Although a last-minute ordeal, Nagasaki had, at least on the official level, revived its image of an historical international past and its present status as a symbol of culture. But the inability of Nagasaki officials to secure a reconstruction law with the word "peace" in the title demonstrated both the city's approach to reconstruction since 1945 and its political weakness in comparison to Hiroshima. Many in Nagasaki could not understand why "peace" did not appear in the title. Tsubouchi argued that there were many issues on which Nagasaki needed to "greatly reflect" in the future, but the main reason that Nagasaki had lost to Hiroshima was that it had not kept up with Hiroshima's peace activism, which had been strong for more than three-and-a-half years. The loss of the word "peace" should serve as Nagasaki's wake-up call, he argued, but the International Cultural City Law was by no means a loss in itself. Rather, Tsubouchi declared, "I truly pray from the heart that with this law Nagasaki emerges internationally as a cultural bridge across the world and sustains lasting development."[63] Overall, city officials and residents were hopeful about their newly defined mission. For Nagasaki in 1949, international culture meant celebrating a vibrant past while embracing a responsibility to work for everlasting peace, even without an official designation as a peace city. Despite the official loss to Hiroshima of the word "peace," the word remained in the local lexicon of reconstruction and commemoration, newspapers referring to the city as "Peace and Culture City Nagasaki," or simply as "Peace City Nagasaki," both of which were interchangeable with "International Cultural City."[64]

From the point of view of city representatives, the law allowed cultivation of Nagasaki's urban identity to include mention of the atomic bombing without being defined by it. In his address to the National Diet, representative Wakamatsu Torao declared that the reconstruction law would make Nagasaki the "central city of international peace," an idea inherent not only in the city's designation as a city of international culture but also in its motto, "Peace Starts from Nagasaki."[65] Emperor Hirohito, too, echoed the interpretation of city officials who linked Nagasaki's destruction and the end of the war, declaring in May 1949 that Nagasaki must "turn the sacrifice of the atomic bombing into the foundation of peace."[66] Being labeled an international cultural city instead of a peace city encouraged this link because from the perspective of city leaders, it allowed Nagasaki to move forward from its tragedy by embracing its history even as it represented the foundation of peace in the present.

Reception and Interpretation of the International Cultural City Identity

Reactions to Nagasaki's 1949 reconstruction law were mixed. The official designation as an "international cultural city" left some residents scratching their heads. Some scholars could not comprehend what made the city more special than other bombed-out cities in Japan or what exactly was meant by international culture, and indeed many residents had a hard time grasping the meaning. Some city officials only slowly discovered what international culture meant. Kino Fumio, chief secretariat of Nagasaki City Council, looked up "international culture" in the encyclopedia but found nothing. He decided to study a bit more about what the term meant so that he could educate his fellow residents who saw the term as an empty designation. In the context of the postwar world, he wrote in 1950, "international culture" meant "freedom and peace," which the 1949 law envisioned with its opening clause that declared the promise to realize "everlasting world peace."[67] The people of Nagasaki would cultivate a city of international culture by resurrecting their past and commemorating the atomic bombing.

Naruse Kaoru, head of the Nagasaki City Construction Office, argued that everyone in Japan was struggling with postwar life and he could "not easily forgive the fact that only Nagasaki would become a good child (*yoi ko*)" through implementation of the special-city reconstruction law. Naruse held the responsibility of implementing projects that focused on concrete activities, such as removing debris, designating land for specific use, and modernizing city streets.[68] It seemed odd to him that Nagasaki had been singled out for "special reconstruction." Writing in 1950, he declared, "I still cannot even comprehend what the devil is meant by the First International Cultural City."[69] "It is a big mistake," he wrote, to think that the city could reconstruct simply because it benefited from a construction law of the national government. To be successful and receive support, the revival (*fukkō*) of Nagasaki had to serve the greater purpose of the reconstruction (*saiken*) of Japan as a whole. But Naruse realized that the revival of the city outweighed the need to debate what seemed to him to be political nonsense surrounding the official designation of the city. International Cultural City did not mean National Treasure City, he declared, and in some cases Nagasaki would have to give priority to "developmental destruction" over preservation of the past in order to remodel itself as an international city that capitalized on Nagasaki's traditional culture.[70]

City residents, however, overwhelmingly embraced the new law. A public vote was held on July 7, 1949, and an historic 73.5 percent of eligible voters showed up at the polls, voting unanimously in favor of the law. Of the 81,637 people to cast votes, 79,220 (98.6%) chose to adopt the law, while only 1,136 (1.4%) voted against it.[71] The law took effect on August 9, 1949, on the fourth anniversary of the bombing, and commemorations were accompanied by celebrations that lasted for three days in honor of the city's progress toward revival. "Today is the birthday of New Nagasaki," declared a headline in the *Nagasaki nichinichi* newspaper. General MacArthur and Prime Minister Yoshida Shigeru sent messages to Mayor Ōhashi and the citizens of Nagasaki to congratulate them on the official new path of reconstruction as a center of international culture.[72]

The international culture of Nagasaki, or its "aroma" (*nioi*), as historian and city planner Shimauchi Hachirō called it, was easily identifiable by its landmarks.[73] Shimauchi boasted of the historic sites that defined Nagasaki in a 1951 article for *Shintoshi* (New Cities), a Tokyo-based journal dedicated to issues of city reconstruction in postwar Japan. Shimauchi included Nagasaki's national treasures, such as the Ōura Cathedral and two (of the city's many) Buddhist temples. The Dutch compound Dejima topped the list of historical landmarks, followed by the Chinese compound, the hill of the Twenty-Six Christian Martyrs of 1597, and the former residence of the British merchant Thomas Glover. Again dubiously linking Glover's mansion to Madame Butterfly, Shimauchi went on to declare that the mansion held special significance because its beautiful garden inspired the opera, which made Nagasaki a place of world-renowned international culture.[74] The city was indeed rich in history, and Shimauchi called on the residents to make the most of it in light of the new reconstruction law. He pointed out in an earlier publication how Nagasaki had two preeminent instances of international culture—three hundred years of foreign trade and the atomic bombing—and he suggested that residents, together with city officials, dedicate themselves to make the most of that history for the most advantageous development possible.[75] Cultivating the city's international history was always a priority for city officials.

Residents boasted of the city's new title by including the words "International Culture" or "Peace" in the names of events and buildings, and they embraced the task given to them by the law to resurrect the past and cultivate peace activism. As an editorial in the *Nishi Nippon* newspaper declared in late August 1949, the basic principle of the law was to make "Nagasaki City a model city of everlasting world peace replete with happiness and peace," and its construction would be re-alized through real activities that promoted peace.[76] This would not be accomplished by the "simple promotion of local culture" or "exclusively through the institution (*shisetsu*) of city planning." The city reconstruction plan, the editorial argued, envisioned at least three things.[77]

> One, as the unique national cultural city of Japan, [Nagasaki] will have facilities (*shisetsu*) that directly promote peace ([i.e.,] facilities for atomic-bombing commemoration, facilities able to carry out assemblies of international peace and culture). Two, [the city] will have educational facilities of higher learning that contribute to the promotion of peace and the advancement of culture. Three, with the general city population in mind, [the city] will equip facilities of a modern city of the highest standard permitted by present-day objective terms and conditions.[78]

Even if city officials interpreted the construction of an international cultural city as refurbishing historic sites, for residents, and especially survivors, it often meant developing infrastructure for peace activism and commemoration of the human suffering of the bombing.

According to commentators, Nagasaki had to look beyond its local, Japanese culture and promote a so-called world culture that blended culture and peace. In 1951, city officials added provisions to the reconstruction legislation to construct appropriate facilities in accordance with the law, which began to shape the architectural landscape of the city. Peace Park, Peace Hall, and other facilities (all located in the Urakami valley) breathed new life into the former wasteland. In some cases, atomic memory gave way to the official urban identity as an international cultural city. Before the 1949 law, there was a municipal Atomic Bombing Museum, but the artifacts on display became relegated to just a portion of the new International Cultural Hall (which became the Atomic Bombing Museum again in the 1990s).[79]

City ambassadors also emerged to spread Nagasaki's image in Japan and abroad. In 1949, the city held a beauty pageant to find an appropriate female ambassador for the city. Kadoki Hisako became the first Miss International (Misu kokusai), and, as the *Yūkan Nagasaki* newspaper put it, she was the embodiment of "a beautiful icon of Nagasaki."[80] In November, Miss International joined Miss Hiroshima (not Miss Peace) in a joint commemoration event organized by youth groups from the two cities, held near the Atomic Dome in Hiroshima—the city's enduring site of memory of the bombing.[81] Among the public representatives of the two atomic-bombed cities, Nagasaki's name was entirely absent, supplanted by its international urban identity. That is, the atomic memory of Nagasaki was again subsumed within the urban identity of the city and the dominant narrative in which Hiroshima was the atomic representative.

Miss International was one of two ambassadors of the new, international Nagasaki who gained visibility in popular media. The other was Nagai Takashi, the Catholic doctor who had survived but lost his wife in the atomic bombing and who helped rebuild his Catholic community.[82] Nagai had risen to fame for the role he played in the reconstruction of Nagasaki long before Kadoki Hisako became Miss International. Many considered Nagai to have advanced the city's postwar culture with his books, a role model in the name of the International Cultural City Law.[83] His Roman Catholic faith was a major component of the city's historic international culture, and the Urakami Catholics fully supported that designation of their city. The promotion of international culture, as they saw it, represented the joining of past and present, namely, their history of martyrdom—exemplified in the annual international commemoration of the Twenty-Six Martyrs of 1597—and the emergence of the age of religious tolerance in postwar Japan. Local officials, such as Prefectural Governor Sugiyama Sojirō, agreed that the history of Christian martyrdom enhanced the cultural city approach.[84]

For national officials, too, Christianity was a characteristic of Nagasaki's international culture that benefited reconstruction. At a press conference on June 25, 1949, Chief Cabinet Secretary Masuda Kaneshichi announced a victory for Nagasaki and Hiroshima: the United States had agreed to contribute all of the resources necessary for the reconstruction of the two cities. This was indeed reason to be pleased, he stated, because "all we have to produce is the labor force (rōdōryoku)." The contribution of the United States, however, was not without condition. A large amount of the money received was tagged for erecting Christian buildings or to otherwise improve the cultural sphere of Nagasaki (and Hiroshima), such as the construction of churches and schools. The United States "installed" (dōnyū) approximately $50 million in private capital to support the special laws of Nagasaki and Hiroshima, including a fund of $12 million for the construction of Christian universities. This proved, Secretary Masuda declared, that "the noble blood spilled in the atomic lands by our fellow countrymen, our brothers, fathers, children, and wives, and their great sacrifice, was not at all pointless. Especially now, we have repaid [that sacrifice]." Masuda continued by referring specifically to Nagasaki, saying, "The shining dawn (shokō) toward the construction of a cultural city is on the horizon (mieta). Our delight that resounds in the atomic wasteland of southernmost Japan, and the zeal of 200,000 residents for the construction of a cultural city, must step in unison in one great march toward world peace."[85] "Yes, 'Peace from Nagasaki,'" echoed the Nagasaki nichinichi after quoting Masuda.[86] Money from the United States aided the realization of a cultural city by contributing to the international aspect of Nagasaki's reconstruction, even if the generosity was partially motivated by the American hope for the revival and cultivation of Christianity in the city and Japan.

For the Urakami Catholics, the International Cultural City Law represented more than a Peace Commemoration City Law ever could. The law revived, through its approach to historical remembrance, Nagasaki's long history with the Christian West, which included the Urakami Catholics' history of oppression and martyrdom. It also gave the city the opportunity to be a "harbinger of peace," as Nagai put it. The defeat of Japan in the war brought unprecedented religious freedom, and aid from the United States promised to aid the revival of Christianity in the city and Japan. The Catholics saw the International Cultural City Law as a call to resurrect and promote Catholicism in Nagasaki, which their leaders, especially Nagai, enthusiastically strived to do.[87]

The Catholics considered their religion essential to the successful construction of an international cultural city. Nagai wrote that Nagasaki lacked the materials necessary to build "a city of beautiful buildings" on par with cities that boasted international cultures, such as Buenos Aires, and that no matter how hard the res-

FIGURE 1.4. A commemorative mass during the four-hundredth anniversary celebrations of the arrival of St. Francis Xavier to Japan, May 1949, taking place among the ruins of the Urakami Cathedral.

Source: Photograph taken by and courtesy of Takahara Itaru.

idents worked to erect such buildings, Nagasaki would rank low in the world and could not be called an international cultural city. Instead, Nagai argued, "Nagasaki must aim to become a great city of spiritual culture (*seishin bunka*)," of which Catholicism had been a vital component for centuries.[88] The Catholics used an international religious celebration to demonstrate that their community enjoyed strong ties to the West. The festival of the four-hundredth anniversary of the arrival of Saint Francis Xavier to Japan, which took place on May 29 and 30, just weeks after the International Cultural City Construction Law was announced, involved more than three hundred thousand people, including numerous missionaries and representatives from the Vatican, who brought with them the holy relic of Xavier's arm.[89] The timing of the event was key to displaying the Urakami Catholics' support of the city's plan to emphasize its international character in its postwar image.

· · ·

By the start of the 1950s, Nagasaki had already made tremendous strides in recovery. The city population rose to 241,818 by 1950, surpassing its 1935 number by more than 15,000 and approaching the 1945 prebombing number of about 270,000.[90] As newly elected Mayor Tagawa Tsutomu proudly put it in a national journal in 1951, the city was building according to its relationship with Western culture, enhancing its history through maintenance of historical sites. A series of photos of these sites displayed the proud scenery of the city, including the Ōura Cathedral where French missionary Petitjean had "discovered" the hidden Christians, the shipbuilding facilities in the bay, for which the city had been famous since the latter part of the nineteenth century, and the so-called Glover mansion of Madame Butterfly.[91] By the mid-1950s, the Nagasaki Mitsubishi Shipbuilding Corporation had once again risen as a world-renowned shipbuilder. The company built a variety of ships, including cargo vessels, oil tankers, and passenger ships, but during the war, it also built all kinds of war vessels, including the famous *Musashi* battleship, completed in 1942. The plant carried its wartime profile into the postwar period, building its first battleship, the *Harukaze*, for the Japanese Self-Defense Forces in 1956, followed by many more, including the *Amatsukaze* (1965), the *Haruna* (1973), and the *Hatakaze* (1986). Royal figures toured the shipbuilding facilities during their visits to Nagasaki, including Emperor Hirohito in 1949 and 1969 and King Baudouin of Belgium in 1964.[92]

Initially, it seemed that the passage of the International Cultural City Construction Law benefited Nagasaki more than the Peace Commemoration City Construction Law did for Hiroshima. The law worked to the advantage of Nagasaki as a site of tourism. Despite its focus on international culture or perhaps because of it, by 1950 Nagasaki had become an attractive destination for people interested in seeing the city's atomic-bombing sites. What appealed to visitors was the combination—or juxtaposition—of natural beauty (of the bay and surrounding mountains), historical sites (such as Glover Park, Dejima, and Chinatown, all of which survived the bombing), and traces of the atomic bombing (such as the Urakami Cathedral ruins).[93] The main museums in the cities, the Nagasaki International Cultural Hall, which served in part as the atomic-bombing museum, and the Hiroshima Peace Memorial Museum, both completed in 1955, also became popular tourist destinations. In the first year of operation, Nagasaki's museum drew in 220,671 visitors to Hiroshima's 115,369. The activities of the two museums were similar, but Nagasaki's greater attraction could perhaps be attributed to—in addition to the city's juxtaposition of histories—its museum's goal to "promote international culture and contribute to the establishment of lasting peace." Hiroshima's museum, by contrast, focused exclusively on the "victim's sufferings as well as their struggle for peace."[94] By 1969, the average number of annual tourists to Nagasaki reached 2.5 million.[95]

Municipal officials received support for their vision from Emperor Hirohito. In May 1949, two weeks after the reconstruction law had passed in the Diet, the emperor traveled to Nagasaki to survey the destruction and view the progress of reconstruction, and, as local newspapers noted, even viewed the quality of the fish at the market. Nagasaki residents were ecstatic. One newspaper headline read, "*Banzai* Cheers of Peace Now Arise in the Atomic Land (*genshi no chi*)," describing the atmosphere of the emperor's visit, during which he charged the citizens of the city with the task of becoming the foundation of peace in the world.[96] The *banzai* cheer, which once expressed patriotism and solidarity with the military goals of the nation in the name of the emperor, now hailed peace at his encouragement. "I am sure it is painful, but I want you to endeavor," Hirohito said. "I am praying," he added, "that a happy and peaceful life comes to you all." He was "deeply touched" by the progress of reconstruction, especially the ability of Nagasaki to revive its past as an international cultural city and find meaning as a "symbolic city of peace and culture." In his parting words to the residents, Hirohito declared the significance of postwar Nagasaki: "Citizens. I am glad that today I was able to experience the revival (*fukkō*) of Nagasaki City and be exposed to the energetic appearance of the residents. I am overcome by sympathy for the sacrifice suffered by Nagasaki residents, but with [the sacrifice] as the cornerstone for the construction of a peaceful Japan, we must work for world peace and culture."[97] The emperor thus appropriated the sacrifice of Nagasaki as the sacrifice of the nation that "we" (*wareware*) must use as a foundation for peace, as he, like city officials since 1945, structured a narrative for Nagasaki that subsumed atomic memory within the municipal vision to revive its distant past.

COEXISTING IN THE VALLEY OF DEATH

American Soldiers and Nagasaki Residents during the Occupation

During the Allied occupation of Japan (1945–1952), the presence of American soldiers was part of the daily life of Nagasaki residents. During the first months of cohabitation, they learned that the former enemy who had destroyed their city with an atomic bomb would be, for better or worse, a lasting and vital force in the reconstruction process. After surrender, fear and anxiety about the occupation abounded in Japan, but as the soldiers flooded into the country in numbers beginning in mid-September, the demonic image of the Americans in popular media was soon replaced by warmer impressions. The transformation of Japanese perceptions of Americans happened in Nagasaki as well. Indeed, in the early months of the occupation, both American occupying forces and Nagasaki residents discovered in each other a common humanity that had been nearly erased by the ravages of war and the waves of propaganda, not to mention the atomic bombing. Amid the atomic ruins, they established a foundation that helped to bring about a successful reconstruction of the city.

Yet in the wake of the bombing, disconnect existed between the American occupiers and Nagasaki residents that was never entirely overcome. For the American occupiers, the war had lasted for three years and eight months, and they arrived in Japan "brimming with pride and self-righteous confidence."[1] For them, the bomb had ended the war and saved American lives that would have been lost in an invasion of Japan.[2] American soldiers in Nagasaki were well aware of the special nature of the city that they occupied, expressing pride in U.S. scientific superiority that had created the bomb and ended the war. The cavalier attitude of the American soldiers in Nagasaki toward everything "atomic" could not have been more different from the views of the locals who had lost their families and who lived with the traumatic aftereffects of the bomb, struggling also to overcome the exhaustion and despair of the fifteen-year war that had destroyed the country.[3] Even though the occupation was rife with tension and misunderstanding, residents have looked back on the period as a positive one compared to what had preceded it—years of war and the destruction of Japanese cities by conventional and atomic bombs.

The reconstruction and revival of Nagasaki began with the presence and the work of the occupation forces. The American soldiers witnessed firsthand how the bomb had turned the northern district of Urakami into the "Valley of Death," as they referred to it, and dedicated themselves to helping in various ways to rebuild the city. The first year of occupation in particular formed the bedrock on which Nagasaki officials and residents rebuilt the city, with cultural exchanges making the biggest impact. The cultural rapprochement between the United States and Japan fit into the orientation of Nagasaki as an international cultural city and left the greatest legacy of the occupation. The importation of new cultural activities, such as American square dancing and beauty pageants, combined with a renewed cultivation of preexisting international phenomena, such as Christianity, to highlight the urban identity of the city as a site of international culture. That is, in the end, the overwhelming presence of Americans in Nagasaki validated and encouraged the municipal vision of reconstruction.

The repaired relationship between the United States and Japan occurred on many levels, but on a human level it took place on the ground, between American occupying forces and Japanese people in war-devastated cities, through such social interactions as culture exchange activities. From serendipitous language lessons on the street that turned into highly popular newspaper columns to a carefully planned square-dancing program and an ad hoc beauty pageant, American occupation officials in Nagasaki worked together with municipal officials, media companies, and local community leaders to curate interactions between American soldiers and Japanese citizens, often to suit the goals of the occupation to demilitarize and democratize Japan. These leaders employed American culture in particular to encourage enthusiasm in order to promote those goals and implement change.

The six-and-a-half years of occupation in Nagasaki influenced reconstruction in a way that did not happen in Hiroshima. First, the Americans had a larger presence, both real and per capita, in Nagasaki. The occupation force, which during the first year reached more than twenty thousand personnel, were American soldiers who sheltered in the city and worked daily with and among the residents. The dormitories of certain local schools and many other buildings, including factories, were requisitioned as barracks or as offices for the occupying forces.[4] Social interactions promoted by American occupiers and local officials increased the contact among Nagasaki residents and the soldiers. The city as a whole experienced an unprecedented amount of engagement with and influence from a foreign culture, at least in the modern age. The timing made the encounter all the more significant. It was during the early, impressionable stage of the reconstruction period that the city began to rise from the ashes, reviving and shaping its urban identity to fit the needs of the present. The Allied military personnel in charge of the occupation of Hiroshima, on the other hand, were not based in the city, but rather in the nearby port city of Kure. From January 1946, British Commonwealth forces from England, Australia, and others took over the occupation of Hiroshima Prefecture, and just three thousand American soldiers remained in the occupation of that area.[5] While regional occupation officials were involved in the reconstruction planning in Hiroshima, the scale of interaction between American soldiers and Hiroshima residents was never equal to that in Nagasaki.

The first four years of occupation were perhaps most important for setting Nagasaki on a path to reconstruction. When the American occupiers arrived in September 1945, they found the city in ruins and its people full of anxiety about their occupiers and their future. The Second Division Marines of the Sixth Army who occupied the city until mid-1946 had their work cut out for them. Working closely with Japanese laborers, the Marines cleared rubble, gathered and destroyed Japanese weapons, and built structures. When they were not working, and after the initial anxiety had worn off, the Marines spent time interacting with and befriending local residents. Occupation soldiers were not always on their best behavior, and, occasionally, interactions led to violence or other unfortunate results, but most of the occupiers left a lasting and positive impact with their stay. When the occupation was transferred to the soldiers of the Eighth Army, the reconstruction and rapprochement that had begun with the Marines continued. From September 23, 1946, to April 2, 1949, Colonel Victor E. Delnore, a Lebanese American who became as popular and admired locally as General Douglas MacArthur was nationally, commanded the Nagasaki Military Government Team (NMGT) and supported municipal officials and their vision for reconstructing Nagasaki as an international cultural city. When Delnore left in 1949, he left behind a city well along the road to reconstruction and recovery and a municipal government emboldened to follow through with their vision.

Americans Arrive in the Valley of Death

George Weller, a respected press correspondent for the U.S. military during the Pacific War, was the first American into Nagasaki. He arrived on September 6, walked out of the train station, and looked in disbelief at the destructive force of the atom: "Walk in Nagasaki's streets and you walk in ruins." As he walked the flattened city over the next several days, Weller observed and described the destruction in his dispatches (which did not survive the military censors but are now a valuable source). On September 8, he traveled north from the Nagasaki Station area toward ground zero and described what he saw. "It is about two miles from the scene of the bomb's 1,500 foot high explosion, where the harbor has narrowed to the 250 foot wide Urakame [sic] River, that the atomic bomb's force begins to be discernible. This area is north of downtown Nagasaki, whose buildings suffered some freakish destruction but are generally still around. . . . The railroad station—destroyed except for the platforms, yet already operating normally—is a sort of gate to the destroyed part of the Urakame valley." Walking in the Urakami valley, Weller explored the devastated scene of ground zero accompanied by Japanese authorities. "The Japanese have heard the legend from American radio that the ground preserves deadly irradiation. But hours of walking amid ruins where the odor of decaying flesh is still strong produces in this writer nausea, but no signs of burns or debilitation." Deeper in the valley, he explored several "ruins which one would gladly have spared," as his guides pointed out to him "that the home area flattened by the American bomb was traditionally the place of Catholic and Christian Japanese." Weller concluded, however, that the destruction of the Mitsubishi factories along the river outweighed any necessity to preserve the valley of the Catholics.[6]

September 11 was a momentous day in Nagasaki. On that day, just thirty-three days after the atomic bomb decimated the city, three American ships docked in the city harbor. The Navy hospital ship *Haven* headed the mission to rescue and aid Allied POWs, and by September 23, around ten thousand POWs from all over Kyushu had been processed and boarded on the ships for evacuation.[7] Nagasaki residents viewed the foreign ships with some anxiety. As the local newspaper reported on September 14, "Nagasaki townspeople temporarily stared wide-eyed as they saw for the first time Allied ships flying the Stars and Stripes on their masts. But, there was not even the slightest bit of the chaos or disturbance that had been expected." In an oddly calm scene, the article continued, locals slowly backed away when they noticed American soldiers making an odd gesture to them with hand motions (the soldiers were waving hello). The newspaper was quick to state that its visitors came in peace. The colonel in charge of the POW mission reassured the reporter, via his proxy Major Arthur, "There is absolutely no need for the Japanese people to fear us. We ask you to continue your ordinary daily lives with a calm attitude." The reporter added that the colonel "wished for the once great country of Japan to again recover that greatness."[8]

But anxiety persisted at the thought of a massive presence of American soldiers. On September 14, nine days before the arrival of American occupation troops in Nagasaki Bay, the city government laid out ground rules for safety in the newspaper for its residents to keep in mind.[9] The heading gave the gist of the rules: "Refraining from Allied Occupation Forces in Nagasaki—Women, stay on your guard! Men, also stay indoors on the day [of their arrival]." The message included fifteen "general instructions," as well as ten warnings especially for women and children. Number nine warned, "When alone, avoid direct contact with the foreign soldiers. If the other party approaches you and speaks, do not panic, do not smile, especially women and children, and do not answer them in clumsy English." Number fourteen advised, "There will be planes dropping rations and other things on the foreigner barracks (formerly the POW camp), so if anything should fall on private houses, definitely turn it in to the police. Absolutely refrain from humiliating yourself by being scorned and having your home searched by the Allied soldiers just because you took some trifling thing." Women, "especially self-aware Japanese women, should not let down their guard." "Do not go outside in your underwear" (no. 2). "Give up being naked or half-naked while indoors and, of course, outdoors" (no. 4). And, "Women, do not pay attention if you are approached with 'Hello' or 'Hey,' or in broken Japanese."[10] The city government hoped for as smooth an occupation as possible by avoiding contact with the American soldiers because they did not expect the Americans to be compassionate.

When approximately twenty ships arrived at Nagasaki harbor at noon on September 23 and occupation forces stepped off the boats, a sigh of relief passed among local residents. It appeared that the Americans were not demons or beasts after all. On the following day, *Nagasaki shinbun* ran the headline: "Harmlessly and Cheerfully, [The Allies'] First Step after Landing in Nagasaki." The paper wrote how the "faces of the occupation soldiers who came ashore were cheerful, with a harmless expression, smiling as they pointed at the [Japanese] reporters and discussed something. There was no dismay and no countenance of concern and anxiety of the residents of Dejima District [where the ships were docked] or other residents on the roadside." The arrival of the American occupation forces that day was a "natural" and "peaceful first step ashore under the autumn sky."[11]

Despite the optimism of the newspaper, it could not have been overtly critical of the arrival of the Americans to Nagasaki in any case. From September 18, Allied occupation officials implemented the Press Code, which outlined the limitations of news coverage: "There shall be no false or destructive criticism of the Allied Powers" (point no. 3); "There shall be no destructive criticism of the Allied Forces of Occupation and nothing which might invite mistrust or resentment of these troops" (no. 4); "There shall be no mention or discussion of Allied troops movements unless such movements have been officially released" (no. 5).[12] The Press Code initiated a system of unofficial censorship, which was conducted through what one historian calls a "phantom bureaucracy" until September 1949, but it continued in various forms until the end of the occupation.[13] Censorship prevented most critical discussion of the atomic bombings by journalists, scholars, and city officials, not to mention the hibakusha, but American troops stationed in Japan were fair material for editorials, as long as they painted the occupiers in a positive light.

As the young soldiers disembarked in Nagasaki on September 23, they were led by a small brass marching band as they made their way to the American Occupation Office a few blocks away from the Ōura docks, near the Ōura Cathedral, which had survived the bombing. One soldier, a young lieutenant who had studied Japanese since high school, turned to a reporter and said in fluent Japanese with a smile, "*Sensō ni wa biiru to gasorin ga hitsuyō desu yo*" (Beer and gasoline are necessary for war). Later that day, curious about the destructive power of the atomic bomb and the damage it inflicted on Nagasaki, some military staff drove around the city ruins in trucks.[14] From September 11 to 24, the number of U.S. Marines arriving in Nagasaki totaled 18,611.[15] Almost immediately, residents grew accustomed to American jeeps in their city and settled into their daily lives with their new coresidents.

The task of the occupation forces was to ensure Japanese compliance with the terms of surrender and supervise local implementation of occupation policy. In other words, they were in Nagasaki to demilitarize and democratize the residents. Approximately 430,000 soldiers from the Sixth and Eighth U.S. Armies arrived in 1945 to occupy Japan, supported by contingents of U.S. Marines and Allied troops from Great Britain, Australia, Canada, and New Zealand.[16] The occupation of Nagasaki was initially delegated to the Second Marine Division, Fifth Amphibious Corps of the Sixth U.S. Army, which boasted a force of 21,469, including army and navy personnel, mostly living in barracks within the city.[17] As the occupation of Japan transitioned to the control of the Eighth Army, the forces of the Sixth Army were relieved of duty and sent home, with the last of the Second Division Marines leaving Nagasaki in July 1946.[18] The Marines had been deactivating forces in numbers each month after it became clear that large troop numbers were unnecessary to carry out the goals of the occupation. General MacArthur decreased U.S. Army numbers to 200,000 in 1946; 120,000 in 1947; and 102,000 in 1948—until 1949 when the Cold War brought a renewed urgency for a large U.S. military presence in East Asia.[19]

The first task of the occupation forces in 1945 was to demilitarize Japan. The Marines in Nagasaki called it "constructive destruction."[20] The Supreme Commander for the Allied Powers (SCAP), which was the American-led military government in charge of the occupation, ordered the Japanese government to collect, record, and destroy weapons and war vehicles, including large stashes that had been hidden in caves and elsewhere in preparation for the Allied invasion.[21] In late September, two Regimental Combat Teams (RCT-2 and RCT-6, totaling around eight thousand soldiers) patrolled Nagasaki and its surroundings for Japanese military supplies and to ensure that demolitions were happening according to surrender terms.[22] Marine demolition teams found a variety of weapons and vehicles, such as midget tanks, DUKWs (amphibious trucks), "baka bombs" ("idiot" bomb, small *kamikaze* plane piloted by a single person), five-man submarines, large-caliber defense guns burrowed into hillsides, and bomb-proof birds nests.[23] Smaller weapons and munitions were collected, inventoried, and given the "deep six" off the coast of Nagasaki.[24]

Other tasks of the occupation forces undertaken during the first months in Nagasaki focused on reconstruction, initially for the purposes of troop activities, but to the benefit of the residents as well. The Marine Engineer Group, aided by the Forty-Third Naval Construction Battalion (NCB), repaired and maintained roads, rehabilitated Dejima Wharf and the ship landing areas of the harbor, fixed petroleum tanks, cleaned up an athletic field near ground zero and built new ones to the west of the harbor where Mitsubishi factories were located, constructed a radio station at Ōmura, and built an airstrip in the Urakami valley. The 1298th Engineer Combat Battalion of the army repaired and maintained all major roads and bridges throughout the city and was tasked with building the Urakami airstrip less than a thousand feet from ground zero. "Atomic Field," as the small airport was called, took twelve days to build with the labor assistance of 350 Japanese workers and opened on October 11.[25] Most projects undertaken by the engineer groups employed at least 150 Japanese laborers per day. The Marine Observation Squadron-2 (VMO-2), flying mostly out of Isahaya Airfield about ten miles outside of Nagasaki, conducted reconnaissance and other flights, including spraying DDT to prevent diseases, such as typhus, among the Allied troops and the Japanese.[26] When the Eighth Army assumed exclusive responsibility of the occupation from 1946 and the U.S. Marines had left Nagasaki after the tasks of demilitarization and initial reconstruction were completed, the primary duties of the occupation forces were surveillance, policing, and reporting to SCAP on the status of occupation policies at the local level.[27]

Living and working within the city presented the same dangers to the occupation troops as to the Nagasaki residents. The Urakami valley remained a landscape of radioactive rubble for months after the arrival of the occupation forces, or as Marine Corporal David C. Milam later described it, the "entire area reeked of decaying human flesh buried under tons of debris."[28] John D. Bankston of the

Second Division Marines explained decades later why they called Urakami the Valley of Death: "As sad and grievously oppressive as it was to the eye and mind, the valley was appropriately named because it was profoundly clear that no one or any living thing escaped this sea of destruction in any form less than invisible micro bits." No photos or souvenir hunting was allowed under penalty of court-martial, although some Marines clandestinely did both. Bankston recalled, "Japanese swords and rifles made great souvenirs for the American troops."[29] As much as possible, though, occupation headquarters in Nagasaki kept the area near ground zero off limits until it had been cleaned up, which took several months. Milam recalled, the "stench of the dead was so overwhelming that you could never become accustomed to it. It even lingered in our clothes. Under the ruins of rubble and waste were body parts and burned flesh, the smell of which subsided only after the winter months offered Mother Nature's cleansing touch."[30] After they cleared off the corpses and the rubble, the Marines built a rifle range, a supply dump, and a football field on which they played a football game on New Year's Day, 1946.[31]

Physical destruction was not the only characteristic of the Valley of Death. Ground zero and surrounding areas were still radioactive when the first Marines arrived, and some servicemen contracted radiation poisoning from working in the rubble. Corporal Milam recalled,

> At first no one seemed to suffer from radiation poisoning. Since nothing was provided to protect us from contaminated air or soil, we assumed that we were not in danger. The first bizarre sign of illness that surfaced was sudden hair loss among the men. It came out in clumps. Then the divisional dentist began to see teeth that came loose without apparent cause. Next came severe headaches. Finally, several men died of leukemia. A friend of mine, Pfc. Morrow, suddenly started getting tired a lot. By the time he finally reported in to sick bay, he was so sick that he died within a few short weeks. Cancer of the blood was something that most of us had never heard of. . . . I felt at the time that Lady Luck had spared me, but years later, after medical tests, I discovered that the radiation had made me sterile.[32]

John Bankston, too, remembered in 2003, "We were never informed of the dangers of being exposed to ionizing radiation fallout, or ingestion of contaminated water in either beer or food." This was especially concerning, considering that the "outside water in the ground holding ponds was highly contaminated with fallout from the Bomb." On returning home to the United States, Bankston suffered constant illnesses that he thinks were due to his exposure to radiation in Nagasaki. He also lost two sons due to health conditions that in his mind resulted from

FIGURE 2.1.   The original caption reads, "NAGASAKI-11/10/45. Marine Capt. Charles D. Barret, Jr., 25, of 1437 44th St., N.W., Washington, D.C., pulls up to the finish line in last place in Nagasaki's first jinriksha [*sic*] race since Marines occupied city. Cheering from the sidelines, right, is Marine 1st Lt. John A. Porter, 28, of 207 South Date St., Toppenish, Wash."

Source: Official U.S. Marine Corps Photograph 138928, Reference Branch, U.S. Marine Corps History Division, Quantico, VA.

his own genes having been ionized.[33] Soldiers like Bankston were exposed to lethal amounts of radiation because occupation officials, if they even knew themselves, did not warn their men of the dangers lurking in the Valley of Death. The "Atomic Soldiers"—as the American personnel poisoned by radioactive fallout from U.S. military atomic and nuclear weapons came to call themselves— understood better than other occupying troops in Japan that victory in the Second World War came at a price.

Despite the dangers of living and working in a radioactive city, the Marines of the first year and the U.S. Army soldiers who came later made themselves at home. During their stay, they organized numerous events in order to brighten the general mood in the postatomic landscape, such as playing American sports and other activities that reminded them of home. Angelo Bertelli won the Heisman Trophy

FIGURE 2.2.   The original caption reads, "HUMAN RELICS IN ATOMIC BOMB AREA—Lieutenant (jg) Robert M. Inglis (MC), USNR, left and Lieutenant Commander Francis Shackelford, USNR, medical officer and intelligence officer, respectively, aboard the escort carrier USS CAPE GLOUCESTER, examine human bones in the atomic bomb area in Nagasaki. The victims were seared to powder skeletons in an instant." Photograph by Pfc. L. F. DeRyke, Nagasaki, Japan, September 16, 1945.

Source: Official U.S. Marine Corps Photograph 137433, Reference Branch, U.S. Marine Corps History Division, Quantico, VA.

in 1943 playing for Notre Dame, but on New Year's Day, 1946, he found himself quarterbacking in the "Atom Bowl," a football game between soldiers from the Second Marine Division that was played on Atomic Athletic Field No. 2 in Nagasaki. Bertelli headed the roster for the Nagasaki Bears, and the Isahaya Tigers featured "Bullet" Bill Osmanski, an NFL fullback who played for the Chicago Bears. In fact, both teams' rosters were packed with seasoned football players. The game grew out of an order from Major General LeRoy P. Hunt to boost morale among the troops who were longing for home during the holidays. Colonel Gerald Sanders, the division's recreation officer, organized the game with the help of Bertelli. The debris on Atomic Athletic Field No. 2 had been removed before the game, but broken glass from the atomic blast remained scattered on the field, so the organizers decided against a tackling game and made a rule of two-hand touch below the waist. A pep band aided the necessary fighting spirit. Despite Bertelli's valiant efforts, the Nagasaki Bears blew a 13–0 halftime lead, losing to Osmanski and the Isahaya Tigers, 14–13. Nagasaki citizens looked on curiously from a distance.[34] And while the American soldiers enjoyed their athletic pastime, occupation officials prohibited the Japanese from engaging in their athletic martial arts, namely kendō and jūdō, because of their association with militarism in the immediate past.[35]

Fitful Rapprochement

Rapprochement did not happen unilaterally or in a straight line, and it was not without its setbacks and challenges. Even so, in the first months of the occupation and resulting interaction between the former enemies, perceptions of one another changed dramatically. Public relations events were one of the ways both the American occupiers and Nagasaki city officials and residents mended wounds and repaired the demonized wartime perceptions of the other. While events like the Atom Bowl entertained the American soldiers, other events—some scripted and some serendipitous—encouraged harmony between the troops and the locals. The encouragement of interaction with the occupiers contrasted starkly with the fears of mid-September 1945, when the locals were advised to stay indoors and to avoid speaking broken English, not to mention the wartime propaganda that had depicted them as beasts. Considering the devastated state of Japan, and especially the destitution of Nagasaki, the practically overnight transformation of the perceptions of American soldiers and Japanese people is remarkable.[36]

In a scene that was common in Japan and occupied Germany, many soldiers lifted the spirits of children with candy and conversation, and in Nagasaki, some spent time with local children to study Japanese.[37] The soldiers often sat among groups of children, armed only with "phrase books" provided by the military and, later, the local newspaper's conversational column, as well as a desire to learn Japanese. After their "lessons" in Japanese, soldiers would be barraged by a bunch of kids yelling, "*tomodachi!*" (friend). Other children who were too shy to participate in the group Japanese lessons were easily won over by soldiers with sticks of gum or chocolate.[38] These encounters perhaps left a greater impression on the American Marines than on the Japanese people.

The American soldiers' interest in learning Japanese and their attempt to interact with the locals attracted the attention and encouragement of the Nagasaki townspeople. Soldiers appeared all over the city saying, "*ohayō*" (good morning), and carrying Japanese conversation dictionaries when they went shopping or out for a stroll.[39] The *Nagasaki shinbun* quickly picked up on the phenomenon and provided a special service to encourage the soldier who wanted to learn Japanese, as well as the Nagasaki resident who wanted to speak English. From October 15, 1945, the newspaper began printing the English Conversation Column. In order to facilitate Japanese (and English) learning as much as possible, the column appeared, respectively, in English, katakana English (phonetic Japanese syllabary used to indicate pronunciation in English), *rōmaji* Japanese (Roman-alphabetized Japanese), and Japanese script. The topic of the first lesson, for example, was "Asking the way" (*Michi wo tanunete* [*sic*]), which included fourteen useful phrases, such as the following:

> Excuse me, can you tell me how I go to Nagasaki Station? (イクスキュ ーズ　ミー　キャン　ユー　テル　ミー　ハウ　アイ　ゴ ー　ツ　ナガサキ　ステシヨン) Sumi masen ga, Nagasaki eki niwa do ittara yoroshu gozai masu ka. (済みませんが　長崎駅には どう行つたら　宜しう　こざいますか) [all *sic*].[40]

Topics ranged from everyday greetings to shopping and bartering and other types of encounters that were possible between American soldiers and locals.

The editors of the *Nagasaki shinbun* knew that communication was the key to mutual understanding, especially in the context of postatomic Nagasaki. They claimed that "Japan-U.S. goodwill starts first from words," and the English column they created encouraged harmonious interaction with the foreign occupiers: "Let's be friendly with the occupation soldiers."[41] Their message was well received—by American soldiers. On October 16, the day after the column's debut, American soldiers flooded the newspaper company with requests for more, leading the editors to conclude that the soldiers' desire for Japanese study was "marvelous." The English Conversation Column was an immediate hit. Within days, American soldiers could be spotted in groups reading the newspaper and practicing the phrases, the paper declaring with emphasis, "*Kaiwa ran dai ninki*" (conversation column immensely popular).[42] The soldiers suggested that the column be made easier to understand for local Japanese. "We understand this well, but isn't it difficult for Japanese people? . . . Please look into how you could make [the English column] easy for Japanese people to understand, too."[43] The paper responded the next day by including explanations of English terms for the locals.[44] The English column in the *Nagasaki shinbun* facilitated communication to a limited extent, but it never served the official purposes of either the U.S. military or the local government. The occupation authorities in Nagasaki hired many local residents to fill various positions, such as doctors and harbor engineers, but there was a mandatory prerequisite of English language skills.[45] Many Japanese who could speak English had hidden their skill during the war for fear of persecution or ostracism, but now they were being called on to act as liaisons to facilitate occupation and reconstruction, and many responded to the call.

Throughout the occupation, the Nagasaki Christians, especially the Urakami Catholics, fascinated the American soldiers. The physical characteristics of ground zero—its mysterious radioactivity and its destroyed cathedral—reminded the Japanese and Americans alike of how little they knew about the historic bombing. The Japanese Christians who had survived were a source of curiosity for the occupiers, and they also provided a sense of familiarity for the Christian Americans who found themselves living in a foreign country, many for the first time. Some Nagasaki residents were quick to point out to their occupiers that Christians lived in their city, and newspapers took an interest in the interaction between the American and Japanese Christians.

Some social events tapped into the history of Christianity in Nagasaki. On Sunday, October 28, 1946, American and Nagasaki Christians alike gathered at the Christian (Methodist) all-girls school, Kassui, for the first meeting between the two groups as a gesture of "cordiality that fosters peace and goodwill" between Japan and the United States. Religious leaders from both groups discussed the past and future of Christianity in Nagasaki, and as the meeting progressed, they "tore down the fence between nations (*minzoku*)." As the local newspaper reported on the event, national interests "melted away in the promise of Japan-U.S. goodwill, as sunlight filled the harmonious atmosphere of the room."[46] Some such events were especially significant for the experience of the Americans. Colonel Gerald Sanders organized a special program for Christmas, 1945, several days before the Atom Bowl, which featured a Japanese children's choir from the Kassui school singing carols in English for their American guests. Some battle-hardened soldiers remained wary of an event with so many locals in attendance, but as Sanders later recounted, even the weathered veteran soldiers "sat there and they cried and they just really found that all Japanese weren't bad that night." In the end, "People felt good and walked out, talking, arms around each other."[47] Christianity had provided common ground for many American soldiers to connect on a human level with Nagasaki residents, who just months earlier were believed to be subhuman.

The significance of Japan's most Christian city being occupied by a largely Christian nation was not lost on the local newspapers. In October 1945, a reporter for the *Nagasaki shinbun* approached a Marine chaplain from Philadelphia who was admiring the Ōura Cathedral near the occupation headquarters, and asked him a few questions. "As a Catholic clergyman," the reporter asked, "is it all the more deeply emotional for you that you have come to occupy Nagasaki, the singular Catholic holy land [in Japan], and not any other city in Japan?" The chaplain replied affirmatively and added that the resilience of the Catholics has inspired his own faith. "Yes," he explained to the reporter, "back home in America, I have heard the name of Japan's holy land of Nagasaki many times. . . . And now that I have come face to face with the city of Nagasaki and the vestiges of its transformation [as a result of the atomic bomb], it impels my human soul along the endless lonely journey (*ryoshū*)." The Japanese reporter bravely pressed the Marine on his feelings about how "your country used the atomic bomb that obliterated the cathedral of Urakami and many Catholic believers"; to which he replied, "As a clergyman, I cannot say anything about that question at the present." He answered instead how he saw the potential in Nagasaki's Christian history to become the bedrock on which Nagasaki residents and Japanese citizens more broadly could "build their future with deep love and understanding."[48]

Many Americans initiated contact with the local Christian communities. Some visited the Ōura Cathedral of their own accord, which had been built by French missionaries in the mid-1800s. On October 5, 1945, two American soldiers asked Father Hatanaka why the Angelus Bell of the cathedral was not ringing. They claimed it was "unbearably lonesome to be unable to hear the sound of the bell at a time when Nagasaki [was] setting out anew." The father explained that the clapper was broken and materials to repair it were hard to come by. The soldiers offered to fix it and did so on the following day; in boasting of their work, they said, "[we] wonder how long the sound of the bell will ring. We have done a truly good thing."[49] The survival of the Nagasaki Christians symbolized for some Americans the resilience of faith. The popular military magazine *Pacific Stars and Stripes* featured a story in early 1946 about the local Catholics, entitled "Christianity Survives Persecution, A-Bomb At Nagasaki." The correspondent, Clement S. McSwanson, wrote,

> There rises out of the debris of this flattened city the atom-butchered bulk of the Urakami Catholic church. Clinging firmly to a knoll overlooking Nagasaki, the shattered red brick stumps of what were once church steeples stab the bleak skyline as a grim reminder to visitors of the inferno loosed by this city's doom bomb. In the miles of rubble that surround the church 80 per cent of Urakami's 10,000 Christians perished.
>
> And yet amidst this scene of terror and death there is no spirit of resignation or defeat among the local clergy. Piles of tile roofing and other building material glisten in the sunlight. Like the sparrows that flit cheerfully about the mutilated place of worship, the Christians of Urakami are rebuilding. Father Francisco Nakada estimates it will take twenty years to reconstruct the once magnificent and imposing landmark. But the Christians of Nagasaki are a stubborn and exceedingly devout lot as history as shown.

The article also stated that the "atomic bomb fell in the heart of Nagasaki's christian [*sic*] settlement," and after mentioning the centuries of religious persecution endured by Nagasaki Catholics, added that the atomic bomb "came as another blow to a long persecuted church." But the Catholics of Nagasaki are resilient, and "show little sign of being squelched even by an atom bomb."[50] McSwanson, presumably a Christian himself, boasted of the invincibility of Christianity in the face of atomic destruction and admired the determination of the local parishioners to rebuild their church in the Valley of Death. However, the article put forth an atomic narrative shared by some Urakami Catholics and municipal officials: the bombing was almost a kind of natural disaster (the bomb "fell"), and it was a tragedy that happened to the Urakami community, not to Nagasaki as a whole.

One American advocated the power of square dancing to promote democracy, in addition to enhancing goodwill relations. By autumn 1946, SCAP officials in Nagasaki had well-established policies of engagement between the Americans and locals that built human ties, and they were willing to try anything as long as it supported democratization. In this spirit, Winfield P. Niblo arrived in September as chief education officer of the NMGT and introduced square dancing, seeking to enhance contact between Americans and Japanese. Although many Japanese were not accustomed to dancing with a partner, the dance became immensely popular practically overnight. According to a December 1946 report by the American military government in Nagasaki, American culture had come to the rescue: "The degree of appreciation and enjoyment which the Nagasakians apparently derive from this activity leads to the conclusion that they have been starving for this type of inexpensive, wholesome, community recreation so much needed to enrich the cultural life of the average Japanese community." By summer of 1947, approximately thirty to fifty thousand residents of Nagasaki Prefecture square-danced. Eventually, the dance spread over much of Japan thanks to a textbook on square dancing prepared by Niblo at the request of the Japanese Ministry of Education, in which he wrote, "Dancing people are happy people, and America is happy that this bit of American culture can bring a portion of happiness to Japan." SCAP officials viewed the quick spread of the American pastime as Japanese willingness to embrace American culture and as a representation of the potential for democracy to take hold in Japan.[51] Square dancing is still popular in Nagasaki Prefecture today.

As Americans extended a hand, Nagasaki townspeople made peace offerings of their own. In October 1945, officials from Nagasaki City; the Nagasaki Prefectural Association of Commerce, Industry, and Economics (Nagasaki-ken shōkō keizai kai); and the Nagasaki Prefectural Society for the Rectification of Goods (Nagasaki-ken busshi kōsei kyōkai) called on all Nagasaki citizens to donate Japanese souvenirs to be gathered and given collectively to the occupation forces as a

FIGURE 2.3. Winfield P. Niblo, chief education officer of the Nagasaki Military Government Team, receiving a farewell bouquet and departing Nagasaki on May 28, 1948.

FIGURE 2.4. Miss Nagasaki beauty pageant, April 1946, which was referred to as the "Miss Atom Bomb contest" in *Pacific Stars and Stripes*, May 16, 1946. Takahara Itaru appears in the center, holding a camera with tripod.

"bouquet of peace." This was just one of many souvenir drives in the city. Even though people were destitute and had little to donate, they gave. But city officials were not picky either. They reassured citizens that almost anything could pass as a Japanese souvenir: clothing, lacquer ware, dolls, footwear, embroidery, glassware, tea sets, postcards with pictures of Nagasaki, or anything else that would serve as a memento. The point was the gesture. Nagasaki residents supposedly would benefit, too, as city officials claimed they would offer a "fair price" for each item.[52] Mementos for the American soldiers of their time in the city represented one method that Nagasaki city officials devised to promote reconciliation.

Pageants, like square dancing, were considered a quintessential piece of American culture that promised to liven the mood of the city while spreading democratic ideas. In April 1946, three major newspaper companies—Nagasaki shinbunsha, Nishi Nippon shinbunsha, and the Mainichi shinbunsha—sponsored and worked closely with municipal officials and the American military headquarters in Nagasaki to organize the first ever Miss Nagasaki pageant. They hoped that the event would "brighten" the city and sought entries from women who might symbolize "Nagasaki rising up from the ruins and who will revive the desolate spirits of the citizens."[53] A classified ad in the *Mainichi shinbun* on April 17 called to Nagasaki women between the ages of seventeen and twenty-five to participate in this rare opportunity to demonstrate the city's budding recovery. Winners would receive a prize. The pageant took place over three days from April 29 at the Takarazuka Dance Hall in the southern part of the city, several kilometers away from ground zero.[54] At the finale on May 1, a panel of ten judges, which included three U.S. Marines, unanimously decided the winner, Yamamura Yōko, as well as the runners up, Kozaka Fumiko, Shimonaga Yoshiko, and Yoshida Nobuko.[55]

Although the beauty pageant may have been well intentioned, it reveals the cracks in the cultural activities enjoyed by the American soldiers and the Nagasaki residents at the time, as well as the nature and reality of the occupation more generally. Yamamura Yōko may have been the first ever Miss Nagasaki, but to the Marines and other soldiers in occupied Japan she became "Miss Atom Bomb." For the occupiers, the contest was not simply the Miss Nagasaki pageant, but rather a beauty contest to find the most beautiful woman in a city destroyed by an atomic bomb. The *Pacific Stars and Stripes* gleefully reported on May 16: "For once, the Marines and the Japanese are in accord" because they decided on the "brunette bombshell" (Yamamura) as "Miss Atom Bomb of 1946."[56] Because occupation soldiers considered everything in Nagasaki "atomic," they viewed the winner in this way, seemingly oblivious to the fact that they were linking female beauty and the horror of the atomic bomb.

The media companies that had organized the event were unaware of the designation of Miss Atom Bomb because for them it was always the Miss Nagasaki pageant. They saw it as a way for the city to demonstrate that the spirits of the residents had not been broken. Takahara Itaru, the *Mainichi shinbun* photographer who covered the pageant, had fond memories of the event, largely because the woman he had asked to enter, Yamamura, took first place, but also because the Marine photographer's flash camera impressed him.[57] The contest was never advertised or discussed in terms of the atomic bombing, and residents presumably never saw the article in *Pacific Stars and Stripes*. Perhaps the residents' view of the American soldiers as beneficent occasionally blinded them to the fact that it was a military occupation. The designation in Japanese as "Miss Nagasaki" suggested that Nagasaki residents wanted to make the occupiers feel at home by proposing a Western-style beauty contest. In fact, the event seemed to entertain the Americans more than it did the locals.

The use of the words "atom" or "atomic" to describe a Nagasaki beauty and residents' later shock at the usage speaks to the politics of words, privilege, and narrative. Nagasaki residents, too, used the adjective "atomic" to label parts of the city, buildings, and events; the local newspaper often referred to Nagasaki as the "atomic" city and occasionally to the residents as "atomic" citizens. For the people of Nagasaki, however, the word was used as a lexical marker of the tragedy of the bombing—its destruction and the suffering of the survivors—not for its supposed beauty. The Americans used the word as a marker of pride in American science, which from their perspective had brought victory and peace, indeed something of which to be proud. Despite the intentions of the organizers, both American and Japanese, the privilege of the soldiers to use "atomic" and "beauty" as interchangeable ideas represented the ultimate victor's justice. The pageant and other such cultural exchanges were crucial to social reconstruction, but they indeed maintained the victor-defeated relationship between the United States and Japan.[58]

The 1946 pageant exemplified the victor-defeated relationship perhaps more than any other cultural activity during the occupation: the contestants were all Nagasaki women, whereas the audience were largely American military men.[59] Moreover, the pageant took place in a building that by early 1946 had already become a notorious spot where the American occupiers could pay money to interact with local women. Before the beauty contest, the Takarazuka Dance Hall served as a site of more direct contact between American occupiers and Japanese women from late 1945, when a local woman named Kogano Tomiko opened it and hired local young women to dance and otherwise fraternize with the young American men freshly arrived in the city.[60] Shortly after the start of the occupation, SCAP began heavily regulating interactions between American soldiers and Japanese women, banning fraternization throughout Japan from March 1946 through September 1949.[61] During that time, public displays of affection between American soldiers and Japanese women would result in a charge of disorderly conduct against the soldier.[62] The Miss Nagasaki contest, a public event sanctioned by American military personnel in Nagasaki, provided the occupiers an approved—and thus controlled—interaction between American men and Japanese women. Whereas earlier the young American men might have visited the dance hall for physical interaction with local women, the beauty contest placed the women on display just out of reach but still allowed the men to objectify them from a distance. The 1946 contest thus added a layer of public presentation to the sexualized nature of the victor-defeated relationship between the United States and Japan during the occupation.[63]

Despite the efforts of the Nagasaki officials and American occupiers to dispel fear and misunderstanding, such feelings persisted. Even if cultural exchange activities helped repair mutual perceptions overall, the feelings of residents were always secondary to those of the occupiers. Residents were often reminded of the reality that the Americans resided in the city as part of a military occupation, not as a cultural exchange program. That is, the American troops were not there simply to enjoy themselves and share their time with Nagasaki residents; this was a military occupation with goals that often made interaction between occupiers and residents, in a word, complicated. Nagasaki townspeople and the American occupation forces indeed found a rhythm in their daily routines over the first year, but the reality of having once been enemies never disappeared. City officials warned locals via the newspapers to behave in the manner of an occupied country and avoid transgressing dangerous lines. During the first year, occasional thefts of Allied supplies, such as clothes and cigarettes, prompted occupation officials to begin body searches of pedestrians and searches of the homes of suspects by Military Police because mere possession of Allied goods was illegal. By August 1948, the frequency of thefts had risen to the point that American officials warned, via the newspapers, "If [we] discover [someone] stealing [they] will be shot to death at once."[64]

Amid the gift giving and the square dancing, some Nagasaki residents did not feel elated, and many found the presence of the occupiers a taxing experience. Among reported incidents involving American servicemen, by the end of the occupation nearly two hundred violent crimes had been committed against Japanese residents, including beatings and knife attacks.[65] Both sides instigated violent clashes to be sure, but some American soldiers' violent assaults of Japanese women, such as rape, and careless driving of jeeps that led to the vehicular manslaughter of residents tended to strain relations.[66] American insensitivity to the bereaved residents was also shocking. Shortly after arriving in Nagasaki, the American troops began clearing debris and building roads for official purposes. A young student who had survived the bomb, Uchida Tsukasa, witnessed the work: "The Americans brought bulldozers to clear up the Urakami area which had been hit by the atomic bomb. There were still many dead under the rubbish. Despite that the Americans drove their bulldozers very fast, treating the bones of the dead just the same as sand or soil. They carried the soil to lower places and used it to broaden roads there. A person who tried to take a picture of what they were doing was approached by the military police. The MP pointed his gun and threatened to confiscate any picture taken." Uchida noted, "Because of the Press Code there was no possibility for us to write about such incidents. Newspapermen did not tell about them and they did not appear even in the readers' columns."[67]

Still other interactions further reminded residents that their American neighbors had official business. During the occupation, Nagasaki residents came to know two kinds of American occupiers: soldiers of the occupation forces and the personnel of the Atomic Bomb Casualty Commission (ABCC), the agency charged with collecting data about the atomic bombing. The ABCC began in 1947, after a survey team of American scientists who visited in December the previous year recommended that the commission undertake research on the effects of the bomb, especially radiation, related to cancer and other illnesses. The ABCC conducted its first research in Hiroshima in April 1947, studying the hematology of survivors. In January 1948, the commission continued with additional funding and research personnel from the Japanese Ministry of Health and Welfare. The permanent ABCC building was completed in Hiroshima in November 1950. In Nagasaki, the commission began its research in July 1948 at the city health center and, by July 1950, had its own facilities. The ABCC continued research in Hiroshima and Nagasaki until 1975, when the Radiation Effects Research Foundation (RERF) succeeded it.[68]

Cooperation with the ABCC was mandatory for those who were selected through a survey, and the experience left an unfavorable impression on many survivors who felt that they were treated as curiosities in a laboratory. City officials on order from Tokyo encouraged the cooperation of the hibakusha "for the good of society." As historian Takemae Eiji puts it: "Informed consent was not on the agenda, and neither the authorities nor the subjects were told the purpose of the experiments."[69] The work of the ABCC was initially impeded by its secrecy during the occupation, the constant turnover of American scientists, and the attitude of Hiroshima and Nagasaki residents who did not trust the commission.[70] The ABCC never provided medical treatment to hibakusha but only tested them, which undercut the image of the Americans as beneficent occupiers and underscored the insensitivity of the occupation and the Japanese government toward survivors.[71]

The rationale behind the ABCC policy of not treating the hibakusha emerged out of an understanding of the survivors that in some ways mirrored the stance of the Japanese government. First, officials in the ABCC thought that the hibaku-sha did not deserve special treatment over the many other people around Japan suffering from the result of the war. As ABCC director Grant Taylor explained to the Hiroshima hibakusha Kikkawa Kiyoshi, who had challenged the ABCC about its no-treatment policy, "I sympathize with you, but you are not the only ones who suffered effects of the war. Therefore there is no cause to render special aid to the citizens of Hiroshima."[72] Second, and perhaps a bigger concern for the Americans, was, as M. Susan Lindee has argued, that to provide such treatment would also appear as acceptance of the responsibility for the atomic bombings and an attempt to "atone" for them. Like the Americans, the Japanese govern-ment, by refusing recognition of the hibakusha as a class of war sufferers distinct from the general public, found a useful way to avoid taking responsibility, too.[73] To take responsibility for the hibakusha, the Japanese government thought, would only lead down a road toward discussions of war responsibility. Such political con-siderations prevented the establishment of a medical system for the treatment of hibakusha until 1957.

· · ·

Despite the complications and contradictions of reconciliation in the wake of the atomic bomb, the work of the American forces in Nagasaki and the everyday in-teraction between occupier and occupied created the basis for successful recon-struction. John D. Bankston looked back on his time in the city, recalling that the "Japanese looked at us with suspicious eyes for some time, and at the same time we were curious and very cautious with them. Both sides showed skepticism as we were greeting each other in a conservative manner." But things quickly changed. "After a short period of time all this changed and we became friendlier to one another. The people of Nagasaki began to realize why we were there and they started to show trust in our daily presence with them. Each passing day it was easy to tell that both parties were becoming more comfortable with one an-other."[74] The American occupiers perhaps found the reconciliation more pro-found than did their Japanese counterparts, who were likely more preoccupied with overcoming the destruction of war and the difficulties of reconstruction. The rapprochement was due in large part to the cultural exchanges, which did much to liven the first six-and-a-half years of reconstruction, when the military occu-pation was an abiding reality for residents.

The American occupiers supported and bolstered the physical and social re-construction of Nagasaki. Shortly after arriving to Nagasaki, Delnore greeted the residents of the prefecture on News Year's Day, 1947, with a hopeful wish for reconstruction. "New Year's Day," he declared, "is a time when we should have a mental housecleaning and remove cobwebs from our minds and dedicate ourselves to worthwhile . . . achievements for the coming year. We should now firmly resolve that the end of the ensuing year shall find [you] much improved as individuals, as families, as communities and as a nation." Nagasaki, he added, "because of its illustrious history and because it has been Japan's gateway to the rest of the Orient [should] take the lead in building a finer and better Japan."[75] Although he had arrived in Nagasaki only three months earlier, Delnore's greeting captured the mood of the city and the direction it had taken since shortly after the bombing. The Americans and Nagasaki residents had settled into an amicable cohabitation, a mood which intensified during Delnore's tenure.

American personnel within and outside of Nagasaki emboldened city officials in their drive to implement a vision of reconstruction that drew on the city's international history. Although Nagasaki did not receive a message from General MacArthur in August 1947 for the two-year anniversary, it did receive one from Colonel Delnore, who praised Nagasaki for its ability to connect to the West.[76] Nagasaki residents "have grasped the significance of western countries in the past, and they should restore this distinctive characteristic of old. I am overcome with gratitude," he continued, that the residents of Nagasaki are exerting "astonishing efforts" to this end. "The exotic atmosphere and beauty of Nagasaki City have long been greatly extolled by western poets and authors. More than any other city in Japan, [Nagasaki] embodies the honor, charm, and beauty of your country." Delnore concluded by assuring Nagasaki residents that American occupation troops would do all in their power to support reconstruction efforts.[77] In an address sent to the people of Nagasaki for the third anniversary of the bombing, General MacArthur said he was pleased to see that residents had produced "exceedingly excellent results in the reconstruction of Nagasaki City."[78] In the minds of city officials, having received nods of approval from the American occupiers, their vision was right on track.

Delnore and other American military personnel in Nagasaki also expressed support for the hibakusha and concern for their plight. For his part, Delnore invested himself in Nagasaki's present struggles as well as in the city's future, understanding that the story of the atomic bombing needed to be openly presented and discussed in order to move forward as a city. In March 1947, Delnore wrote to American occupation censors in Fukuoka in support of publishing two accounts of the bombing by survivors, *Masako taorezu* and *Chichi no omoide o kataru*. He wrote, "We of the Nagasaki Military Government Team feel that publication of these books . . . is of importance in these post-war years." Closing his letter, he emphasized, "For us to properly realize the significance of the atomic bomb, to experience vicariously the feelings that so many thousands of Japanese people experienced is desirable in these propitious times."[79] Open discussion of the bombing held the potential not only to allow Nagasaki as a city to move forward during its reconstruction but also to enlighten the world at the moment of the dawn of the atomic age.

Through his dedication to Nagasaki and its residents, Delnore left an impression as the greatest foreign benefactor in the city's recent history. When the occupation ended and Delnore departed, among the many farewell gifts he received, such as a scrapbook with letters of gratitude for his work, photographs, and other memorabilia, the city showed their gratitude and commemorated his tenure by naming a street after him: Derunoa dōri. While the street was not officially changed to his name by the city government until 2011, an unveiling ceremony for Derunoa dōri took place before he departed in mid-1949. City officials were perhaps especially grateful to Delnore because, from the moment he arrived in late 1946, he supported the municipal vision of reconstruction, which officials had been developing since before the first ships of American troops landed at Ōura Harbor. The work and presence of the American occupation helped catalyze the city's revival as it emboldened municipal officials who envisioned rebuilding Nagasaki as an international cultural city.[80]

Local community leaders were also key to ensuring that the municipal vision took root. Nagai Takashi, who became a representative for the Urakami Catholics soon after the war, promoted the reconstruction of Nagasaki as a venture of international culture. Municipal and national officials employed Nagai's image in discussions of Nagasaki's bombing and reconstruction, with officials such as Kino Fumio declaring that he was a perfect exemplar for an international cultural city. Thanks to Nagai's books, Kino said in 1950, "the cultural nature of Nagasaki is being conveyed forcefully and widely." Kino further declared that when others finally emerge in Nagasaki who rank with Nagai and "bathe in the true limelight of the world in science and art, or intellectually and politically," only then can Nagasaki be said to have achieved the "prestige (*menboku*) of an international cultural city."[81] Members of the National Diet evoked Nagai's name during the May 1949 meetings when they passed the special-city reconstruction laws of Nagasaki and Hiroshima, and other legislators agreed that Nagai was exemplary because of his contributions to the reconstruction of Nagasaki.[82] Indeed, Nagai came to play a central role in much of the discourse surrounding the bombing and reconstruction.

3

THE "SAINT" OF URAKAMI

Nagai Takashi and Early Representations of the
Atomic Experience

Nagai Takashi (1908–51) was, perhaps, the most unlikely representative voice of
Nagasaki to emerge in the early postwar years. He was a Catholic, a historically
oppressed minority in Japan for centuries, including within Nagasaki, and he was
terminally ill with cancer since before the bombing. But he also seemed a natural
choice. As the popular memory of the bombing in local and national narratives
became localized as an Urakami tragedy, the Catholic leader who lost his wife in
the bombing, lay dying of cancer, and lived in the bombed-out region defined
for many, especially those outside Nagasaki, the suffering of the city as a whole.
Furthermore, municipal officials found Nagai useful because he promoted an
atomic narrative and a vision of reconstruction that complemented, and at times
mirrored, their own. Among all of the figures to emerge in the first years of postwar Nagasaki, no single person affected the reconstruction of the city and shaped
its atomic narratives on local, national, and international levels as did Nagai.

Nagai's leadership among the Urakami Catholics came in three stages. First,
during the Second World War, Nagai represented for his community a paragon
Japanese Catholic, who served both God and the emperor by dedicating himself
to the war effort; on his return from military service in China, he became the
parishioner representative. Second, from 1945 to 1947, Nagai led the Catholic
survivors into recovery from the atomic bombing, providing for them an explanation for the bombing that drew on their religious beliefs and gave meaning
to the loss of their loved ones and their personal suffering. Third, from 1948 to
1951, Nagai acted as the representative voice for Urakami and the city more
generally, by publishing prolifically; explaining the atomic experience to local,

5

national, and international media; and making large monetary donations to the city to aid in the reconstruction. During the last phase especially, Nagai's writings and persona supported the municipal vision of reconstruction.

A confluence of circumstances allowed Nagai to rise as the representative of Nagasaki. Nagai benefited from the occupation being primarily an American venture as Christianity increased in importance, strengthening his position as a Catholic and giving visibility to his religious rhetoric. The focus on reconstruction throughout his books, which encouraged community revival, religious themes such as forgiveness of one's enemies, and the recovery of a historic Nagasaki in which Catholicism played a part, served the purposes of local and national politicians, as well as the American occupation, not to mention the Nagasaki Catholic community. Nagai's ruminations on the relationship between God, destruction, and revival also advanced the image of the church in Japan. Nagai exerted efforts in support of recovery through literary and monetary means, drawing national and international attention to the history of Nagasaki, especially its Christians, its plight among the other war-torn cities in Japan, and its desire to fully recover from the tragedy and become a voice of peace. Nagai's point of view as a witness of the bombing, combined with the postwar benefits of his religious position, propelled him to the top of the literary world when the nation thirsted for information regarding the atomic bomb.

Nagai's Catholic interpretation of the atomic bombing became the central motif of his postwar writings. Nagai, drawing inspiration from Mark 8:34 in the Bible, thought that because God loves the Urakami Catholics, they had to walk in the footsteps of Jesus Christ as martyrs for a greater cause, a sacrificial lamb to end the war.[1] Nagai developed this interpretation shortly after the bombing, but his public declaration of it from November 1945 was timely in that it provided comfort to his fellow Catholic survivors, who struggled to make sense of the destruction of their community in the face of anti-Christian sentiments among townspeople. In the weeks and months after the bombing, some in Nagasaki declared that the atomic bomb that decimated the Urakami valley exemplified divine punishment because the Catholics had not made sufficient pilgrimage to Suwa Jinja, the main Shinto shrine in the southern part of the city. In response to this claim, Nagai declared that it was not divine punishment, but, rather, the love of God that directed the bomb to Urakami.[2] In this way he sought to give meaning to the suffering of the Urakami Catholics. Appearing in his best-selling books from 1948, this interpretation drew the attention of national and international readers, not to mention the American occupiers, and helped shape both the Christian image of ground zero and Nagasaki's place in popular memory more generally.

Within months of publishing his first books in 1948, Nagai, the "saint" of Urakami as some chose to call him, enjoyed overwhelming national and international popularity. Letters of admiration and support poured in to his small hut from actors, community leaders, government officials, and everyday citizens from all over the world, including some American occupation officials and the Vatican. The National Diet took note of Nagai, commending him for his "contributions to reconstruction" and even referencing him and his writings in discussions of postwar issues such as war orphans and the tax code. But not everyone was a Nagai fan. Some argued that Nagai deserved no special attention because everyone in Japan was suffering. The Communist Party criticized members of the National Diet for co-opting Nagai's fame for their own personal gain by attempting to whitewash the memory of the government's militaristic past.

Nagai embodied the Christian image of ground zero. He was a devout Catholic and leader in the Urakami community who suffered the atomic experience and dedicated himself for the revival of the city. Through his writings, he interpreted the bombing as an Urakami sacrifice, not a Nagasaki one. Nagai was always careful to write "Urakami" when discussing ground zero and the atomic destruction, even if decades later translators have replaced the word with "Nagasaki."[3] Urakami figured in all of his best-selling books as a historical center of Christian martyrdom and sacrifice, the atomic bombing having been one more instance on that timeline. His books outsold all others from Nagasaki, creating a popular discourse on the bombing that drew on his voice above others. In the eyes of local, national, and international media and publishers, as well as municipal and national officials, not to mention the American occupiers, Nagai spoke for Nagasaki's atomic experience. Thus, in their treatment of Nagai, these groups enhanced the Christian image of ground zero and, as a result, encouraged the disparity between Nagasaki and Hiroshima in popular memory.

Nagai Takashi as a Community Leader in War and Suffering

Nagai Takashi was not born in Nagasaki. Nor was he originally Catholic. He was born in 1908 in Matsue City, Shimane Prefecture, where his ancestors had lived for generations in the region of Izumo, or as Kataoka Yakichi once wrote, "the land of the foundation myths of Japan."[4] Izumo is home to one of the most historically and spiritually important Shinto shrines in Japan, the Izumo Taisha, and Nagai's father Noboru was a devout worshipper at the shrine.[5] Growing up in Izumo and in a strictly Shinto household gave Nagai a solid patriotic foundation, which later underlay his encouragement of fellow Catholics in Nagasaki to embrace the cause of the nation in the war. Nagai left his hometown at the age of twenty to attend medical school at Nagasaki University, located in Urakami. On a hill near the medical school stood the grand Urakami Cathedral, which mes-merized Nagai with its red bricks and the sound of its Angelus bells. When offered a room for rent, he moved to the second floor of the house of the Moriyama family, which stood directly in front of the cathedral.[6] The Moriyamas were direct descendants of the hidden Christians (*kakure Kirishitan*), Japanese Christians who took their faith underground after enduring persecution from the early 1600s and practiced their faith in secrecy for almost 250 years. The Mori-yama family had been the *chōgata* (keeper of the calendar), the most important task of Catholic leaders during the centuries underground.[7] While living with the Moriyama family, Nagai learned the history of the Urakami Catholics and was drawn to Christianity.

When he was drafted into the military as a medic in 1931 after the Manchu-rian Incident, the young daughter of the Moriyama household, Maria Midori, sent Nagai a book entitled *Kōkyō yōri* (Catholic catechism) in a care package. Nagai received Midori's gift under the watchful eye of his commanding sergeant, who was immediately suspicious of the book and sent it to be examined for subver-sive ideas. Three days later the sergeant returned the catechism to Nagai, saying, "This is a Christian book, so there are many areas in it that make no sense, but because it does not seem particularly socialist, I guess you can hang on to it. How-ever, if you have time to read stuff like this book of a Western God, read the Im-perial Rescript to Soldiers (*Gunjin chokuyu*)." Nagai had already memorized the *Gunjin chokuyu*, so he decided to devote his time to studying the Catholic cate-chism.[8] It was on the battlefield in China studying the principles of Christianity that Nagai began to understand the essence of Catholicism and decided to em-brace the Christian God. On his return to Nagasaki, he converted to Catholicism.[9] On June 12, 1934, Nagai was baptized a Roman Catholic and received the name "Paulo."[10] Two months later in August, Paulo Takashi married Maria Midori, thereby becoming a member of one of the most important Catholic families in Nagasaki.[11]

Nagai rose in the community, becoming a role model of an Urakami Catholic who balanced the duties of a devout believer and a patriotic subject. After Nagai was again drafted into the military as a medical officer (lieutenant) when Japan entered all-out war with China in July 1937, he sent letters back home addressed to the entire community and meant for publication in the *Katorikukyō hō* (Catholicism bulletin), a bimonthly publication that kept the parish informed on religious matters and national news, as well as international Catholic affairs. In the letters he stressed the importance of balancing the duties of an imperial sub-ject and a Roman Catholic. On August 29, 1937, when his group was fighting near the Great Wall, he wrote a letter that was published in the September 15 issue of the *Katorikukyō hō*. In it, he encouraged the Catholics to exert all efforts possible for the war. The battles in China were gruesome, he wrote, and "the corpses of Chinese soldiers" lay everywhere. He shared, "Tomorrow we are finally going over the Great Wall and advancing the attack. I'm glad."

He then put the war in the context of the role of Nagasaki:

> I've mentioned the bombing of Tianjin [in previous letters], but the aerial bombing of that city was actually quite tragic. You had to see it to believe it.[12] I did not take pleasure in Tianjin's condition, but looking back, my heart shivered (*samukunatta*) when I thought what if Nagasaki were bombed. . . .
>
> I want Nagasaki to more seriously build its air defenses. There is nothing more pitiful than a city with no air-defense facilities.
>
> First, you must actively build (*ken'nō*) patriotic airplanes to secure Japan's command of the air. Then comes building air-defense facilities.
>
> Everyday, planes come and the sounds of the Great Wall being bombed ring on. We all raise our hands and shout, "*banzai!*" It feels great. I wish I had a plane.[13]

In retrospect, the letter conveyed an eerie premonition of the city's fate in 1945, but Nagai's point was to encourage his community to mobilize for the war effort, build airplanes, and defend the homeland. Although Nagai was a fervent Catholic, patriotism for his Shinto homeland pervaded his letters from the battlefront. Nagai's patriotism was not atypical of Japanese Christians, his letters from the battlefront echoing the calls of Catholic leaders in Nagasaki to be patriotic.

He spoke of the patriotic duty of the Urakami Catholics again in a New Year's greeting written from Nanjing in December 1937, after the Japanese Imperial Army had occupied and devastated the city from the thirteenth of that month. Although Nagai acknowledged years later that he "saw all kinds of crimes being calmly performed on the battlefield" in China, the mood of his letter was cheery.[14] "I respectfully wish you all a Merry Christmas and a Happy New Year from the battlefield," he wrote. "We have greeted this year along with grave current events, but especially this year Japan will soar. This is the perfect opportunity for Japanese Christians to display that essence. As I pray for the activities of everyone on the home front, I, too, will render the duty of a warrior of Japan and repay the kindness of the emperor."[15] Nagai reveals here that the duties of believer and subject are compatible, but separate, as he prays for the Catholics but fights for the emperor. Furthermore, Nagai encouraged his fellow Urakami Catholics to see themselves not simply as subjects, but as "warriors of Japan."

Although Nagai's letters conveyed a proud and cheery sense of unbreakable patriotism, the reality was of course grim. Three years of encountering the violence of war in China shaped his views of death. He witnessed bloody battles and treated countless wounded soldiers, Japanese and Chinese alike; faced with the daily reality of war and death, Nagai turned to the Bible for guidance. He always carried with him a 1910 copy of Emil Raguet's translation of the New Testament (he thought the newer translations had too many errors), and he repeatedly read a particular passage for comfort: "We all face death for the Lord, and through it we are akin to the sacrificial lamb."[16] Nagai wrote years later that during his time in China he realized that "death is never coincidence. It is according to the Providence of God (*Tenshu*)."[17] Nagai later evoked this view of death to give meaning to the atomic bombing.

After he returned from China in 1940, Nagai settled back into a routine at home. He had returned to Nagasaki on March 5 as a decorated soldier, having received the Order of the Rising Sun for his bravery in China, and he continued to wear his military uniform to work at the hospital to show his patriotism and promote military preparedness among his community.[18] He continued his work as a radiologist at Nagasaki University Medical School. Because of wartime scarcity, X-ray film was in short supply and he could no longer take indirect photographs of patients, but he could also not stop his work. Nagai continued working with X-rays, exposing his body to dangerous amounts of radiation, and in May 1945, he began feeling ill.[19] In June, Nagai was given three years to live. His colleagues estimated that he had contracted leukemia as early as 1940, since he had been living with the pain for five years.[20] Nonetheless, Nagai continued to teach at the university and treat patients.

During the war, Christians all over Japan sought to prove their dedication to the Japanese war effort to allay doubts surrounding their patriotism. Even so, Christians, including decorated war veterans such as Nagai, were under constant suspicion from their fellow citizens and the government of being American sympathizers. In July 1945, the military ordered Catholic leaders to report to army headquarters in Nagasaki for a meeting to address their loyalty to the nation. Military officials had long suspected Japanese Christians of being fifth columnists, but they grew more concerned once American planes began bombing the main islands in late 1944. At the meeting in July 1945, officials berated the Catholics and demanded they report to police headquarters immediately if they discovered any Americans landing.[21] Nagai and the Catholics never had the opportunity to warn of the arrival of the Americans to Urakami on August 9, 1945, when the atomic bomb decimated the only place in Nagasaki that the Japanese military suspected would be sympathetic to the Americans. Even amid the atomic destruction, Nagai's patriotism manifested, when, on the evening of the bombing while he and his medical staff were treating the waves of wounded that flooded their relief station, he took the bandage from his own bleeding forehead and used it to draw a red circle in the middle of a large white cloth. He planted the makeshift flag of the rising sun with a bamboo pole on the hilltop above the university which overlooked the flattened and burning landscape of Urakami.[22]

When the war ended on August 15 and less than two thousand of the ten thousand Urakami Catholics remained alive, the community turned to Nagai to help them understand the loss. In the months following, Nagai established himself as the leading voice for the surviving Urakami Catholics. The atomic bomb had exploded in the northern part of the city, not the main part of the city in the south, which led some southern residents to form explanations of the bombing that revealed a historical tension between the disparate regions of the city. The northern, Christian district of Urakami had long contrasted with the southern part of Nagasaki with its mostly Buddhist and Shinto population.[23] The disparity was such that Nagai referred to Urakami and "Old Nagasaki" as the "City of Maria" and the "City of Eros," respectively. Both Nagasakis were cities of love, Nagai declared, but the "city of the god Eros" was filled with earthly love in contrast to the supernatural love of the "city of Holy Maria."[24] The disdain between the two parts of the city was mutual and did not disappear with the bomb. Instead, the bombing reaffirmed for some residents that the gods disliked the Urakami Catholics because they refused to worship at shrines.

In October, two months after the bombing, Nagai moved back into Urakami from the relief station in Mitsuyama in defiance of the so-called seventy-year sterility theory, building a small three-meter-squared shack to live with his two children. In January 1946, Nagai and his children moved to a more stable makeshift hut, and in March 1948, they moved into a better hut built and donated by many in the Catholic community, where he and his children lived until his death in 1951. Nagai named the humble hermitage "Nyokodō," which he derived from the words of Jesus, "Love thy neighbor as thyself."[25] Nyokodō, the "smallest house in the prefecture," as Nagai claimed, represented for him the unrelenting faith of the Urakami believers, including those killed in the bombing. The hut served as the headquarters of Nagai's reconstruction activities, through which he continued to spread his interpretation of the bombing of Nagasaki.[26]

The tragedy of the atomic bombing and especially the death of loved ones challenged the Urakami Catholics' faith in God, and so the first priority for Nagai was to use religious explanations for the destruction to put it into a context that they could understand. A friend of Nagai, Yamada Ichitarō, returned home to Nagasaki to find his wife and five children killed in the bombing. Yamada believed what people were saying, agonizing, "Everyone I meet says so: the atomic bomb was the wrath of God (tenbatsu); those who were killed were sinners (warumono); those who survived received a special grace from God. So, does that mean that my wife and children were sinners!?" Yamada was torn because he could not believe that God, to whom he had dedicated his life, had killed his wife and five

FIGURE 3.1.   Nagai Takashi with his two children, Makoto (left) and Kayano (right).

Source: Photograph courtesy of Nagai Tokusaburō, son of Makoto.

children for being sinners, especially considering that it was he who had been a soldier in the Imperial Army. Nagai reassured Yamada that such thinking misunderstood the workings of God. "That the atomic bomb fell on Urakami was great Divine Providence. It was the grace of God," Nagai declared to his troubled friend. And instead of lamenting the destruction and losing faith, Nagai argued, "Urakami must offer thanks unto God" for having been chosen as a sacrifice to end the war. The survivors, he claimed, had failed the entrance exam into heaven and had to remain on earth to continue their studies through suffering. Yamada understood and, feeling reassured of God's love, left Nagai's hut, saying, "I am a sinner (*tsumibito*), so more than anything I look forward to the opportunity to suffer and pay for my sins (*baishō*)."[27]

Shortly after this episode, Nagai shared and expounded his interpretation of the bombing as Providence at a mass funeral among the ruins of the Urakami Cathedral on November 23, 1945, which was attended by survivors as well as some Catholics from around Japan who had returned to help in recovery. As the parishioner representative, Nagai presented the eulogy.[28] On a hill overlooking the devastated landscape of the Urakami valley in front of thousands of Christians gathered near the cathedral ruins, Nagai spoke words of comfort, reassuring them of the exceptional love of God for Nagasaki Catholics and linking the atomic tragedy with the history of Christian martyrdom in the city. The eulogy was the first instance in which Nagai spoke publicly of the atomic bombing as a providential tragedy.

The eulogy blended religious and historical interpretations of the tragedy to proclaim the exceptional character of Urakami in the eyes of God. For Nagai, the bombing exemplified atonement for the sin of world war. The sin, however, was not the Catholics', or even Japan's, but rather humanity's; that is, responsibility for the war belonged to all of humankind equally, including the victorious Allies. Because Japan had initiated the "fifteen-year war" with the "Manchurian Incident," he said, the war had to end in Japan, but the numerous cities that the Allies firebombed in the last year of the war were "not suitable for the sacrifice." Only Urakami possessed the qualifications to become a sacrificial lamb because the community had endured persecution "for four hundred years, shedding the blood of numerous martyrs." In light of this history of sacrifice, he asked, were not the Catholics of Urakami "chosen from among the world as a flock of pure lambs that should be offered on the altar of the Lord? Alas, the great holocaust (*hansai*) that was made in the presence of this cathedral on August ninth and duly ended the darkness of the great world war and shined the light of peace! Even in the nadir of sadness, we reverently viewed this as something beautiful, something pure, and something sacred." More to the point, he claimed that "the church of Urakami was placed on the altar of sacrifice as atonement for the sin of humankind (*jinrui*) that was the world war. It was chosen as a pure lamb, slaughtered, and burned." Nagai created a theodicy for his community in that he claimed God worked through them in order to expiate the sins of humankind.[29] He hoped that the belief in the exceptional love of God for his community would comfort the few who had not been "summoned to His side" and that they would take comfort in knowing that their loved ones who died were not punished, as some Nagasaki residents had claimed, but rather chosen by God because of their purity and righteousness. The atomic bombing of Nagasaki was not divine punishment. It had ended "darkness," bringing peace and freedom of religion to Japan. Urakami's sacrifice, Nagai declared, "saved billions of people from the calamity of war."[30] Although the rationale and context differed, Nagai's interpretation of the bombing as having ended the war and saved lives echoed the narrative of the United States.

The surviving Catholics took to heart Nagai's message about the bombing as holocaust.[31] Nishida Hideo, who attended the funeral, remembers that when Nagai read the eulogy "in a loud voice," everyone wept. "We were persuaded" (*nattoku*) by Nagai's interpretation of the bomb, Nishida says, "even the people who had thought it was divine punishment." Nagaoka Some, too, remembers Nagai as having inspired the Catholic community. "He was such a good person," she says, "that some people thought God had delivered him to us (*unde kureta*)."[32] To evoke the words of the poet Rainer Maria Rilke, the "eulogy entrusted [him] with a mission" to "gently remove the appearance of injustice about their death—which at times slightly hinders their souls from proceeding onward."[33] In other words, the interpretation of the bombing as an Urakami sacrifice gave meaning to the community's suffering in a way they could comprehend. In the wake of the destruction and misery of the war, the atomic bomb, and defeat, Nagai's voice seemed like a light illuminating a path to recovery. In the months after the November eulogy, many people in and outside of Nagasaki venerated him as a paragon Catholic and Japanese citizen. From early 1946, newspapers in Nagasaki and from around Japan also began to take notice. Reporters came to Nyokodō and turned to Nagai to speak for the residents of the Urakami valley and about the atomic experience of the city. Nagai used every chance to convey his understanding of the bombing as an act of Providence.

In February, a reporter from the *Nagasaki shinbun* interviewed Nagai, who took the opportunity to reiterate some of the ideas that he had advanced in his November eulogy. The article began by describing Nagai's leukemia and how he had contracted it, going on to explain how it improved after the atomic bombing, when his white-blood cell temporarily decreased from two hundred thousand to one hundred thousand. Even so, little changed for Nagai, the reporter pointed out, as a healthy person's count is around seven or eight thousand, and "according to common medical knowledge today," Nagai's sickness was still serious and he had "less than three years to live." Despite his severe leukemia, Nagai performed his duties as a doctor, and, considering that his terminal condition resulted from work as a radiologist, the reporter concluded, Nagai had made an enormous "noble scientific sacrifice." The Ministry of Education's promotion of Nagai to full professor in 1946 was the first of many awards that, the reporter declared, recognized his dedication as a doctor and his ability to inspire strength in his fellow citizens. The reporter went on to extol Nagai: "As an ardent Christian, he makes a point to participate in Church functions no matter how busy he may be with work, and he stands in a position of leadership" in his community, always showing love and affection as he guides them through destitute and painful times. When the atomic bomb exploded, he suffered a severe injury, the reporter explained, but he treated numerous patients with one hand pressing a cloth to his wound to keep the fresh blood out of his face. Nagai "performs abilities (*hataraki*) that a normal person could not possibly do, as if he is doing the work of God (*Kamiwaza no gotoku*)."

The reporter's flattering descriptions preceded Nagai's explanation of the significance of the bombing. "The damage of the atomic bomb is the tragedy of the century," began Nagai. "Eight thousand believers died because of it. However, those people are blessed. Bearing the greatest gift of the Temple of Heaven (*jōdo no tenshudō*), they were chosen as atonement for sin to bring about peace for humankind, and they ascended to the foot of God." The reporter concluded, "A man of passion. A man of love. An object of reverence by his colleagues and acquaintances. And just the fact that he is a rising professor of much promise, the thought that [his success] will be short-lived is unbearable, and the Doctor will be missed."[34] The article, appearing just six months after the bombing, depicted the bombing in a way that had become typical in media since September 1945; that is, the bombing was framed as an Urakami tragedy. Furthermore, neither the reporter nor Nagai mentioned the other sixty-five thousand or more Nagasaki residents who died in addition to the "eight thousand believers," illustrating the local narrative of the bombing taking shape around Urakami, not Nagasaki as a whole.

As the article affirmed Nagai's status as a notable figure in Nagasaki, it also echoed the discourse of postatomic Urakami that Nagai had initiated with his eulogy, giving visibility to his interpretation of the bombing beyond his fellow believers. The Ministry of Education's elevation of Nagai to full professor suggests that officials saw the promise of Nagai's strength and fortitude to inspire Nagasaki residents to endure the road of hardship. By February 1946, the image of Nagai and Urakami in postwar popular media was established. Local and national reporters depicted Nagai as pious and undeterred by the atomic bomb, almost superhumanly so, and as someone for all Japanese to emulate as they attempted to overcome defeat and destruction. The fame enjoyed by Nagai from early 1946 led to the next chapter of his life as the voice of Nagasaki that transcended local and national borders.

Nagai's November 1945 eulogy attracted national and international attention after the first part of it was translated and published in 1947 in an American magazine, *The Field Affair*, along with one of his poems. The translated portion of the eulogy included Nagai's declaration that the atomic bombing of Urakami exemplified atonement for the war and that the Catholics were the sacrificial lambs that expiated the sin of humankind. An American named Ruth Giblin wrote to Nagai from Concord, Massachusetts, in March after reading the article, to express solidarity and sympathy as a fellow Christian; she offered to help the Urakami community in any way she could. Nagai requested of Giblin only a holy cloth for the church altar, which she enclosed with a letter two months later, along with some soap. The altar cloth and the soap, however, never made it to Nagai, who thought that both had probably been confiscated on entry to Japan, which caused him to "feel sad."[35]

By 1947, Nagai had established himself as the public voice of Urakami's Catholic community and of Nagasaki's atomic bombing. The *Nagasaki nichinichi* newspaper declared in 1947 on the second anniversary of the bombing that Nagai's "religious love that transcends national borders" had allowed the knowledge of the tragedy of the bomb to reach international audiences, as evidenced by the letter from an American admirer. His writings on the medical effects of the atomic bomb, which he began producing and presenting as early as 1946, using himself as a research specimen, would soon be translated into English, the newspaper asserted. Nagai's achievements by 1947 had positioned him to become the "vanguard of international goodwill," not to mention a key to Japan-U.S. relations. The newspaper commented that "Nagai of Nagasaki" had become "Nagai of Japan," and now, at last, he was the "Nagai of the world."[36] From 1948, Nagai used his position in the spotlight to publish numerous books and help in the reconstruction of Nagasaki, leaving a lasting imprint on the city and discussions of its bombing.

Writing Nagasaki

If Nagai worked for the spiritual revival of Urakami from 1945 to 1947, then from 1948 until his death in 1951, he worked for the physical reconstruction of Nagasaki through his writings and in his role as representative voice of the city. From 1948, Nagai wrote and published prolifically on the bombing, Christianity, and the dawn of the nuclear age, donating his royalties to reconstruction projects in Urakami and other parts of Nagasaki. The books brought him considerable domestic and international renown, which he used to advance the image of Nagasaki and improve the position of Catholics in Japan. Despite Nagai's controversial interpretation of the bombing, religious leaders such as Pope Pius XII and others in the international Christian community applauded the "saint of Urakami" for his literary, spiritual, and financial contributions to the postwar revival of the city.

Nagai's fame became a key component of the municipal vision of reconstruction. As the only atomic-bombing author to appear in major circulation and to be read widely, Nagai symbolized the prosperity of Nagasaki as an international cultural city. No representative emerged as equally influential in Hiroshima. In total, Nagai published nine books and numerous medical reports, poems, paintings, and editorials in newspapers and journals. Two additional manuscripts of his were published posthumously as books.[37] Reviewers praised his books for describing the nuclear age and educating the populace on the truths about radiation and the peaceful uses of atomic energy.[38] "Dr. Nagai is quite famous" for his dedication to atomic science (*genshigaku*), wrote Ono Tomoaki, and the way in which he connected the narrative of the atomic destruction of Urakami to the region's history of Christianity and his own faith demonstrated how Nagai "conquered atomic power with faith."[39] Nagai's persona also became a shorthand way to discuss matters related to the bombing in national media, which served the purposes of the municipal government because it located the bombing in Urakami, displayed the Catholic history of the city, and portrayed the special nature of the city that had entitled it to special reconstruction funds above the other bombed-out cities. In many people's eyes, the international nature of Nagasaki's history gave hope to the city's reconstruction efforts, and for them, Nagai exemplified that hope.

The many books that Nagai wrote drew on his experiences after the bombing. A month after collapsing in front of Urakami Station in July 1946 from complications of his leukemia, Nagai produced his first book manuscript. Less than a year had passed since the bombing, and with the experience fresh in his mind, Nagai wrote candidly about the physical destruction, his medical relief team and their futile efforts to treat irradiated patients, the physics of the atomic bomb, and the impact of the bombing on his community. He also included his November 1945 eulogy address as representative of his community's interpretation of the bombing. The manuscript, entitled *Genshi jidai no kaimaku: Igakusha no taiken shita genshi bakudan* (Raising the curtain on the atomic age: The atomic bomb as experienced by a physician), promised to inform readers outside Nagasaki (and Hiroshima) of the effects of the atomic bomb. Nagai hoped to publish the manuscript as soon as possible, and because he did not criticize the United States for dropping the bomb, he did not expect any problems in passing censorship.

He was wrong. The institution of American censorship was not fully understood by authors in mid-1946, even if some knew enough to self-censor. From early in the occupation, Nagasaki newspapers reminded citizens: "Remember without exception to submit publication materials for censorship."[40] Authors did not always know what might be considered unpalatable to the occupiers, and Nagai submitted *Genshi jidai no kaimaku*, in manuscript form, to officials for approval in early 1947. After a lengthy review process that involved several departments of SCAP, the censorship bureau suspended the decision on Nagai's manuscript for six months. While waiting for the decision, Nagai continued to write from the perspective of an atomic-bombing survivor, doctor and physicist, Catholic, and father. Those books easily passed censorship and were published in 1948, soon topping the best-sellers charts. *Kono ko o nokoshite* (Leaving these children behind), *Itoshigo yo* (My beloved children), *Rozario no kusari* (Rosary chain), and his autobiography *Horobinu mono o* (Grant me something eternal) established Nagai as the first author to emerge prolifically and successfully from the atomic-bombed cities. One bookstore in Tokyo advertised Nagai's autobiography as the "bible of the modern era" (*gendai no seisho*).[41] His books sold hundreds of thousands of copies. Not bad for "a frail little Japanese doctor who awaits death in a tiny hut on a Nagasaki hill," and who also happened to be "Japan's most popular author-doctor," as Nagai was described in a June 1949 article in the Associated Press.[42]

Kono ko o nokoshite was a huge success, selling 220,000 copies in the first year of publication.[43] Written from the viewpoint of a father contemplating what will become of his two children, Makoto and Kayano, when he dies of leukemia, the book makes several references to the bombing of Nagasaki. At one point, Nagai recounts the treatment he applied to the wounds of a little boy with whom he discussed the hundreds of dead schoolgirls whose corpses lined the riverbed. But the way in which Nagai wrote this account, couching the depictions of destruction in lofty religious language, made it acceptable to the occupation authorities. It began with Christian sentiment:

> The Lord giveth and the Lord taketh away. Let us always praise the name of the Lord! . . .
>
> That night, I medically treated Kozasa-*kun* and the others, but according to their story, it appears that in the dead of night on a riverbank two hundred meters east from the [Jōsei] all-girls school, a Latin hymn sung by several people could be heard joining then ceasing, joining then ceasing. When the night expired and we looked, the nuns were clumped into a group and had become cold.—Could it have been these nuns who were singing last night's hymns? Or, couldn't it have been a flock of Angels, come to welcome the souls, who were singing?—Looking at the pure faces of the dead that were lined in a row made you think that way.
>
> Those of us left living who saw the dead thought that the atomic bomb was not divine punishment at all, but that it was no different from the expression of some profound plan of Divine Providence.—That same day I too had become a weak, penniless person and had embraced two small children in the fire ruins. I don't know what it was, but I believed and didn't doubt that this was the expression of Love's Providence.
>
> I have endured three years since that day, but the fact that my faith that day was correct will gradually come to be proven.
>
> Because of the atomic bomb, the obstruction that was blocking my righteous path was removed, and I became able to taste true happiness.
>
> "Death" that will come to me soon is also the greatest gift of love that I confront, I who am God's and who increases in His infinite love.[44]

The chapter in which this excerpt appears, entitled "Providence," revealed a transformation in Nagai's views since 1945. No longer was Nagai professing the idea of the providential tragedy as his own, but rather as "ours"; specifically, "Those of us left living," *we*, consider the atomic bombing an "expression of Divine Providence." As parishioner representative since 1945, Nagai spoke for the entire Urakami community, but after the publication of *Kono ko o nokoshite* in 1948, he began to represent the "we" of Nagasaki to the people all over Japan and the world. In addition, the Christian words Nagai used to express the bombing of Nagasaki in the book outweighed the potential of the book to arouse anti-American sentiments. After all, in the eyes of the censors, "they" of Urakami were uncritical of the atomic bombing and even grateful. The book thus posed no threat to the image of the Allies.

Kono ko o nokoshite brought Nagai's Catholic ideas to a wide segment of the population. The book connected with readers both because of his Christian message and because many around Japan related to his experience of hardship in recovering from the ravages of war. The writer Inoue Hisashi wrote that when he lived in an orphanage in Sendai in the north of Japan as a child after the war, he received a piece of chocolate whenever he brought home a book written by Nagai Takashi because of the Catholic message in his books.[45] *Kono ko o nokoshite*, especially, was popular in orphanages, because in it Nagai expresses the unconditional love of a father in the valuable advice he gives to his soon to be orphaned children. An advertisement in the *Nagasaki shinbun* declared that "the saint of Urakami, Dr. Nagai," had produced in *Kono ko o nokoshite* "a memoir of passionate paternal love, written from his sickbed for his beloved children. It is also a book of love bequeathed on behalf of the mothers and fathers of the world." The ad insisted, "Tears! Tears! [Your] tears will soak this emotional book."[46] Another ad said that *Kono ko o nokoshite* was the representative work of Nagai, which "extracted the sorrowful tears of the nation (*zenkokumin no netsurui*)."[47] Nagai's voice represented the anxiety of his generation, who contemplated the future of their children in a war-ravaged society that had witnessed the violent emergence of the atomic age.

Nagai's books also appealed to people in Japan because he drew attention to social problems facing the reconstructing nation. In a 1949 essay, one scholar admired Nagai's ability to illuminate broader social issues such as the war orphans. Reflecting on the fate of his own children after his death, Nagai drew attention to society for its failure to properly address the problem of orphans in postwar Japan. When Nagai discussed the dire state of orphanages in a story of an orphan who drowned while attempting to escape from an institution, the scholar felt "sharp regret (*hansei*) boil to the surface, as if I had committed some kind of great crime. Ahh, if only the many bourgeoisie of the world, the directors of social service institutions, and related government authorities—no, the entire nation of Japan—understood orphans even just half as well as Dr. Nagai does, then might we have been able to prevent an extremely large number of tragedies and crimes" against the orphans of Japan?[48] Nagai's discussion of orphanages reached the ears of policymakers in the National Diet. At a meeting of the House of Representatives on March 31, 1949, representative Fukuda Masako pointed out the destitute conditions of orphanages and argued for the revision of the Juvenile Social Welfare Law (Jidō fukushi hō) and the improvement of facilities throughout the country. The words of Nagai in *Kono ko o nokoshite* emphasized for Fukuda the failure of current facilities to allow for the proper nurturing and psychological cultivation of children.[49]

Japanese actors, artists, and novelists also expressed their admiration for Nagai in personal letters.[50] Actor Chiaki Minoru, who starred in several Kurosawa Akira films, including *Rashōmon* and *Seven Samurai*, and who played Nagai in a 1949 play version of *Nagasaki no kane*, wrote to Nagai on March 14, 1949, after visiting him in Nagasaki.[51] "As a public figure, Nagai-sensei is now everyone's sensei," declared Chiaki. "You are everyone's Nagai-sensei, [including] ordinary people and the many admiring readers from the time [you published] *Rozario no kusari*."[52] Nagai represented the exemplary sensei and a role model for the nation.

At one point, Nagai became the most read author in Japan. In early September 1949, the Mainichi shinbun newspaper company conducted a national survey of readers. The Third National Public Opinion Poll of Publications posed the question: "Among the books you read in the past year, are there any that you consider notable books (*ryōsho*)?" The previous year, Dazai Osamu's *Shayō* (*The Setting Sun*) and *Ningen shikkaku* (*No Longer Human*) had dominated the *Mainichi*'s charts, but the 1949 results revealed a change. Three books by Nagai Takashi appeared in the rankings: *Kono ko o nokoshite* stood at number one, surpassing the number-two book by 30 percent of the votes; his *Nagasaki no kane* (The bell of Nagasaki[53]) won out over Yoshikawa Eiji's popular historical novel *Miyamoto Musashi* for fourth place; and his *Rozario no kusari* was sixteenth. Nagai's books placed far ahead of the Japanese translation of John Hersey's *Hiroshima*, which was nineteenth, and that only in the votes of men. Nagai's books equally dominated sales in bookstores across Japan.[54] Although he was the most read author in the 1948–49 publishing year, he was not the most popular. Nagai did not even appear in the top ten of the "favorite author" category. Number one in that category was Yoshikawa Eiji.[55] The subject matter of Nagai's books had made them popular.

Some dignitaries took note of Nagai. On May 27, 1949, just two days before the Saint Francis Xavier festival, Emperor Hirohito paid a visit to the sickbed of Nagai, who had moved to an office in the Nagasaki Medical School to allow for more space during the visit. A few months earlier, Nagai had presented the emperor with a copy of *Nagasaki no kane* through his publisher Shikiba Ryūsaburō.[56] Hirohito asked gently, "How is your illness?" "I am fine," replied Nagai in a respectful tone (*"Genki de orimasu"*). "I hope for your quick recovery," added Hirohito. As the emperor spoke, Nagai brought his hands together silently and replied, "My hands still move. I will continue to write as long as my strength allows." Hirohito, smiling, told Nagai, "I saw your novel (*shōsetsu*)."[57] The emperor then turned to Dr. Kageura, the chief physician caring for Nagai and said, "Please take care [of the patient]."[58] The *Nagasaki minyū* newspaper wrote that the kindness of the "human and scientist emperor echoed strongly in the heart of the bedridden Dr. Nagai."[59] Before leaving, Hirohito encouraged Nagai's children, Makoto and Kayano, "Please study hard and become fine people."[60] Nagai was excited to receive a visit from the emperor. Years earlier, he and so many others had fought in China in his name, and as Nagai saw it, the sacrifice of Nagasaki had convinced Hirohito to end the war. Nagai was overwhelmed with gratitude and humility, wishing that the encounter had occurred under better circumstances.[61] Nonetheless, May 27, 1949, was a special day for Nagai, and he composed several poems as mementos of the imperial visit.[62]

The meeting between the emperor and Nagai exemplified the delicate juxtaposition between the wartime empire and the defeated nation. The emperor seemed to understand the significance of Nagai and his books. As one historian writes, the "emperor skillfully tapped" into the "Nagai boom" that swept the nation in the late 1940s and early 1950s.[63] Hirohito, the icon of Japanese imperialism, and Nagai, the "saint of Urakami," came together for a photo opportunity that embodied the hope of a postwar transition. With the issue of the war responsibility of the nation (and of the emperor) left unaddressed, the two men seamlessly combined the wartime and postwar legacies of Japan.

The Nagai boom extended beyond the borders of Japan. By the time *Nagasaki no kane* was published in 1949, Nagai Takashi was already famous. His best sellers had made him an international figure as a voice of Japanese who repented for the sins of war and struggled to rebuild their nation in the hope of world peace. For Christians, Nagai's ability to find God in the destruction commanded admiration and attracted notable visitors, such as sixty-nine-year-old Helen Keller, who made a pilgrimage to his bedside on October 18, 1948.[64] Eva Peron sent Nagai a statue of Mother Mary from Argentina in winter of 1950.[65] Letters from publishers, editors, and admirers abroad poured in. His fame was such that some letters arrived at his small hut in Urakami without a correct address, as long as the sender had managed to include Nagai's name in some form. One letter was addressed simply to "Dr. Paul Nagai, Nagasaki, Japan," but no matter the language or the address, the letters seemed to arrive safely.[66] The correspondence Nagai received from America, Italy, Spain, Mexico, Brazil, and other countries praised him for his books, his courage in the face of leukemia, and his ability to relate the devastation of the atomic bombing in the language of his faith. The success of *Kono ko o nokoshite* caught the attention of foreign publishers, who thought they could sell the Christian aspect to their readers. Indeed, Roman Catholics around the world admired Nagai for his ability to see the love of God where others saw only death and despair; Pope Pius XII sent Nagai a wooden rosary in May 1950. Representatives from the publisher Editorial Marfil in Spain asked Nagai for permission to publish a Spanish version because "we think that publication of this book in Spain would be very interesting for the large mass of the Catholic people of our country."[67]

Other foreign publishers sought to tap into the Nagai boom. In 1949, Duell, Sloan and Pearce of New York approached Kodansha publishers in Tokyo about the possibility of translating *Kono ko o nokoshite*. For the American press, the book had value for readers because of its "Catholic aspects (*nioi*)" and scientific approach to discussing the bomb, both of which the publisher hoped to intensify in the translation.[68] But the deal never came to fruition. Instead, Duell, Sloan and Pearce became interested in an account of eight Nagasaki survivors written by Nagai for an American audience, which Kodansha sent them in November 1949. Charles A. Pearce replied in February the following year that the manuscript, "Genshiun Senjo Shinri (Atomic Battlefield Psychology) [*sic*] . . . has been carefully examined and read by several reliable advisers. As a result, I am happy to report that we wish to proceed with the translation and publication of this manuscript by Dr. Nagai." The press had already secured the necessary translators, "a professor at Columbia University and one of his colleagues," after having promised to pay them "a substantial royalty on the first 10,000 copies."[69] Ichiro Shirato and Herbert B. L. Silverman translated the book as *We of Nagasaki: The Story of Survivors in an Atomic Wasteland*, which was released in early 1951. Thus Nagai's voice and that of the Urakami Catholics spoke for all of Nagasaki to the English-speaking world.

Duell, Sloan and Pearce hoped that Nagai's reportorial account of the experience of the Nagasaki survivors—which had been tentatively titled in English *The Fate of Man at Nagasaki*—would outdo the success of John Hersey's *Hiroshima*. In a fall 1950 press release, the publishers declared that thanks to the "acuteness and reportorial detail" with which Nagai told the story of the survivors, the "narratives probably surpass any existing reports, not excluding the Hersey account of Hiroshima." The release pointed out the contribution of the Nagasaki survivor accounts: "Cumulatively, they lead to a moving statement of Nagai's major theme, that the dangerous spiritual degeneration which an atomic war must inevitably beget is being lost sight of in the concern with material loss, physical death,and suffering [spacing *sic*]."[70] Charles Pearce wrote in his letter, "We believe that this book of his is one of the most sincere, impressive and thought-provoking message[s] that could be presented to the world today."[71] Nagai, too, dreamed that his works would garner American sympathy for Nagasaki, just as Hersey's book had done for Hiroshima.

The significance of *We of Nagasaki* as envisioned by Nagai and the American publishers was not lost on its readers. Ruth E. Giblin, who had visited Nagasaki and met Catholic Fathers Nakashima and Nagata, wrote to Nagai after reading *We of Nagasaki*: "I hope all readers cannot fail to see that those of Nagasaki have carried the cross and suffered the crucifixion for all the rest of us weak ones." Giblin agreed that Nagasaki was the sacrificial lamb on God's altar that ended the war. But the greatest impact of Nagai's book for her was that it forced recognition of "our American responsibility for it all," which, she added, "weighs me down. But now we, on our side, are in fear of the bomb being used on us, but most are in great ignorance and have no idea what it could be like." Nagai's book promised to educate Americans on these matters, she thought.[72] Other letters to Nagai noted the importance of the book in teaching the world of the destructive power of the atomic bomb. Mary Rutherford, too, wrote, "I hope many people throughout the world read [your book] and become more aware of the far reaching horror and destruction caused by such a weapon."[73]

The international translations of Nagai's books carried abroad the Christian image of Nagasaki's ground zero. Sister Mary Ambrose, BVM, of Mundelein College in Chicago reviewed *We of Nagasaki* for a journal and expressed her admiration for it in a letter she wrote to Nagai. "I am very sorry that you are ill for your cross of suffering is heavy indeed. When I knew that the bomb had struck Urakami where Christian families, who have so loyally preserved and suffered for their faith since the days of St. Francis Xavier lived, I recognized again the mission of those whom God calls to share the sufferings of Christ, His Only Son. . . . *We of Nagasaki* are doing that—and your reward will be exceedingly great."[74] That Nagai found God in the atomic destruction did not surprise Ambrose. Rather, as a fellow Christian, it assured her that Nagai understood the workings of God. God requires the faithful to "share the sufferings of Christ, His Only Son," Ambrose wrote, agreeing with Nagai that the residents of Urakami were a natural sacrifice. Like Nagai, she based her views on Catholic theology that sees suffering as the manifestation of God's love for the ardently faithful, "those loyal enough to give everything." For Ambrose and other readers of Nagai's books in translation, the "Christian families" of Urakami who endured numerous historical martyrdoms exemplified the atomic experience of Nagasaki. Other American publishers were interested in books by Nagai, including *Nagasaki no kane*, but *We of Nagasaki* was the only English translation published during his lifetime.[75]

The overwhelming number of printings of Nagai's works brought overwhelming royalties, most of which he donated to fund reconstruction projects in Nagasaki. He began this practice from the time of his first major publication in the postwar period, which had nothing to do with the atomic bombing but everything to do with his religion.[76] The book, a 1947 cotranslation of the Scottish author Bruce Marshall's Catholic novel and international best seller, *The World, the Flesh, and Father Smith*, earned Nagai around ¥40,000 in royalties, of which he donated ¥38,000 to the funds to rebuild Nagasaki's famous St. Francis Xavier Hospital, three schools, and the Urakami Cathedral. Among the contributions was a ¥10,000 organ for the cathedral, which was rebuilt in 1959. The ¥2,000 that remained went to feed his family.[77] Nagai hoped that the book would help propagate "the fact that Christianity forms the foundation of democracy."[78] The immediate benefit of the book was not ideological, but material. The donation of his royalties for reconstruction efforts set a precedent for Nagai when his own books began selling in the late 1940s.

Nagai's best sellers produced substantial profits for him and his publishing companies, but rather than keep the wealth for himself, he gave most of it to the city. During the 1948–49 fiscal year, Nagai Takashi's books earned ¥2,176,333 in royalties.[79] In mid-1949, when *Kono ko o nokoshite* had sold 220,000 copies and the rest of his books followed closely behind, Nagai experienced a sudden and enormous gain in wealth.[80] The royalties catapulted Nagai to the eighth-highest income earner in Nagasaki City, yet he remained in his Nyokodō hut and continued his daily life in poverty. Nagai cherished the humble life, but, more importantly, he never viewed his books and their royalties as his alone—he thought they always belonged in some way to Nagasaki. Indeed, he claimed he wrote "for the sake of Nagasaki," for its culture and history, and so that atomic-bombing "literature by Nagasaki writers will not lose out to Hiroshima."[81]

The majority of Nagai's after-tax income went directly to city reconstruction projects, but taxes presented a challenge to Nagai's charity. Out of the ¥2,176,333 earned in 1948–49, he paid nearly 90 percent in commercial, national, and city taxes, leaving him with around ¥20,000 to donate to the city.[82] The previous year was not much better: Nagai paid around ¥400,000 in taxes on a royalty income of about ¥800,000.[83] While the city taxes that Nagai paid probably went in some way to reconstruction efforts, the fate of his national and commercial taxes was less clear. But Nagai never had a problem with paying taxes. "I want to pay all taxes," he said, "because the payment of tax is a shared responsibility for the reconstruction of Japan."[84] When Nagasaki residents and journalists expressed their surprise and confusion at the government exacting exorbitant amounts of tax from Nagai, he told his close friend Kataoka Yakichi, "Taxes are the oil for the reconstruction of Japan. I am working for reconstruction and there is no way I would not pay taxes. I gathered my income documents and filed a tax return without a mistake of even a single *sen*. I will pay my taxes in full."[85] Nagai did, however, sometimes disagree with the way the government used his and other citizens' taxes. "When I hear of [our] hard-earned taxes being misappropriated (*tsumamigui*) or being wasted on banquet expenses, my desire to pay taxes weakens." As he wryly said to Kataoka, at first "I wrote to eat. I then had to pay taxes because I wrote. Now, I must write only to pay taxes."[86] "It's as if my legs are stuck in a bog."[87] Even so, he took his position as a kind of role model in Nagasaki seriously, encouraging all residents to be sure to pay taxes in support of the International Cultural City Construction Law that was set to make Nagasaki "a beautiful town" and a city of culture.[88]

Nagai dedicated himself to supporting the reconstruction of Nagasaki as envisioned by municipal officials. He declared in May 1949 that he wished to donate all of his royalties to the Nagasaki International Cultural City Construction Fund for projects such as building a medical treatment facility for atomic-bombing survivors, an orphanage, a museum, or a Peace Cultural Hall, as long as it improved the infrastructure of the city. In this way, he believed that donating to the larger city fund would also allow for the revitalization of the Urakami community. But tax law threatened to bleed dry his hopes.[89] Large monetary donations were subject to additional taxation, and Nagai's donations were indeed massive. Newspapers noted that his recently published books, *Horobinu mono o*, *Seimei no kawa*, and *Hana saku oka* (Hill of blossoming flowers) promised to bring in around ¥5 million in royalties, but income tax would claim around 80 percent. Of the remaining ¥1 million, Nagai hoped to put away ¥100,000 for his family after he died and donate ¥900,000 to the main city reconstruction fund, but after a hefty donation tax the amount the city received would be reduced to around ¥400,000.[90]

When the tax system compromised Nagai's efforts to donate, he abandoned the large, single donation and continued to donate to smaller projects that were not subject to as much taxation. Whatever money remained after taxes, Nagai gave most of it to the Urakami community or Nagasaki City because he thought that his children Makoto and Kayano would benefit from improved infrastructure instead of individual family wealth. Nagai explained to Kataoka Yakichi, who had asked him why he did not save any money for his children, "We must raise the general level of the area. If everyone improves, then my children will also improve. The revitalization (*fukkō*) of Urakami and the reconstruction (*saiken*) of Nagasaki are our serious responsibilities."[91] For Nagai, writing books not only helped the reconstruction of the city, but it also laid the foundation for the future of his children and the other children of Nagasaki.

Nagai's charitable spirit produced tangible results for both the Catholic parish and all of Nagasaki. Nagai intended Our Bookcase (Uchira no honbako), a library aimed at educating the children of Nagasaki, and the Monument for Those Children (meaning those killed in the bombing) to advance social education in the city and improve the commemorative landscape of the atomic-devastated area.[92] His support also made possible the planting of one thousand cherry trees in the Urakami valley, which were meant to rejuvenate the area in time for the third Christmas after the bombing.[93] Initially called the "Thousand Urakami *sakura* (cherry trees)," the hill of cherry blossoms later came to be known also as the "Nagai *sakura*."[94]

The Politics of Fame

Nagai's work led to numerous awards. In November 1948, the Kyūshū taimuzu (The Kyushu Times) conferred on Nagai the Kyushu Times Culture Award—an award in recognition of contributions to the cultural reconstruction of Japan (*Nihon bunka saiken*)—for his dedicated research on atomic sickness (*genshi byō*) in which he used himself as a subject.[95] On December 3, 1949, Nagasaki City Council voted unanimously to name Nagai an "Honorary Citizen" (*meiyo shimin*) for his efforts to realize the vision of Nagasaki as an international cultural city through his books and for "spreading the spirit of love to the world."[96] Among other things, the title of *meiyo shimin* entitled Nagai to a municipally sponsored funeral.[97] The list of awards was long, but not everyone in Japan had boarded the Nagai award train. Some saw his national recognition as undue, or they used their criticism of Nagai to point out how some groups appropriated his suffering and status to serve their own political ends. Nagai's loudest critics were members of the Communist Party, but many other citizens around Japan shared their opinions as well. Criticism of Nagai in the late 1940s presents a window onto the relationship between national politics and nascent narratives of the war, while also providing us with a more complete picture of Nagai as a person and revealing cracks in the saintliness of his popular image in postwar society. In general, it reveals the way in which various groups in the postwar period, such as the National Diet and SCAP, co-opted Nagai's influence for their own purposes under the guise of promoting a role model for the nation during the recovery period. In reality, they saw Nagai as a medium to help in reshaping Japan's national image from a soldier to a saint, much like Nagai's own life trajectory. At the heart of the criticism of Nagai and his place in burgeoning war narratives was a call for Japan to remember its past and not to whitewash it through false postwar narratives; only by confronting its past could Japan realize true antiwar culture.

One award in particular sparked a debate over the qualifications of Nagai and his contributions to the nation, revealing, also, a tension between democracy and communism, as well as the presence of an anti-Catholic undercurrent in postwar society. In mid-1949, the National Diet formed the Special Investigation Committee of the House of Representatives (*Shūgi'in kōsa tokubetsu i'inkai*) to search out and nominate people for the first award for "persons whose deeds have contributed to the reconstruction of the nation" (*Kokka saiken no kōrōsha*). The committee chose two men. The first nominee was Yukawa Hideki, who had won the Nobel Prize in Physics in 1949, the first Japanese person to receive the honor. The other nominee was Nagai Takashi. By then, the Nagai boom had reached most of Japan and parts of the world, and members of the National Diet were no exception. Yet not all Diet members shared a reverence for Nagai. The Communist Party and the Socialist Party objected to Nagai's nomination on the grounds that he had no qualifications or "academic achievements" (*kōseki*), especially when compared to Yukawa.[98]

A Diet meeting was convened on September 12, 1949, to present the findings of the special committee and to discuss the concerns of the dissenters. The two dissenting parties argued, firstly, that if the Diet sought to commend a Japanese scientist for his work, someone with a higher level of achievement (*gyōseki no suijun*) would be more appropriate, such as the bacteriologist Nakamura Keizō for his research on leprosy or the pathologist Oka Harumichi for his work on tuberculosis. Secondly, one of Nagai's books, *Rozario no kusari*, showed him to be no humanist at all because he revealed his feudal mindset in the way he treated his wife like a slave (*reizokuteki*). Thirdly, the dissenters argued, "This same doctor had supported the Pacific War until the very last moment." Lastly, they pointed out that Nagai's books having become best sellers did not necessarily mean that he contributed to the reconstruction of the nation.[99] Nonetheless, the majority of the special committee concluded that the "famous achievements" (*gyōseki*) of Nagai from his various books, such as *Kono ko o nokoshite* and *Nagasaki no kane*, "have contributed (*kiyo*) to culture and science, and contribute (*kōken*) substantially to the reconstruction of Japan."[100]

Eventually, the Communists remained the only dissenting party, because for them Nagai did not sufficiently represent the antiwar culture of postwar Japan.[101] Kamiyama Shigeo, leader of the Communist Party, summarized the viewpoint of the opposition in an article, entitled "Leave Matters of God in the Hands of God (*Kami no mono wa kami no te ni*)." He expanded on the opinions of the original dissenters, concluding that the issue was a political problem, not a cultural or religious one, even as he employed culture and religion in his own analysis.[102] He hoped that an argument against Nagai's nomination would reveal the machinations of a corrupt capitalist government seeking to exploit Nagai for its own gain. Kamiyama criticized the nomination of Nagai on five grounds, echoing the breadth of criticisms that others had also held of Nagai at the time. First, Nagai failed as a scientist. Kamiyama pointed out that his work did not compare to the significant contributions of Nakamura Kenzō, Oka Harumichi, and the biophysicist Tasaki Ichiji. In the field of physics, especially, Nagai could never compare to the "giant" Yukawa Hideki, who was "always devoted to the development of science, from the prewar through the war, and intellectuals the world over also recognize him as a scholar who is the pride of the Japanese nation (*Nihon minzoku*)." Even the special investigation committee, Kamiyama pointed out, had no choice but to admit that Nagai as a scientist cast a relatively "small shadow."[103]

Second, Kamiyama argued that because the publishing world created best sellers, Nagai's books having become best sellers did not necessarily reflect the true interests of the masses. The best-seller rankings in newspapers, he argued, were flawed: "We must point out the extremely unscientific nature of the polling method" that was used, for example, by the Yomiuri shinbun company. The newspaper's poll, he said, provided no scientific basis for the special investigation committee to conclude that Nagai's books were indeed best sellers that made a major contribution to society. Giving the example of Yoshikawa Eiji's best-seller *Shinran*, "which contains extremely feudalistic and out-of-date subjects," Kamiyama argued that it is "completely simplistic (*keisotsu*) to see books as influencing the minds of people in society just because they appear on the best-seller list, or because they were advertised on the radio or in newspapers as having done so. This may be forgivable for a journalist, but we must emphasize that it should not be a stance taken by the National Diet." The fact that Nagai's books appeared on the best-seller lists simply meant that they had sold well, and it did not mean they contained anything truly scientific or that they had contributed to "public morals and human spirit" (*sedōjinshin*) (73–74).

Third, Kamiyama thought that Nagai was wrong in his understanding of war, and his religious interpretations of it damaged the peace movement more than they advanced it. In other words, Nagai's outlook on the war and defeat did not demonstrate enough regret for Japan's wartime aggression. No doubt Nagai contributed "not a few things related to 'peace,'" Kamiyama conceded, but "we also know that Mr. Nagai's peace ideology (*heiwa shisō*)—if there is such a thing—is far removed from the ideology for real peace." Kamiyama never explained what constituted "real peace ideology" in his or the Communists' eyes, and even he discussed the war in terms of the conflict with the United States. He argued that Nagai did not embody peace because he "does not know, nor makes any attempt to know, the reactionary and aggressive nature of the Pacific War." Nagai had always been a strong patriot and believed in the immortality of the land of the gods, Kamiyama pointed out. As a result, Nagai mistakenly interpreted the defeat of Japan as a regrettable event, "lamenting that the 'Yamato race (*minzoku*) had been thrust into the lowest hell (*naraku*)'" by the defeat, and that "he envies

the people who found happiness by 'leaving the world without knowing defeat.'
He cries that 'We who survived are miserable.' "[104] Kamiyama believed that even
Nagai could not ignore the fact that "defeat taught us so much more than war
ever did." Even though Nagai "weeps to himself as a survivor in the defeated country of Japan, 'What pleasure is there in having lost the war?,'" Kamiyama knew
that "Mr. Nagai" (not "Dr. Nagai," as he was generally referred to in public media)
was undoubtedly "grateful for the return of peace and for the freedom of religion"
that stemmed from the defeat (74).

Religion, however, represented for Kamiyama the biggest weakness of Nagai's
"peace ideology" because it contributed nothing tangible to the promotion of
peace. Prayers and hope are not only powerless, he claimed, but they become "instruments that dull the battle for peace." This was no coincidence, Kamiyama
thought. In Japan, among Christian activists in the antiwar movement who had
tried to make a difference, from the time of the Russo-Japanese War through the
Pacific War, and even in the postwar international movement, everyone had been
a Protestant. The Catholics, Kamiyama argued, had largely been absent, and the
behavior of Nagai exemplified that of an "old-fashioned Catholic" (75).

The eulogy of November 23, 1945, represented the perfect example for Kamiyama of how Nagai's Catholic ideas "anesthetize the anger of the Japanese people
against the true war criminals," and it demonstrates how little Nagai understood
"the nature of war." The complete eulogy appeared in revised form in Nagai's best
seller, *Nagasaki no kane*. Kamiyama declared that the eulogy in fact did not con-
stitute a commemoration of those sacrificed in the war, but rather exemplified
the forced resignation of the will of the people because everything—including national defeat and the atomic bombing of Urakami—was due to Providence. That
may be fine for someone like "Mr. Nagai" who lived his life according to a deep
faith in Catholicism, Kamiyama explained, but "when such a thing is spread as
propaganda to the masses, we must think about it." Nagai's promotion of the omnipotence of God in world affairs produced a dangerous mindset, he argued. If
Nagai was correct to assert that God punishes the unjust with defeat and bestows
His blessing on the victorious, and if "There is no possibility of victory in a war
that is not just before God," then the "victories of the aggressive, imperialistic
wars—the Sino-Japanese War, the Russo-Japanese War, and the First World War—
become rationalized in the name of God." Kamiyama considered this mode of
thinking as lacking knowledge of the nature of war by ignoring the facts of history, which would prove useful for contemporary war provocateurs, such as the
reemerging fascists. If World War III were to erupt today, he asserted, "it would
not begin or end according to 'God's Providence.'" Prayers will not stop it. "War
does not fall from heaven. . . . It is an invariable product of society," and it would
be through the collective action of myriads of people who have realized this that

we will defend against the coming of a third world war. In order to truly contrib-ute to the fight for peace, Kamiyama thought, Nagai needed to elaborate on and explain to the masses several of the points that appear in his books, such as how the use of atomic weapons is contradictory to humanity, that the atomic weap-ons currently in existence should be destroyed, and how the peaceful use of atomic energy could greatly contribute to world society and human history. However, "hopes and prayers will not protect peace" (74–75).

Fourth, Kamiyama attacked Nagai's character, claiming that he was a selfish person, not a paragon of humanism, and deserved no national honor. This was a response to Nagai's criticism of and opposition to communism in a 1949 article in the *Tokyo shinbun*, which Kamiyama thought demonstrated that Nagai's "opin-ions are extremely narrow." Nagai had never hidden his dislike of communism; he had written during the war of the danger of communism consuming China and eventually Japan.[105] The *Tokyo shinbun* article signified for Kamiyama and his Communist colleagues that "Mr. Nagai is completely ignorant about the labor movement," and they could not help but "smile wryly" as they read it. For them, Nagai was in no position to criticize the Communists because he continued social practices that were outdated relics from the days of feudal Japan. Kamiyama turned to one of Nagai's own books, *Rozario no kusari*, to support his argument, because in it, he claimed, Nagai treats his wife inhumanely.[106] In the book, Nagai wrote that his wife Midori, who had perished in the atomic bombing and whose ashes he found with a melted rosary, was a "simple woman" and that the main reason for marrying her was to have children. However, "with a farmer's daughter, who did not have the education that I had, clinging to me would only hinder success in life. Is that kind of person worthy of being the woman (*ojōsan*) of a university professor?" Kamiyama thought that Nagai did not respect Midori, and because he viewed her as inferior and as a subservient person who was meant to care for the household, Kamiyama accused Nagai of perpetuating feu-dalism. In short, Kamiyama explained, because of Nagai's "feudal," "inhumane," and "narrow-minded" qualities, he and the Communists could not concur with the findings of the special committee that declared Nagai an "incarnation of humanism" (75–77).

The final point that Kamiyama made put Nagai at the center of the struggle between communism and capitalism for the "peace, freedom, and independence" of Japan. Kamiyama accused capitalists of using the "saint of Urakami" as a political tool to appease the working class, and it was therefore capitalism that had corrupted the Diet. The Democratic Party, which Kamiyama accused of having used the Nagai debate to attack the Communists, was the biggest culprit with its "misgovernment" of the Diet, which pushed forward a course of recon-struction that benefited the capitalists. In this respect, the Democrats had the most to gain from the Nagai award. "They say that through this 'saint' they give consolation and strength to the 'workers' and the 'weak,' and they 'arouse the will to reconstruct,'" when in fact, Kamiyama insisted, the Democrats were simply working to "preserve their own system of rule." What they were actually doing was "crushing the industry of the nation, creating widespread unemployment, tormenting the peasants, causing the mountains and rivers and seas of our beloved ancestral land to fall into ruin, and giving only pain and suffering to the 'workers' and the 'weak.'" In Kamiyama's mind, the capitalists were "non-Japanese" (*hi-Nichi*) and would destroy the nation in their greedy quest for money and power. In other words, the National Diet was appropriating the fame of Nagai in order to overwrite memory of the recent past for their personal gain (77–78).

Kamiyama denied the Democrats' accusation that the opposition to Nagai stemmed from a hatred of Catholicism, which grew out of a centuries-long battle between Catholicism and communism that began "hundreds of years before Kamiyama's fatherland, the Soviet Union, gained political power." The policy of the Communists in bringing "peace, freedom, and independence" to the people of Japan promised the best future for the country, Kamiyama declared, as his party would "strive to create a comprehensive democratic national front by transcending ideology (*shisō*), faith, gender, and nationality." The Democrats failed to recognize, Kamiyama went on to say, that "religion is a personal affair" and should not influence national issues. In conclusion, he pleaded, society must leave Nagai and his Catholic community to live according to their religion and not embroil them in the things of society that do not concern them: "Let God govern the matters of God." Religion and politics needed to be separated. Kamiyama believed that Nagai himself could not disagree with the political critique put forward by the Communist Party in light of the political motivations of the Diet in bestowing him with the national award (78–79).

Kamiyama was right. Nagai felt that the Diet had made a mistake by choosing him because he thought they had overlooked more qualified candidates. Shortly after the nomination, Nagai wrote, "It is a national disgrace that the National Diet would award someone like me, who is a failure at life and a citizen of a defeated nation. There are so many worldly persons (*sekaiteki jinbutsu*) who have truly worked for the reconstruction of the nation, and [the Diet] would do better to award those people." Nagai added, for good measure, "I agree with Representative Kamiyama's dissenting opinion."[107] Nagai's humility had no effect on the special committee and they moved forward with their vetting process for the award, which consisted of interviewing people close to Nagai, as well as scientists and other academics.

Other critics of the "saint of Urakami" emerged outside the political realm and included normal citizens and scholars, who did not agree that Nagai was the best choice for their country's honor. Konno Setsuzo, a "company employee" in Tokyo, echoed some of the general points of opposition, stating, "I do not think Dr. Nagai is the most eligible for the honor." It must be recognized that "Japan still is in the process of reconstruction; it has not yet been 'reconstructed.' Accordingly, no [single] person can be credited with contribution to its rehabilitation." In addition, "There are many scientists much superior to Dr. Nagai." Nagai's books, Konno concluded, are indeed "replete with his humanitarian sentiments but that is all. He has done no positive service for moral rehabilitation of the Japanese people. What made his books the best-sellers of the year are nothing but the beautiful style, the peculiar circumstances in which he has been placed and the publicity whipped up by publishers."[108] Although the Nagai boom embroiled most of the nation, some people in Japan maintained their skepticism of the circumstances surrounding his sudden fame and recognition.

Opposition to Nagai's nomination was out-voiced by popular opinion that agreed with the Diet that Nagai had made substantial contributions to the reconstruction of the nation. Some artists showed their support of Nagai by satirizing the opposition of the Communist Party. In the September 15, 1949, *Tōkyō taimuzu*, cartoonist Shimokawa Ōten depicted the "achievements of Dr. Nagai" as a giant "stake driven into the heart of the reconstruction of Japan," with a Diet member presenting the award to the stake, which extended up to the clouds. On the other side of the stake stands a blindfolded "Materialist [Diet] Representative" who "can't see" the massive contributions of Nagai in front of him.[109] In December 1949, the Diet voted unanimously to bestow the award on Nagai, and on June 1, 1950, he received the Prime Minister Award and the Imperial Silver Cups.[110] In the end, however, the Diet members decided not to award Nagai on the grounds of academic achievements, which the Communists had contested, but rather for his contributions to social reconstruction.

· · ·

The circumstances surrounding the National Diet's recognition of Nagai in 1949 represented more than a disagreement over his qualifications. They reflected a general stance against communism and a political loss for the Japanese Communist Party. The Communists had a point regarding the insistence on awarding a seemingly unqualified Nagai: the 1949 award for "persons whose deeds have contributed to the reconstruction of the nation" was also an attempt to appropriate Nagai's persona to depict Japan as a nation victimized by the atomic bombings. Instead of a former aggressor in East Asia, Japan could be linked to the image of a saint amid the atomic ruins. The emperor's visit to Nagai's bedside earlier that year was a literal photo opportunity to juxtapose the wartime leader with the atomic-bombing survivor, depicting Nagai's suffering as something to be shared by both the emperor and the Japanese nation more broadly. Regardless of how Nagai felt about his fame and awards, many groups sought to appropriate him to promote their own war narratives. The American occupiers, too, promoted Nagai's books to cultivate a narrative of the war in which it ended with punishing Japan for its war crimes through retribution by atomic bombing.

Nagai, who originally intended to console his community, based his interpretation of the bombing on specific religious and geographical contexts, but his writings shaped the formation of atomic narratives in at least two ways. First, the dissemination and promotion of Nagai's interpretation of the bombing in the immediate postwar era prevented other narratives of personal trauma and suffering from emerging, including among the Catholics, some of whom did not agree with him. One book, *Masako taorezu* (Masako shall not perish), written by a Nagasaki survivor and published in 1949, was no less heartbreaking in conveying the tragedy of the bombing than *Nagasaki no kane* published the same year, but it failed to compete with any of Nagai's books. In other words, the hype surrounding Nagai blinded Japanese readers and politicians, not to mention international audiences, to the other narratives and voices emerging from the atomic experience of Nagasaki. A self-proclaimed martyr replaced the individual experiences of tens of thousands of survivors. Second, in Nagai's formula, the United States did not factor into the bombing—it was all due to the work of God—which impeded discussion of the events surrounding the decision to drop the atomic bombs. Occupation-period censorship also contributed to the lack of discussion, of course, but Nagai's writings supported a view of history in which American responsibility was a nonissue. American censors realized the value of Nagai's writings and sought to use them to promote their own atomic narrative.

Nagai Takashi died from leukemia on May 1, 1951, at forty-three years of age, leaving behind his son Makoto (sixteen) and daughter Kayano (nine). Nagai donated his body to science to advance research on radiation-related illness. An autopsy revealed that his organs were badly affected, with his spleen thirty-five times larger than normal and his liver five-times larger. Despite the severity of his leukemia, Nagai had lived three years longer than expected. On May 3, the Urakami Catholics held a funeral mass for him, and on May 14, as a privilege of the first Honorary Citizen of Nagasaki City, awarded in 1949, he received a second, city-sponsored funeral, which attracted a crowd of around twenty thousand people.[111] Among the attendees was Prime Minister Yoshida Shigeru, who gave the funeral oration. Nagai's "achievements are truly remarkable with many implications for morality and faith," declared Yoshida. "Today, at the Nagasaki City Public Funeral Service, I extol the virtues of [his] life and reverently present this memorial address." Mayor Tagawa Tsutomu spoke as well, recounting Nagai's many contributions to science on the effects of radiation on the human body and his many books that garnered him and the city so much international attention. A representative from the Vatican attended the funeral and read a message from Pope Pius XII, who had sent Nagai a rosary together with a portrait containing a handwritten note in August 1950, and in December had bestowed on him an "exceptional blessing." "I extend my deepest sympathies to the bereaved family of Dr. Nagai," the pope stated. "Dr. Nagai, who had a deep understanding of Catholic doctrine and who transcended (*yoku shinogareta*) poor health, resides now in heaven as a grand protector of your nation."[112] In the first year and a half after Nagai's death, six books were published: two that he had written, one that he had edited, and three about him by other authors.[113] Among all of the books that bear his name, however, *Nagasaki no kane* provides the clearest window onto the relationship between discourse on the bombings, occupation-period censorship, and atomic narrative formation.

WRITING NAGASAKI

The Occupation Publishing Industry,
Nagasaki no kane, and Atomic Narratives

During the Allied occupation, SCAP control of the publishing industry contin-ued the psychological warfare against Japan that had thrived during the last year of the Second World War. The United States sought to refashion Japan from an enemy into an ally through its goal of democratization, thinking that, in order to do so, they first needed to fundamentally reform the psyche of the Japanese people. This approach, which informed official policy, made sense to SCAP officials, including chief of psychological warfare operations during the war, Brigadier General Bonner F. Fellers, who was one of MacArthur's closest advisers. After the war, Fellers's Psychological Warfare Branch (PWB) of the Office of War Informa-tion (OWI) became the Information Dissemination Branch (IDB) of the Civil Information and Education Section (CI&E) of SCAP.[1] Indeed, American offi-cials sometimes phrased the work of the occupation in wartime terms as a strug-gle for the minds of the people, a position which led them to create a "reorientation program" in the Office for Occupied Areas in the Department of the Army. The goal of the program was to bring the "peoples of the occupied areas into the main-stream of democratic life," seeking to "instruct and guide 90 million people in the ways of democracy" by tapping into and controlling "informational media" such as "motion pictures, press, periodicals, books, fine arts and exhibits." Through this program, they hoped they could achieve the "long-range task of *developing in the minds of the people a genuine understanding*" of American ideals of democ-racy (emphasis in original).[2] The IDB disseminated materials to this end within Japan.[3] Control of the publishing industry provided one means to control the flow of ideas. This is not to say, of course, that the American occupiers succeeded in influencing the minds of the Japanese people. The psychological warfare approach of the Americans did, however, shape the content of the material produced and published during the occupation. In other words, Japanese people produced books, films, and various other cultural media that might not have otherwise emerged or been as successful in other contexts.[4]

Many strategies of the psychological war against Japan during the Second World War continued into the occupation. In both contexts, the United States dedicated massive amounts of paper to disseminating ideas favorable to the Americans and their allies in the hopes of influencing the minds of the Japanese people. In July 1945, the PWB dropped 22,244,000 leaflets and newsletters in various languages over Southeast Asia, urging Japanese soldiers to surrender, explaining the evils of Japan to the peoples of this region, or generally trolling Japanese soldiers and citizens by boasting of American victories in the Pacific. In just fifteen days, from August 1 through the end of the war on August 15, American bombers dropped 11,225,972 so-called paper bombs over Japan and Southeast Asia, 8,111,856 in Japanese alone.[5] Japan, on the other hand, did not have access to large supplies of paper during the war, and thus they did not have equal ammunition to fight the psychological war on this level.[6] The scarcity of paper continued throughout most of the occupation and so SCAP and the government maintained a strict system of rationing, which offered one convenient method of information control.[7] While the demonstration of American power through firebombing and atomic bombs ended in August 1945, the bombardment of Japan with paper bombs continued throughout the occupation through control of the publishing industry. SCAP hoped that control of paper allocation and printing would help shape ideas in Japanese society and mold the nation in ways that suited the interests of the United States. Narratives of the war initially took shape within this context.

Among the tens of thousands of books published during the first five years after the war, the books by Nagai Takashi stand out as products of the policies of the Allied occupation. In other words, Nagai wrote his books within a historical context that allowed for their emergence in the literary world, as well as for their influence on Nagasaki's atomic narratives. After detailed review processes, American censors cleared all of Nagai's books for publication, which contained graphic accounts of the bombing as well as descriptions of the bomb and atomic energy from a physicist's perspective. In the case of *Nagasaki no kane*, SCAP even supplied substantial amounts of paper to print the book when paper was still scarce in Japan. American officials allowed Nagai to publish because his works offered a medium through which ideas inherent in the goals of SCAP, both official and unofficial, could reach Japanese citizens: Nagai perpetuated strong Christian morals; he did not criticize the use of the atomic bomb by the United

States, but rather expressed gratitude for it; he professed anticommunist ideas; and despite having witnessed the terrifying power of atomic science, he praised the future of atomic energy and related it to world peace. In other words, Nagai's books became best sellers because they coincided with the work of the Allied occupation to craft a narrative of the war and the bombings that suited the United States.

The publication of *Nagasaki no kane* illuminates the ways in which SCAP involvement in the publishing industry shaped discussions of the war. First, SCAP did not seek to eliminate all discussion of the atomic bombings, but rather to control the discussion as much as possible in order to shape the narrative of war, of which the atomic bombings were a part. Censors did not always object to discussion of the bombings per se, but rather to passages that might "invite resentment" against the United States, as they put it, or otherwise undermine that narrative or the goals of the occupation more generally. SCAP did not suppress discussions of the atomic bombings if they supported the American narrative(s) of the war. Second, Nagai's discussion of the bombing as a necessary sacrifice to end the war countered discussions of the bombings as crimes against humanity. Nagai's interpretation exempted American responsibility for the Nagasaki bombing, specifically, strengthening the American argument that both bombings were necessary for ending the war. Third, SCAP officials sought to shape the Japanese narrative of the war to match, or at least to complement, the American perspective, and the publication of *Nagasaki no kane* with an appendix detailing Japanese atrocities in Manila promised to do just that. Lastly, discussions among censors of Nagai's manuscript demonstrate how the machine of censorship depended on the opinions of individuals who were not always on the same page, resulting in a bureaucracy of information control replete with cracks through which discussions of the bombings trickled to the masses and narratives began to take shape.

Nagai's books provided an opportunity for SCAP to release a pressure valve in regards to popular interest in information on the bombings, while not jeopardizing the American narrative of the war (or so they hoped). The year 1949 marked a significant opening for the flow of particularly graphic discourse on the bombings, with *Nagasaki no kane* starting it off and several books by survivors from both Nagasaki and Hiroshima following shortly after. This did not mean that censorship ended; rather, it took on other, less obvious forms than outright suppression, yet still maintained the same objective of influencing the formation of narratives of the war and the atomic bombings. Partly because of SCAP's preference for Nagai over other Nagasaki authors, his books became the representative voice of the bombing during the occupation and for decades after it ended in 1952. The journey of the manuscript of *Nagasaki no kane* through the occupation-period publishing industry reveals, most important perhaps, that such atomic-bombing literature and narratives about the Nagasaki bombing in general were never pre-determined, but rather were a by-product of an American occupation. This is not to say that the United States won the psychological war or had a decisive influence on the minds of the Japanese people. Rather, SCAP control of the publishing industry shaped the flow of information regarding the war and the bombings, thus contributing to the early formation of atomic narratives and popular memory. The psychological war that continued into the postwar period produced the final version of *Nagasaki no kane* and provided a platform for the book in a way that no other book on the bombings enjoyed, ensuring the dominant presence of Nagai and his works in discussions of Nagasaki's bombing.

The Postwar Publishing Industry

The publishing industry was one of the first commercial sectors to recover after the war. As John Dower puts it, "as if a dam had broken, defeated Japan was engulfed in words," creating a "great river of communication" caused in large part by the lifting of the heavy wartime censorship of Japan's military government and the Japanese people's "hunger for words."[8] Just as the Allies did in wartime and postwar Europe, the Americans sought to tap into that hunger and make use of the "great river of communication" flowing among the people.[9] In Japan, the American occupiers controlled all aspects of publishing, from intellectual content to materials including glue, ink, and paper, creating a bureaucracy of control that spanned numerous departments and incorporated various methods not limited to conventional censorship. Occupation officials viewed censorship as a way to nurture the "seeds of democracy planted by SCAP," as they put it. During the first five years, SCAP had a hand in the publication of 77,019 books, including 49,268 first editions. Its goal was to put the publishing industry to work to help achieve the goal of democratization, an idea that found its way to the core of the industry. The opening lines of the 1947 Publishers' Code of the Japanese Publishers' Association declared that the "responsibility of the publishing industry is very significant in establishing a democratic society. Our publications must be such as to help our people understand the principles of democracy, and establish for themselves their own democratic institutions and practices."[10]

The publishing industry in occupied Japan evolved over three periods. The war had set the stage for the first period, the recovery phase, which lasted from the end of the war until mid-1947. In the last two years of the war, printing establishments had decreased from 18,225 to less than 4,000. The overall decline in the publishing industry during the war was due to a combination of factors, including wartime censorship, which had shut down publishers not directly contributing to the war effort; shortage of supplies such as glue, ink, and paper; and damage from Allied bombing in the last year of the war. In the first eight months of the recovery phase, the number of book publishing companies rose from 203 to 1,750. The "hunger for words" was at its peak, and, as a SCAP publication put it, for "the first two years of Occupation a seller's market prevailed. Publishers could dispose of practically every book printed." In terms of censorship during this phase, the Americans touted freedom of expression but suppressed discussion of ideas deemed counter to the work and goals of the occupation. Censorship targeted militaristic and ultranationalist thought, as well as anti-American sentiment, which included mentions of the atomic bombings that were critical of the United States. The process of censorship was conventional review of all prepublished material, which was called precensorship.[11]

The second period, 1947–49, was a relative heyday for the publishing industry, when the number of companies more than doubled to 4,600. In terms of censorship, this was the tapering period, when conventional, prepublication review was replaced with other methods of censorship. The target of suppression became leftist and communist ideas, instead of purely militaristic thought, leading to a policy from April 1948, at the start of the cold war, for the Press, Pictorial and Broadcast Division (PPB) of the Civil Censorship Detachment (CCD) to review 100 percent of communist media. The methods of the CCD also evolved. From 1948, SCAP ordered undesirable materials to be held without a decision in order to stall or suppress the writing from being published. Nagai's *Nagasaki no kane* was the first instance of this method. SCAP also began the process of postcensorship, whereby publishers who had earned the trust of SCAP could publish without review by CCD, but they were still required to self-censor unfavorable words and ideas should they be discovered by SCAP at a later date. Depending on the severity of the infraction of the published book, SCAP could order it pulled from store shelves. As John Dower notes, the economic danger inherent in the move to postcensorship had a "chilling rather than a liberating effect on many publishers, editors, and writers."[12]

While some publishers still had to submit for precensorship during the heyday, regional publishers enjoyed relative autonomy as long as infractions were minimal and publishers dealt with them accordingly. In the case of a 1948 book by Nagai Takashi, *Horobinu mono o*, which was subjected to postcensorship, the publisher, Nagasaki nichinichi shinbun sha, had to ensure that the term "Manchurian Incident" was redacted with ink from the final copies; however, Nagai's descriptions of the bombing were left untouched, including comments on patients who died of "radiation death" without external injuries and an account of discovering the charred bones of his wife among the ruins of his house.[13] Books intended to be published and disseminated on a national scale were still subject to the precensorship design, but the SCAP censorship apparatus on the local levels showed leniency, and sometimes support, to writers and publishers. SCAP use of the paper allotment to either reward or punish publishers emerged as another method of censorship. Because paper was scarce throughout most of the occupation, control of paper served as an effective way of controlling information. In early 1949, SCAP and the Japanese government decided to decrease the monthly allotment of paper for communist publications from 86,000 to 20,000 pounds, because by that time it was clear that such writings worked against nurturing the seeds of democracy. A reduction in paper meant that the valve of free-flowing communist ideas was being closed off. Months later, SCAP shut down thousands of communist publications entirely.[14] On the other hand, many of Nagai's books received generous allotments of paper from SCAP because they worked to strengthen the stance of the United States.

The third period began in 1949 and reflected the general poor state of the Japanese economy. By 1951, the number of publishing companies had fallen to about 1,900. SCAP dissolved the CCD in 1949, bringing to a close the official censorship apparatus, but leading to an unpredictability of a system of information control that lived on in other forms. Precensorship continued in some instances, but the bulk of publishers were put on the postcensorship list. If SCAP disliked a publication, however, it ordered it pulled from stores at an economic cost to the publisher, which encouraged further self-censoring. SCAP also wielded a heavy hand at times. In summer 1950, at the start of the Korean War, it ordered thousands of communist publications to shut down.[15]

The constant changes in policy and method made it difficult for writers, publishers, and even SCAP censors to know what was off limits and what was publishable. The subject of censorship was often a moving target, and so the methods of suppression, too, evolved with the times. As SCAP officials made adjustments to their methods of wielding power over the publishing industry, they sought to shape narratives of the war and the atomic bombings as published by Japanese authors that suited the purposes of the United States. Despite the unpredictability of censorship, the sensitivity and approach to public portrayals of the atomic bombings stayed constant. SCAP did not outright ban general discussion of the atomic bombings, as even a cursory look at local newspapers in late 1940s Nagasaki reveals. Rather, they suppressed materials related to the bombings that described or portrayed the human destruction in detail because it might "invite resentment" against the United States, as one censor put it, or if they outright criticized the United States for dropping the bombs. In other words, it was not the subject of the atomic bombings per se that was suppressed; context was important. In fact, occupation officials in Nagasaki thought that discussions of the bombings should not be censored but rather that the hibakusha should be supported in their efforts to speak of their experiences. At any rate, top SCAP leaders knew that discussion of the atomic bombings would eventually be out of their hands, and so they selectively approved books in an attempt to cultivate a narrative of Nagasaki and Hiroshima that did not explicitly indict the Americans. Nagai's book *Nagasaki no kane*, especially, provided them with the perfect opportunity to shape the narrative of the Nagasaki bombing.

It was during the heyday period that Nagai published most of his books and had the greatest success. During that time, the United States became increasingly concerned about the threat posed by communist activists in Japan, some of whom they worried were seeking to form a united front with the Chinese Communist Party. Indeed, SCAP worked to counter the rise of what they considered propaganda from such communist periodicals as *Akahata*.[16] When the occupation lifted the ban on criticizing the Soviet Union after the "reverse course" in policy that sought to dampen the communist political voice in Japan, books such as Nagai's were appealing. Writer Inoue Hisashi charged that Nagai's anticommunist approach to the atomic experience—in addition to his Christian rhetoric—led to his becoming a minion (*chōji*) of SCAP. The works of Nagai met the demands of "this internationally vigorous culture" (i.e., anticommunism), Inoue wrote, and proved their usefulness to SCAP after the reverse course in occupation policy. In other words, Nagai's rise to literary fame was not predestined; or, as Inoue noted, "books have a reason why they sell, and then they sell for that reason."[17]

Nagai openly opposed communism, and he envisioned the cold war as a struggle between Christianity and communism.[18] He had been openly expressing anticommunist feelings since the 1930s, continuing to relate what he saw as the dangers of communism in his postwar writings. In the number-one selling book of 1948, *Kono ko o nokoshite*, he made his case against communism by comparing "America and Western Europe where Christianity prospers" to the "wretched condition of the masses in Eastern Europe where Christianity is persecuted." He described how "when citizens become poor, anti-Christian communism becomes prosperous. For communism to flourish, it becomes necessary for [the communists] to make their citizens poor." To preclude communism taking root in Japan, Nagai advised his readers, "It is necessary that we, through the neighborly love of Christianity, give food, clothing, housing, new jobs, and preach the word of God to those poor people who will be pulled away by the evil hand of communism."[19]

Published from 1948, as the cold war intensified, Nagai's best-selling books conveyed anticommunist rhetoric to hundreds of thousands of readers. He condemned communism in another work, *Heiwa tō* (Peace tower, 1949). He argued that "the red leaders of materialism tame the masses to live only on bread; in other words, they train them to be domestic livestock that are the property of the nation."[20] In his 1948 best seller *Rozario no kusari*, Nagai illustrated how to be charitable in order to keep one's neighbors from falling into the hands of the communists and becoming "the property of the nation," by observing red ants near a jar of sugar. Nagai had taken out the sugar to sweeten some coffee that he received from Captain W. F. Deal of the U.S. Liberty Ship *George L. Farley* docked in Nagasaki.[21] The "pitiable red ants," Nagai wrote, approached the jar while periodically stopping to do "what appears to be praying." They then arrived at the sugar at which they look with sorrowful eyes. They did not look for an opening in the jar in order to steal the sugar, but simply looked up at the jar in awe of the beauty of the sugar, like monks (*shūshi*) singing hymns. Nagai, feeling pity for the red ants, gave them a pinch of sugar from the jar and exclaimed, "Oh, the surprise and gratitude of the red ants!"[22] The anticommunist message in Nagai's books, whether direct or through metaphor, was clear: if we help and love our communist neighbors, they will see the error of their ways, become enlightened, and turn to Christianity.[23] In part because Nagai's ideas on communism and Christianity coincided with the politics of the late 1940s, his books avoided suppression. But Nagai's role as Nagasaki author held value beyond his anticommunist appeal. Eventually, American occupation officials discovered that Nagai's ideas, especially those related to the atomic bombing of Nagasaki, could bolster the American narrative of the war, and they, too, set out to tap into the Nagai boom.

The Road to Publishing *Nagasaki no kane*

The majority of occupation-period discourse on atomic bombs focused on atomic energy and only incidentally on the significance of the bombings of Nagasaki and Hiroshima. In the postoccupation period, the national government and peace movements evoked the experience of the atomic bombings to portray Japan as a nation of victims of the war rather than its aggressors.[24] The transition from aggressor to victim began during the occupation period, with the publication of the books of Nagai Takashi playing a part. An examination of one of his books shows one of the ways that atomic victimization came to dominate the postwar story. The first manuscript that Nagai completed after his collapse from leukemia in 1946, *Genshi jidai no kaimaku* (Raising the curtain on the atomic age), received SCAP permission to be printed in January 1949 under the title *Nagasaki no kane* (The bell of Nagasaki), but only after Nagai had agreed to include an American-prepared appendix. By October, the book had become the fourth most-read best seller in Japan, behind the number-one *Kono ko o nokoshite*, also by Nagai.[25] The road to the final version of *Nagasaki no kane* reveals much about the publishing industry under the control of SCAP.

Occupation authorities understood that information regarding the atomic bombings could not be contained indefinitely. The books of Nagai provided them a way to slowly lift the ban, and lift it in a way that might work to their advantage. *Nagasaki no kane* detailed day-by-day the experience of the bombing and its aftermath, Nagai's medical musings, and his Christian rhetoric, including his November 1945 eulogy. Even though Nagai made revisions to the eulogy for publication, he stayed true to his main point: that the atomic bombing exemplified God's Providence. Before the eulogy in the book, Nagai depicts an encounter with his friend Yamada Ichitarō to whom he declared, "That the atomic bomb fell on Urakami is great Divine Providence. It is God's grace. Urakami should offer gratitude unto God."[26] Similar to his 1948 best seller *Kono ko o nokoshite*, *Nagasaki no kane* portrayed the atomic bombing of Nagasaki as the result of the grace of God.[27] Nagai's formulation of the atomic bombing as a providential tragedy in *Nagasaki no kane* caught the eyes of SCAP censors soon after the publisher, Tokyo Times Company, submitted the manuscript for censorship on March 24, 1947.[28] Seven days later, the Economic and Scientific Section (ESS) expressed "no objection to the publication of the physical and chemical information disclosed in this document."[29] The Public Health and Welfare Section (PHW) concurred, stating on April 10, "PHW has no objection" to the "physical effects on humans of the atomic bomb explosion at Nagasaki" because the descriptions put forth by Nagai in the manuscript "are of common knowledge and have been repeatedly publicised in newspapers and other stories."[30] The publisher Shikiba Shunzō remembers that when he submitted the manuscript earlier under its original title, *Genshi jidai no kaimaku*, it had elicited an abrupt "No, of course we can't publish this!" kind of reaction from the censors because of the book's references to "hell," "eruption of innards," "stomach ripping open and exposing intestines," and "eyeballs flying out."[31] But the nature of censorship was changing, and this time the manuscript, with its new title, translated as *The Bell Tolls for Nagasaki* in SCAP documents, seemed to be moving along quite smoothly.[32]

Nagai's blend of Christianity and antiwar sentiment in the book excited some censors. As early as April 29, 1947, SCAP censor Richard (Dick) Kunzman recommended that *Nagasaki no kane* pass censorship and be published in its entirety, noting in his report two significant passages that demonstrated why the manuscript was eligible. The first was a lesson by Nagai about the Bible to two of his former students who had fought in the war, in which Nagai advised them to throw away silly ideas of revenge and of "rising again like Germany did with our swords in our hands." Kunzman pointed out that Nagai explained, in "the Scriptures one reads the words of God, 'Vengeance is mine, I will repay.' God punishes those who are unjust in His eyes, without regard to gains and losses in battles fought on earth. The question of revenge lies beyond us."[33] Nagai encouraged his readers to embrace defeat without feelings of vengeance and exert themselves to maintain peace. He offered, through his manuscript, a potential tool for precluding ultra-nationalist ideas of revolt against the occupiers, but more important, Nagai promoted antiwar sentiment. The second passage that Kunzman singled out also rang a familiar Christian tone. He reported that the "author includes an oration read at the funeral service for those who died by the bomb: 'It is God who gives, and God who takes. Praised be his name. And let us offer thanks to Him that Urakami was chosen for the sacrifice. Let us be thankful that through this sacrifice peace was restored to the world, and freedom of belief given to Japan.' (Urakami is a section of Nagasaki)." The importance of this passage had appeal beyond the Christian tone. Because Nagai was "thankful" for the atomic bomb ending the war through the martyrdom of his community, he removed the United States from discussion of the morality of the atomic bombings. Kunzman concluded in regard to the censorship of *Nagasaki no kane*: "Recommend book be passed in entirety."[34]

Another censor, John (Jack) Costello of the CI&E, vehemently objected. Costello could not understand how *Nagasaki no kane* had been recommended for publication, and he was perplexed by the incompetency of the censorship apparatus. "I could not believe this document had been given deliberate censorship examination after I read only a few pages," wrote an incredulous Costello. "It is clear to anyone who reads it that some parts must be deleted, if the book were allowed to pass at all." Furthermore, Costello added,

> I asked Dick [Kunzman], who recommended that it be passed in its entirety, if he had read it. He had "skimmed through" the first part, he said, and read the last part, described in his memo, thoorughly [sic]. I asked if anyone in PPB I had read the entire book. He didn't know, but "thought that Mr. Takata (head of Book Department) read it." . . . In other words, no one in PPB I read it before bucking it to me. I can understand that it is quite a chore, because I had to read it. Careful censorship, of course, is not spectacular, but it is certainly a sine qua non. This is not the first instance, or only instance, of tedious, time-consuming routine being avoided by PPB I.[35]

The same day, May 5, 1947, Costello sent a memo directly to Kunzman, chastising him for what he saw as laziness, and he advised Dick to do his job: "It is impossible to censor material without reading it or a completely satisfactory brief."[36] But rather than simple laziness, Kunzman's work on *Nagasaki no kane* illustrates the nature of censorship during the occupation: not everyone understood what the work of censorship entailed, nor was it always clear what material should be suppressed. But some censors, like Costello, did not think there existed any grey area in regards to censorship.

Costello pushed hard to stop the approval of *Nagasaki no kane*. In his May 5 report, after acknowledging that the ESS, PHW, and Kunzman all recommend the book for publication in full, Costello stated, "I recommend the book be suppressed, on grounds that it would invite resentment against U.S. If desired, will prepare IOM [interoffice memo] for forwarding to CIS [Civil Intelligence Section of SCAP] or G-2 [Intelligence Division] for action." His main reason for recommending suppression was that the book "describes at length the scenes of horror, and the great death toll, as well as the destruction of irreplacable [*sic*] medical personnel and equipment, by the atom bomb, and the painful injuries inflicted on the victims."[37] On May 15, Costello sent the interoffice memorandum to General Charles A. Willoughby, the head of G-2. He conveyed his concerns as outlined in the May 5 memo, but went on to point out a significant omission in Nagai's book: "No mention is made of destruction of military objectives."[38] General Willoughby concurred with Costello "because [the book] described the horrors and the great death toll and thus was likely to disturb public tranquility and create ill will toward the United States."[39] For Willoughby and Costello, the danger in *Nagasaki no kane* was not that it discussed the atomic bombing per se, but rather because parts of the book depicted the human destruction caused by the bomb, which would remind Japanese people of the human destruction caused by the United States.

However, the book was not suppressed. Instead, G-2 decided to *suspend* publication for six months, which changed the nature of censorship of the bombings as well as other sensitive topics.[40] A memo dated May 16, 1947, ended the controversy over the fate of Nagai's book, at least for the time being:

> A manuscript of a book entitled "The Bell Tolls for Nagasaki" was referred in the following order to: MTT, RRZ, RHK, RRZ, Masuda, ESS Tech Intel, PHW, ESS, Hank Masuda, RRZ, RHK, JJC, Col Putnam, JJC, Col Myrick of CIS, Col Blake of CIS, Gen Willoughby, Col Bratton, Col Putnam, JJC, RHK, RRZ and now you [probably RMS, meaning Captain Shaw]. There were various recommendations made in connection with it, including "Pass in Entirety", "Pass With Deletions", "Suppress",. [punctuation *sic*] The last comment, and the significant one for your reference in future censorship action, was made by Col Putnam who stated:
>
> "*Costello*: Book is not suppressed, only suspended for 6 mo. as will all articles or books of this nature. We propose to allow publication at a future date. WBP"[41]

And so *Nagasaki no kane* was granted permission to be published, albeit "at a future date" and under to-be-determined conditions. When Colonel Putnam had ordered that the publication not be suppressed, but rather suspended, Costello thought that was "pretty slick, 'cause we never did that before."[42] A new technique for SCAP to control the "great river of communication" was born.

When the six months had passed, a representative from the local district censorship bureau visited Nagai in January 1948 to confirm his illness.[43] Nagai's publishers had pleaded to SCAP censors from early on for a quick and positive response to the matter of publication because "the author (Nagai) desired to see his book published prior to his death." Indeed, as the censors understood, Nagai "was near death (acute leukemia) in Jan 48."[44] According to the representative's report, Nagai explained that he wrote *Nagasaki no kane* in response to Hiroshima having garnered so much attention and sympathy from American readers, while Nagasaki was largely ignored. Nagai claimed that the bombing of his city was vastly more significant than Hiroshima, and he hoped that American readers would acknowledge that fact.[45] The story of the atomic bombing of Hiroshima had captivated the sympathy of American readers as early as 1946 when John Hersey published his account of six survivors in the *New Yorker* as "Hiroshima."[46] Costello, in his May 5, 1947, detachment concerning *The Bell Tolls for Nagasaki*, acknowledged the similarity of the writings, noting that Nagai's book was "an eye-witness account of bombing of Nagasaki, resembling Hersey's article in New Yorker."[47]

Yoshida Ken'ichi, scholar of English literature and son of Prime Minister Yoshida Shigeru, translated *Nagasaki no kane* into English at the request of Shikiba Ryūsaburō at Hibiya shuppan sha, and published an abridged version in the *Japan Review* 12, no. 16, April 17, 1949.[48] Earlier, SCAP censors, who were already familiar with Yoshida, noticed with some irritation his involvement with the book: "YOSHIDA Kenichi [*sic*] is in the act here too, just as in the Battleship of Yamato deal," of which Yoshida was the "ringleader."[49] Despite opposition from SCAP, Shikiba intended to publish the entire translation in America because, he argued, even though Hersey's *Hiroshima* was the first book and an immensely valuable piece of literature on the atomic bombings, *Nagasaki no kane* was the first account written from the point of view of a Japanese person.[50] A complete translation would have to wait because Nagai wanted to first publish the book for Japanese readers, who were his primary audience.

Nagai's publisher resubmitted a request for *Nagasaki no kane* to SCAP in January 1948.[51] In March, after it had been sitting for nearly a year without an official decision on publication, General Willoughby and the censors began reexamining the book.[52] Willoughby decided to allow publication by Hibiya shuppan sha on the condition that the author include the appendix about Japanese atrocities in Manila. At first, Nagai's publishers refused because, they claimed, "the purposes of the publications are entirely different." The publishers in charge of Nagai's manuscript, Shikiba Ryūsaburō and his younger brother Shunzō, even pointed out how with "great meekness the author admits the justification for dropping of the atomic bomb" in the book. But Willoughby demanded that the "other side of the story" be given "or the book would be suppressed in the future as well."[53] The Shikiba brothers and Nagai eventually acquiesced to SCAP's demand to include the appendix, *Manira no higeki* (Tragedy of Manila), which accompanied the publication of *Nagasaki no kane* in January 1949.[54] In February 1949, less than a month after its debut, the initial 30,000 copies of *Nagasaki no kane* sold out, and five months later in July the number had reached 110,000.[55] In March, it was the number-six best-selling book in Japan behind Yoshikawa Eiji's popular historical novel *Miyamoto Musashi*.[56]

Before publishing his November 1945 eulogy in *Nagasaki no kane*, Nagai made edits to it that reflected the American narrative of the war and the bombing. The original eulogy framed the war in terms of the "fifteen-year war" that had begun with the Manchurian Incident in 1931, but both terms were scrubbed in the 1949 *Nagasaki no kane* version, leaving more room for his conclusion that there had been many chances to end the war but only Urakami suited God for a sacrifice.[57] The elimination of the context of the Second World War in East Asia perpetuated the American narrative of the war as a conflict between the United States and Japan, that is, the Pacific War, which began ten years after the Manchurian Incident. The target of the bombing, too, changed in the published version. In the original eulogy, Nagai had noted that the American bomber "aimed for the vicinity of the prefectural office in the heart of Nagasaki City," or, in other words, a residential and nonmilitary hub of the city.[58] In *Nagasaki no kane*, Nagai changed the passage to read that the American bomber had "aimed for war plants (*gunju kōjō*)."[59] Although Nagai mentioned an original target in the sentence in both versions in order to argue that the bomb drifted to Urakami because it was a more significant "sacrifice" to end the war, the change in wording reflects the American claim that the targets were military installations, not residential areas. Nagai was, of course, correct in his initial assertion because the American bombers indeed aimed for area "114061" on their target map, or the residential area of the city that included the prefectural office.[60]

The Manila Appendix: Creating an Atomic Narrative

The 1949 publication of *Nagasaki no kane* was a milestone for the spread of information about the atomic bombings as well as for the American narrative of the end of the war. The book seemed useful to occupation officials because they thought they might piggyback on Nagai's popularity to spread their own message. As the Civil Intelligence Section (CIS) pointed out in January 1948, "The book is well-written and will undoubtedly sell well. . . . Recommend we do *not* suppress it."[61] A potential best-selling book about the bombing of Nagasaki did not worry SCAP officials about the spread of information about the atomic experience; rather, it excited them. With this book, they thought, they could shape discourse surrounding the bombing, and perhaps of the war more generally. The atomic narrative of the book, in which God dropped the atomic bomb and brought an end to the war, complemented and bolstered the narrative put forth by the United States that the bombed ended the war and saved American lives. A potential best-selling book could convey that message to readers all over Japan. Furthermore, to divert any possible criticism of the United States for dropping the bombs, SCAP placed the account of the Japanese attack at Manila at the end of the book to explain to Japanese readers the reason for the destruction about which they just read. The placement was crucial: having the Manila account as an appendix instead of, say, a preface would leave readers with the Japanese attack fresher in their minds than the American attack on Nagasaki.

Among the many known atrocities committed by the Japanese military during the war, the "Manila tragedy" was, for American officials, the natural choice to append to a book about the Nagasaki bombing. General MacArthur had a deep connection with the Philippines, of course, but more than that, the Americans considered the people of the Philippines "our nationals," as one official put it. The Japanese attack on the Philippines, then, was personal. The Americans were also not interested in portraying Japanese atrocities per se; if so, the Nanjing massacre would have perhaps made the more obvious choice. In 1948, when Nagai's book and the appendix were under consideration, the Americans were not interested in portraying the Chinese as victims because, much to the chagrin of the United States, the Communists were on the verge of a complete takeover in China. Furthermore, the Manila attack fit into the American narrative of the Pacific War in which the Chinese factored relatively little. The Americans had nothing to gain by portraying the Chinese as victims of the Japanese, but depicting "our nationals" as victims promised, they hoped, to rationalize the American use of the atomic bomb(s). SCAP officials hoped that inclusion of the Manila appendix would be understood by Japanese readers as retribution that had been rightly meted out to Japan for its war crimes and that the atomic bombing(s) exemplified Japan's redemption for its past aggression. That is, the atomic bomb(s) had given the Japanese people a new start by wiping the slate clean, as it were. From the perspective of the United States, cultivating postwar Japan in this way suited their needs as they attempted to fashion Japan into a cold war ally.

To ensure that their narrative of the war and the atomic bombing reached a wide audience with the book's publication, SCAP turned to a familiar strategy of psychological warfare: the careful and planned use of paper. To help the book become a best seller, SCAP set aside enough paper for the Japanese publishers to print 30,000 copies in its initial release.[62] In other words and in wartime terms, the 330-page book's first printing equaled 4,950,000 double-sided sheets worth of "paper bombs"; by July 1949, the book had sold 110,000 copies, delivering 18,150,000 sheets of paper bombs to Japanese readers. Furthermore, the paper allotted for the initial printing was not the usual rationed *zara* (pulp) paper, but rather *senka* (reclaimed) paper, which was classified as nonrationed because it was of (slightly) better quality and therefore of more value to all interested parties.[63] SCAP used paper allotment as a form of punishment or reward in its censorship method, and so the large allocation of paper to the *Nagasaki no kane* project rewarded Nagai and his publishers for the favorable interpretation of the bombing and their overall cooperation. It also served the agendas of SCAP. The investment of paper supported the atomic narrative that the United States was hoping to cultivate: the bombing was divine retribution for the Japanese atrocities during the Second World War. The SCAP investment in Nagai's book also gave life to the American-written Manila report. Produced by the OWI, just as were the pamphlets during the war, the Manila appendix was another form of paper bomb, also written during the war, to be dropped on the minds of the Japanese people.

SCAP allotted Nagai's publishers generous amounts of paper for the initial printing of his books, often more than they allocated to other books about the Nagasaki bombing. His *Genshiun no moto ni ikite* received paper for ten thousand copies (three thousand zara and seven thousand senka); a simple pamphlet Nagai produced to raise money for the rebuilding of the Urakami Cathedral, received zara for five thousand copies. Incredibly, *Hana saku oka* (June 1949) received enough senka for thirty-five thousand copies, which was perhaps a reward to the publisher, Hibiya shuppan sha, for cooperating with SCAP on *Nagasaki no kane*. By contrast, a 1949 volume of twenty-two hibakusha accounts published by Nagasaki City was allotted zara paper for only three thousand copies.[64] In this way, SCAP controlled the flow of paper out of Nagasaki (and Hiroshima) as one way to control the story of the atomic experiences.

The release of *Nagasaki no kane* differed from Nagai's previous books in that the inclusion of the appendix presented the Nagasaki bombing as a justified attack. During the occupation, American officials feared that the atomic bombings must appear to others to be an atrocity. Indeed, several intellectuals all over the world shared the sentiment that the atomic bombings were crimes against humanity, but U.S. officials defended the bombings and combated the notion that they were a war crime.[65] The purpose of the Manila appendix, as Willoughby saw it, was to show the "other side of the story," or, in other words, the reason for using the atomic bombs against Japan. Willoughby argued that the appendix would clearly demonstrate that "we used the bomb to terminate a war *which we did not start*," so "if and when American military acts were described (as the bombing), then Jap military acts *that were provocation or motive will have to be shown*" (emphases in original).[66] The Americans viewed the atomic bombings as an appropriate response to Japanese aggression during the war, and the Manila appendix gave them an opportunity to justify the bombings as retribution.[67] Nagai had already argued in many of his books that the bombing represented atonement for the sin of war. If the "saint of Urakami" included the appendix, then Japanese readers, too, might begin to view the atomic bombings as just punishment for the sins of their nation during the war. Or so the American occupiers may have hoped.

The appendix, which had been prepared long before Nagai ever wrote *Nagasaki no kane*, portrayed the Japanese attack on Manila as an attack against the United States. The first page of the Manila appendix contained a memo from Senator Elbert D. Thomas, chairman of the U.S. Senate Committee on Military Affairs, to Senator Carl Hayden. The memo, dated June 16, 1945, nearly two months before the atomic bombing, summarized the significance of the account of Manila in the eyes of the U.S. military: "Since the Japanese atrocities in Manila were committed on territory under our flag, and against persons who are our nationals, it is felt that our official condemnation of Japanese atrocities can be effected only through the most formal kind of censure." Thomas wrote that because the account derived from military documents, it provides "the solemn pledge of the national honor in attestation of the truth of these reports."[68] The Japanese attack on Manila equated to an attack on American soil, which called for retaliation. The date of the memo suggests that the military had wanted to publish the information about Manila for years. Nagai's detailed account of the Nagasaki bombing gave them the opportunity to present to the Japanese people their own military's atrocities committed against American nationals. For the Americans, the Manila account was the more important part of the publication, illustrated also by the imbalance of photographs included in each account. The appendix included seven photographs, all depicting human suffering and death in Manila, whereas the account of Nagasaki included only four photographs, with one simply showing a large cloud of smoke with no destruction at all.

Atrocities committed against the peoples of Asia who were not considered American nationals, however, were not mentioned. Indeed, the narrative being put forth in the *Nagasaki no kane*–"Manira no higeki" publication was that of the conflict between Japan and the United States. In the preface to *Nagasaki no kane*, Shikiba Ryūsaburō pleaded to Japanese readers: "As we lower our heads to the tragedy of Nagasaki, we must also deeply reflect on the Manila Incident (*jihen*). Mr. Nagai's record will be looked upon by the people of the world as the first account of the atomic bombing experience in the world, and will definitely leave its mark on the world. That is why we Japanese, along with [*Nagasaki no kane*], must read the Manila Incident with solemn feelings."[69] Japanese readers, that is, should reflect on their country's role in the Pacific War, not the conflict with China. Indeed, Shikiba, Nagai, and SCAP officials effaced Japan's conflict with China and the country's aggression in East Asia more broadly through publication of the book. The only atrocity that mattered to American officials, and on which they required the Japanese deeply reflect, was one of their own interest. With the *Nagasaki no kane*–"Manira no higeki" publication then, Nagai, Shikiba, and SCAP officials encouraged Japanese readers to understand the necessity for the American use of the atomic bombs as punishment for the crimes of their nation in war. However, SCAP's logic for including "Manira no higeki" unintentionally reaffirmed what they had wanted to prevent all along: that the atomic bombing of Nagasaki was an atrocity visited on a civilian population.[70] SCAP intended to illustrate the reasons for the use of the bombs, but the appendix of one tragedy to the book about another appeared as an admission that the atomic bombing of Nagasaki, too, was an inhumane act. Yet, allowing *Nagasaki no kane* to be published by itself seemed a greater threat to the occupation because, as General Willoughby had put it, it had the potential to "disturb public tranquility and create ill will toward the United States."

SCAP officials hoped that the appendix would bolster another war narrative that it had worked to cultivate during the occupation: that the Japanese military government had led the country astray. The preface to the appendix declared, "The primary responsibility for the crimes lies with the Japanese Supreme Command and the Japanese Government which re-presented [*sic*] the Emperor. Moreover, the Japanese people cannot escape the responsibility for the terrible crimes. The Japanese are, morally speaking, accomplices and are, therefore, guilty."[71] SCAP hoped to divert the "ill will" about the bombings from being directed at the Americans to being directed at the wartime government of Japan.[72] In fact, framing the war and the country's destruction as the sole responsibility of Japan's military leaders had been a key goal of Fellers's Psychological Warfare Branch during the war as well. In summer 1945, for example, a key objective of the "Weekly Military Plan for Psychological Warfare" against Japan was to "show responsibility of militarists for national disaster," and, furthermore, to "drive a wedge between the people and the Emperor on the one hand and the militarists on the other."[73] The publication of *Nagasaki no kane* brought a wartime objective into the postwar culture of Japan, providing a way for American officials to keep their psychological warfare alive through the maintenance of a wartime narrative.

The tragedy at Manila had long exemplified the aggression of the Japanese wartime government in the eyes of the Americans. The June 16, 1945, memo to Senator Hayden that prefaced the Manila appendix reflected the desire to inform people about the Japanese military's savagery in Manila. Frank Capra's 1945 film for the U.S. military, *Know Your Enemy—Japan*, served the same purpose. Capra includes the Manila tragedy as testimony to the barbarity of the Japanese enemy, depicting images of the dead juxtaposed with sarcastic narration explaining that this exemplified Japan's assertions to "peace," "co-prosperity," and "enlightenment."[74] Relating the story of the massacre at Manila was for American officials the best way to then illustrate the wartime barbarity of the Japanese military, which had, in their eyes, necessitated the bombs. President Harry Truman's comment to the Federal Council of Churches in defense of the use of the atomic bombs had reflected that wartime view of the Japanese: "When you have to deal with a beast you have to treat him as a beast."[75] Although the Manila appendix evoked the stereotype of the wartime Japanese enemy as savage and subhuman to justify the dropping of the bombs, it did not reflect the occupation's attitude toward the Japanese people.

The concern of SCAP was not what impact the depiction of the wartime Japanese people might have, but rather how the actions of the United States during the war appeared to the Japanese public. Shortly after *Nagasaki no kane* was published in January, SCAP prepared a summary report on the book and the Manila appendix, showing its top-down process from G-2 against the dissent of the censors. Captain Shaw (RMS) wrote in February 1949 that the "joint Nagasaki-Manila" publication represented the American bombings of Nagasaki and Hiroshima as atrocities. "Coupling of these accounts in publication," he noted in the report, "is direct demonstration of what the Japanese mean when they claim that Nagasaki-Hiroshima was just as bad as, if not worse than, the Japanese atrocities in Manila & Nanking, and that our action cancels out their guilt."[76] SCAP officials realized, albeit too late, that the Manila appendix equated the two American atomic bombings to two of the most infamous Japanese war crimes. The coupling of Nagasaki and Manila in fact appeared to have canceled out the guilt for atrocities that Japanese readers were supposed to have felt by intensifying the sense of victimization by the atomic bomb.

The way in which SCAP dealt with writings on Nagasaki also contributed to the Christian image of ground zero. In the case of the dual *Nagasaki no kane*– "Manira no higeki" publication, both events were framed as Christian tragedies. The content of *Nagasaki no kane* included discussion of the history of oppression, persecution, and martyrdom of Nagasaki Christians, setting up the context for the Providence of the bombing. The residents of Manila, as discussed in the appendix, were not just "our nationals" in the colonial sense. They were Christian. The Japanese slaughter of Christian nationals of the United States, as some

American officials saw it, constituted an attack on the Christian religion, a theme that became a tool of propaganda. The narrator of Capra's *Know Your Enemy—Japan* argues that "Shinto seems to be a nice, quaint religion for a nice, quaint people," but its doctrine "is now evil," and the Pacific War is a fight to save "Christian humanity."[77] This statement echoed utterances in the West, such as the claim by British Lord Halifax that the war equated a "struggle to save Christian civilization."[78] Reminiscent of such remarks, the Manila appendix echoed the view of the war as a religious crusade.

SCAP sought to put forth the narrative of the Nagasaki bombing as a necessary act, both as retribution for the attack on Christian Manila and as a means to end the war, as though that were the plan all along. The preface to the appendix discusses the oppression of Christians and Christianity in Japan as a precedent for the actions of the Japanese military in the Philippines: "The Japanese sought to wipe clean every last drop of the stench of Christianity in the Philippines. . . . Churches, schools, and the property of [Christian] groups were indiscriminately destroyed. The result of the Japanese attempt to extirpate (*nekosogi jokyo*) the vigor of Christianity in the Philippines surpasses the pain endured by Christians in Nagasaki and Shimabara four hundred years ago."[79] The English translation of the "Preface to Tragedy of Manila" in SCAP documents differed slightly from the original, but stressed how "One of the incomprehensible things about Japanese policy was that the Japanese wanted to eliminate all that was under Christian influence. Pastors, missionaries, nurses and orphans in monasteries were all murdered. Not only the Catholics, but anyone who has connections with Christianity, whether he was Catholic or Protestant, all had to suffer."[80] The SCAP translator had replaced a sentence about the beheading of eleven Baptist missionaries with mention of Protestants, who did not appear in the original Japanese version of the text, perhaps to appeal to SCAP officials such as General MacArthur who were Protestant.[81] The translator added that in the account of Manila, "Several examples of atrocities against Christians are given," including the "Murder of children in Catholic schools."[82] The preface concluded that "America and the entire world had no other choice but to drop the atomic bomb" to end these indiscriminate acts of atrocity, and in doing so "saved the countless souls of Japan and other countries."[83]

But occupation officials and censors did not observe that the bombing meted out the retribution for an attack on Christian Manila on the largest population of Christians in all of Japan. Nagai wrote clearly about the bombing as a Christian tragedy in *Nagasaki no kane*, especially in the eulogy of November 1945, which the censors had taken note of from early on. Not only were the Americans then unwittingly equating one atrocity with another, but they were also framing the Nagasaki bombing as an eye-for-an-eye retaliation, one act of Christian destruction as retribution for another.

Other Voices from Nagasaki and Hiroshima

Books on the atomic bombings which did not suit the goals of the occupation did not fair as well as Nagai's writings. Hibakusha authors in Nagasaki and Hiroshima attempted to publish narrative and poetic accounts of their atomic-bombing experiences, but their readership remained limited during the occupation, if they were able to avoid censorship at all. The other survivors who did write and manage to publish presented a narrative of the bombings that contrasted with Nagai's Catholic interpretation; they conveyed the horrifying realities of atomic destruction instead of religious interpretations that seemed to undermine the significance of the tragedy. However, regional presses in or around Nagasaki and Hiroshima published much of the early atomic-bombing literature, including the lesser-known works of Nagai such as *Horobinu mono o*. Indeed, for the first eight or so years after the war, the atomic bombings remained a local literary subject.

The hibakusha writers who did publish faced challenges that Nagai had seemingly transcended. In addition to basic censorship, dissemination of and interest in Nagasaki/Hiroshima literature remained limited because the genre of atomic-bomb literature (*genbaku bungaku*) was not welcomed into the Japanese literary tradition. Well into the 1950s, as John Treat notes, "atomic-bomb literature was generally regarded as a local literature restricted to the provinces, a minor literature concerned with a minor theme."[84] Many publishers thought that books and other writings by hibakusha would not be popular and chose not to publish them. Even the magazine *Hiroshima bungaku* (Hiroshima literature) ignored hibakusha writings. The hibakusha claimed that their writings formed a new genre, but literary circles disagreed, including the Hiroshima bungaku kai (Hiroshima Literature Society). Kurihara Sadako and other survivors found it irritating that such pretentious groups determined the fate of writings on the atomic bombings. In 1953, Ōta Yōko spoke out against the *bundan*, which were exclusive, bourgeois groups consisting of writers, critics, and editors, who had historically determined what constituted *bungaku* (literature), and who denied Ōta and other hibakusha a position in the literary world as authors of a new genre. Debates on the atomic bombings as a subject of literature waged for several decades.[85] Perhaps what made Nagai's books successful, at least in part, was that he never identified his writings as a new genre or purported them to be so; he intended them to serve as a record of the bombing of Nagasaki to convey the experience of the city and the significance as he saw it, often employing literary conventions to these ends, as did most hibakusha authors. However, Nagai had also benefited from the backing of municipal and national leaders, not to mention the occupation government, and so his works found avenues to reach audiences in ways that the works by other Nagasaki/Hiroshima writers did not.

Despite debates over the bombings' place in the Japanese literary tradition, SCAP controlled the publishing industry during the occupation, and thus they controlled which writings on the bombings would be published. Nagai's antiwar message appealed to SCAP officials, who hoped that the message would appeal to a wide audience, and also helped bring his books to print. As he wrote of Nagasaki's place in postatomic Japan, Nagai promoted the phrase "Peace starts from Nagasaki" (*Heiwa wa Nagasaki yori*) in his books, spreading an antiwar message to a nationwide audience at a time when Japan set out to create a so-called peace-loving nation, perhaps best exemplified in Article 9 of the country's constitution (1947), which committed Japan to pacifism. For SCAP, of course, Nagai's writings offered a steam valve for information on the bombings through prose couched in religious and antiwar sentiment, while his books also helped fashion the American narrative of the war and the bombings as necessary to end the war and punish Japan for its wartime aggression. The Hiroshima writers and the other writers from Nagasaki did not offer the same package.

Some occupation officials were sympathetic to the hibakusha and thought that eyewitness accounts of the bomb were important testimonies about the dawn of the atomic age, even if they depicted the human destruction and thus appeared critical of the United States. When Ishida Masako, a teenage survivor in Nagasaki, sought to publish her account, *Masako taorezu* (Masako shall not perish) in March 1947, American officials supported her. Captain Irvin W. Rogers recommended to the CCD in Fukuoka that Ishida's book and her father's book-length account be published without censorship. The Nagasaki Military Government Team, he wrote, "feels that the books . . . are worthy of publication. They are true and gripping depictions of a vivid personal experience." Furthermore, he asserted, "The books were examined in manuscript form and were found to contain nothing censorable." Colonel Delnore also attached a note to the letter saying that the two books were valuable in conveying the truth of atomic experience: "They show the reactions of the members of one small family in the holocaust; they show the heartbreak and the pain." Furthermore, Delnore pointed out, "For us to properly realize the significance of the atomic bomb, to experience vicariously the feelings that so many thousands of Japanese people experienced is desirable in these propitious times."[86]

After initial rejection, Captain Rogers sent another letter in June. The district censor in Fukuoka, Major George P. Solovskoy, replied that the book indeed violated the Press Code and could therefore not be approved for publication. "This District believes," Solovskoy wrote in summer 1947, "that the novel, 'MASAKO TAOREZU', would disturb public tranquility in Japan and that it implies the bombing was a crime against humanity." The differing opinions between Rogers and Solovskoy about the content of the book revealed, as in the case of the censors of *Nagasaki no kane*, disconnect among personnel in the censorship bureaucracy about what was off limits. Rogers had argued that Nagasaki-based American personnel found nothing censorable, but Solovskoy figured that such descriptions of the bombing as "Flesh raw from burns, bodies like peeled peaches" could not be published in a book to be sold "to the Japanese public." Had the book remained "merely for the personal records of the writer's family," Solovskoy implied that it would not have been censored. The book was suppressed, "at least for the time being," or as Solovskoy also explained it, "publication in Japan should be postponed until some future time when it would be less apt to tear open war scars and rekindle animosity."[87]

As a last-ditch effort, however, the local publisher, Fujiki hakuei sha, collected and submitted statements from prominent Nagasaki residents who petitioned for the book's publication, among them Mayor Ōhashi, Governor Sugiyama, and Urakami Catholic bishop Yamaguchi Aijirō. The supporters all testified that the book did not stir in them any anti-American feelings.[88] These efforts were to no avail in 1947, but *Masako taorezu* was finally published by a different company, Fujin taimuzu sha, on February 20, 1949, a few weeks after Nagai Takashi's *Nagasaki no kane* (January 30).[89]

Masako's book, however, never attained the popularity of Nagai's book. For one, it did not receive a special allotment of paper for its initial printing separate from its standard allotment of rationed zara paper, which was for two thousand copies, far below Nagai's thirty thousand copies of nonrationed (NR) senka paper. Furthermore, in an updated version of *Masako taorezu*, published by Hyōgen sha in August 1949, the book included a photograph of Masako visiting Nagai, a copy of a letter he had written to her, and a new six-page preface written, of course, by Nagai.[90] Nagai did not appear in the original 1947 version, which was ultimately rejected by Solovskoy, nor in the early 1949 version, which included thirty photos of Nagasaki's destruction and recovery. Nagai's *Nagasaki no kane*, by contrast, only included four photos of the destruction.

Other than Ishida Masako, few others published in Nagasaki until the mid-1950s, but in Hiroshima, many hibakusha wrote about their trauma, which, if it appeared in smaller publications, generally went unnoticed. Hara Tamiki's famous story, *Natsu no hana* (Summer flowers, 1947), appeared in an obscure journal that escaped the eyes of the censors and, as John Treat notes, "fell, so to speak, between the cracks."[91] But SCAP censors based in Tokyo rarely took note of these smaller publications even if they were well known around Japan. Indeed, Hiroshima writers produced relatively abundantly, and in 1949 several received national recognition in a special issue of the journal *Shūkan asahi* dedicated to "No More Hiroshimas." Among the books mentioned were Hara Tamiki's *Natsu no hana*, Ōta Yōko's 1948 *Shikabane no machi* (City of corpses), Ogura Toyofumi's

Zetsugo no kiroku (Letters from the End of the World), Koromogawa Maiko's *Hiroshima*, Tamai Reiko's *Watashi wa* Hiroshima *ni ita* (I was in *Hiroshima*), and Agawa Hiroyuki's 1947 *Hachigatsu muika* (August sixth).[92] The body of atomic-bombing literature produced by Hiroshima writers was impressive. In Nagasaki, it took decades for the hibakusha to strengthen their collective voice and challenge Nagai as the representative of the city's atomic experience by building their own body of atomic-bombing literature.

· · ·

The process that led to the publication of Nagai Takashi's *Nagasaki no kane* illuminates the history of the Allied occupation in at least three ways. First, it reveals how censorship evolved over the period 1947–49, when SCAP first outright suppressed it, then held the book without decision, and then dedicated a large allotment of paper once Nagai and the publishers acquiesced to their demands. Second, the contribution of paper for the initial printing exemplifies the experimental nature of SCAP's attempts to control the "great river of communication" during the occupation, in this case by rewarding publishers who disseminated ideas favorable to the American narrative of the war. Third, SCAP's attempt to influence Japanese society in this way betrayed a continuation of the American psywar through which it sought to fashion Japan into an ally. The dual *Nagasaki no kane*–"Manira no higeki" publication fit into SCAP's goals of democratizing Japan because it helped make the case that, because Japan had been punished, it could now become a peace-loving and democratic people.

The published version of *Nagasaki no kane* helped shape war narratives as well. The book confirmed the status of the people of Nagasaki and Hiroshima as victims of war, and the people of Japan as citizens of a hibaku-nation. The suffering of a few hundred thousand became the suffering of millions. The removal of the Manila appendix from the printings of *Nagasaki no kane* after the occupation ended in 1952 underlined the move from victimizer to victim. After the removal of the appendix, an *Asahi Graph* poll of August 6, 1952, showed that "that which shocked the citizens of Japan in the seventh year after the war was the victimization of the atomic bombings of Hiroshima and Nagasaki, not the Japanese military's invasion and victimization of Asia and the Pacific."[93] The appendix did not appear in a Japanese version of the book published in the United States by Saikensha in Denver, Colorado, in March 1949. By the end of the occupation, the Japanese narrative of the war was becoming defined in terms of the experience of the atomic bombings.[94] In other words, *Nagasaki no kane* served as a bridge between the early postwar repentance and the postoccupation silence about wartime aggression that came to define a nation of atomic-bomb victims.

Nagai and his books influenced and reflected the course of events that created a democratic Japan struggling to come to terms with its role in the war. The sentimental prose found in all of Nagai books helped Japan appear as a repentant nation opposed to the inhumanity of war, which supported the goals of the occupation and reflected the atmosphere of postwar Japan. When director Ōba Hideo made *Nagasaki no kane* into a film in 1950 for the Shōchiku film company, Nagai's ideas on the bombing found an audience beyond his readers. The film version did not include an account of Japanese atrocities in Manila, nor did it shy away from depicting the Japanese as victims of the Second World War more generally, as popular wartime musical artists Koseki Yūji and Fujiyama Ichirō provided the sentimental soundtrack.[95] As John Dower notes, in postwar Japan, "war itself became the greatest 'victimizer,' while the Japanese—personified by the saintly father/doctor/scientist [Nagai] dying in a nuclear-bombed city—emerged as the most exemplary victims of modern war."[96] In other works, too, Nagai depicted the Japanese as victims of war, broadly speaking. He explained the death of their mother to his children in *Itoshigo yo*, writing that the atomic bomb "is a clump of atoms. Atoms did not come to Urakami to kill your mother. What killed your mother—that loving mother—was war."[97] The Americans benefited from this interpretation because they also "did not come to Urakami to kill" the Japanese people, war did.

The occupation's preferential treatment of Nagai and his books built walls and reinforced others around discussions of the bombing. In subsequent decades, Nagai's works and persona continued to be the voice of Nagasaki's atomic experience, fostering a popular image of the city as having responded to the destruction by praying for peace but performing little real action in the antinuclear and antiwar movements compared to Hiroshima. This view presented a challenge to survivors who disputed the interpretation of the atomic tragedy as providential and were able only in the 1960s to begin shaking Nagai's hold on the popular memory of the bombing. For more than the first two decades after the bombing, the memory activism of the Nagasaki hibakusha worked to break down the walls of silence that had emerged during the occupation.

WALLS OF SILENCE

The Postwar Lives and Memory Activism
of the *Hibakusha*

For the Nagasaki hibakusha, the first two postwar decades were, in a word, difficult. During this time, municipal officials pursued urban reconstruction policies that gave priority to the city's historical urban identity over its atomic experience, leaving the hibakusha with little official support in matters of commemoration, psychological working-through of their trauma, and medical care for their atomic-bombing related illnesses. The books of Nagai Takashi spoke to national and international audiences on behalf of the Nagasaki survivors, who had not chosen him as their representative; indeed, he did not convey the atomic experience as they lived it. Furthermore, the story of the Nagasaki survivors seemed to be drowned out in popular discourse on the bombings by a preference for Hiroshima. The years 1945 to 1957, in particular, have become known as the "dark era," when no national system of recognition, compensation, and medical benefits existed for the hibakusha of both cities.[1] The national government refused to recognize them as different from other war survivors, therefore preventing them from receiving government support for their medical costs. Moreover, atomic-bombing survivors—especially those with scarred bodies—initially did not fit into reconstruction discourse because, as Yoshikuni Igarashi argues, "hygienic" bodies came to represent the nation as Japan cultivated an alliance with the United States. Scarred bodies found their place in the "discursive space of postwar Japan as signifiers of war experiences only insofar as they confirmed the official narrative."[2] Hibakusha in particular often endured the scorn of their fellow citizens because, in addition to their scarred bodies serving as reminders of the defeat of the war, their postatomic illnesses caused fears of contagiousness and led to their ostracism in society. Their bodies became relevant in discussions of the war and the atomic bombings only after antinuclear activism and nuclear victimhood became key components of national narratives.

Many hibakusha chose to fight for political and social acknowledgement of their experience from early on. Survivors and nonsurvivors alike came together and formed special-interest groups, becoming activists fighting to improve the lives of all hibakusha by seeking medical relief from the government and promoting peace activism through a focus on individual and collective memories of the atomic experience. They worked against the custodians of memory in Nagasaki, the municipal officials, who had created a postwar narrative of the city that emphasized its history of an international past over the memory of the recent atomic trauma. In contrast, the hibakusha promoted an atomic narrative that focused on the human suffering and remembrance of it. The evolution of the activist groups was gradual and improvements in the lives of the hibakusha developed slowly over decades. The political voice of the hibakusha and other activist groups grew in strength from 1954 with the burgeoning of the antinuclear peace movement, achieving small but important victories along the way. The first medical relief law that passed in 1957 improved little for the daily lives of hibakusha, but it was the fruit of social activism that had begun to pick up steam. In Nagasaki, where municipal officials did not always see eye to eye with the atomic-memory activists, the presence of the hibakusha voice remained muffled for decades, and so progress came more slowly there. In the late 1960s, the Nagasaki survivors turned to literature—testimony, narrative, and poetry—as their primary vehicle of memory activism, seeking to promote their narrative and resuscitate their collective experience in the popular memory of the bombings in both the city and the nation. Their first task was to seek assistance from the government in the treatment of their atomic-bombing related illnesses.

The Dark Era and the Fight for Medical Relief

Hibakusha and activists in Nagasaki encountered the most obstacles to their recovery during the so-called dark era, 1945–57. Not least among the challenges they faced were government regulations and approaches to alleviating the suffering of the nation's citizens. Change on this front happened only gradually. Shortly after the war, survivors of the Allied aerial bombings, including the atomic bombings, were confronted with a difficult situation. Medical relief from the Wartime Casualties Care Law (WCCL), implemented in 1942, lasted for only two months, expired in October 1945, and left them without a national system of care. The WCCL provided no special exception for residents of the atomic-bombed cities, meaning that the relief stations operating under the purview of the local and national government had to close. The relief center in Mitsuyama that Nagai Takashi had overseen shut down as well, the wounded having to seek medical care elsewhere at their own expense.[3]

The cities did their best to make up for the closures. Officials in Hiroshima designated a number of school buildings as hospitals for the treatment of hibakusha under provisions set forth in the National Medical Care Law of 1942. Nagasaki Medical University, whose main buildings were largely destroyed in the bombing, designated two satellite facilities to care for hibakusha, one initially located at Ōmura Naval Hospital and then moved to Kawatana Naval Hospital in Isahaya, and the other at the Shinkōzen Elementary School. After the start of the Allied occupation, the U.S. military provided medical supplies, including medicines not common in Japan, such as penicillin and sulfaguanidine. Some of the medicines provided by the United States effectively treated subacute infections related to bombing injuries, which were difficult to treat because of the biological complications induced by radiation poisoning. In December 1945, the occupation official in charge of overseeing medical activities in Nagasaki, Captain Hohne, converted a former army hospital into Blair Hospital, stocked it with medical supplies, and donated it to the residents of Nagasaki. The facility became a charity hospital and was later renamed the Nagasaki Citizens Hospital.[4]

The government closure of the relief stations in October 1945 despite the severity of the atomic bombings and the medical needs of the wounded represented for some hibakusha the start of the Japanese government's apathy for and abandonment of the atomic-bombing survivors. In essence, as scholar and hibakusha Yamada Hirotami argues, the closures shut them out and ushered in the "dark era of the hibakusha." He says that the Japanese government may indeed have been too overwhelmed with the chaos of the postwar period to consider the welfare of hibakusha, but he thinks that it was only part of the reason for their neglect. He claims that the Japanese government "ingratiated (geigō) with the occupation forces, who strove to conceal the destruction of the atomic bombings, especially the radiation damage." Yamada points to a September 1945 statement by General Thomas F. Farrell at a press conference at the Tokyo Imperial Hotel as the origin of the official stance of the occupation regarding the damaging effects of radiation in Hiroshima and in Nagasaki, a stance to which Japanese government officials catered. Farrell, who was a key member of the Manhattan Project, declared after visiting the two cities that no one there suffered from radiation poisoning and that residual radiation was not harmful to human health. In response, Yamada argues, the Japanese government "deliberately abandoned relief for the atomic-bombing victims (higaisha)."[5] Whether or not the abandonment of the hibakusha was deliberate, it was undeniable. As a result, survivors organized and fended for themselves in the early years after the bombings, engaging in relief efforts to help one another, such as creating associations to provide daily necessities to those in need.[6]

The postwar living standards of hibakusha began to brighten from the early 1950s, when local governments began to acknowledge their medical needs. In May 1953, a group led by Mayor Tagawa Tsutomu, which included representatives from Nagasaki University, prefectural and municipal offices, medical associations, and social groups, formed the Nagasaki Atomic Bomb Casualty Council (a similar council had been created earlier in Hiroshima) and launched a system of free medical examinations for hibakusha. The council also conducted surveys of hibakusha and undertook research of atomic-bombing related illnesses. Yet the general livelihood of hibakusha was slow to improve. Relief developed through the survivors' own efforts and the support of other members of the peace movement.[7]

A United States nuclear weapons test on Bikini Atoll in March 1954 brought national attention to the plight of the atomic-bombing survivors. Radioactive fallout from the test fell for six hours on the Japanese fishing boat Lucky Dragon No. 5, located about one hundred miles east of the explosion, and the twenty-three crew members contracted radiation poisoning before their return to Japan two weeks later. In September 1954, one crewman died. The incident converted the dangers of nuclear weapons into a national crisis, reviving the atomic bombings in national consciousness, which emboldened the hibakusha medical relief activists to seize the moment. Citizen groups and the casualty councils in Hiroshima and Nagasaki, backed by the mayors, city council members, and National Diet members from each city, petitioned Tokyo for "payment by the national government of all medical costs of the A-bomb victims." The petition, an initiative of the Nagasaki Atomic Bomb Casualty Council, stated that the number of hibakusha in Hiroshima and Nagasaki that required medical care was six thousand and three thousand, respectively, but the activists also demanded special provisions to aid their livelihood. For the first time, the Ministry of Health and Welfare acknowledged that it was necessary, "as demonstrated by the Bikini incident, for the state to make all haste in providing compensation to the victims of atomic bombings." The government responded to the demands of the petition by distributing ¥3,522,000 to medical institutions in the two cities, with ¥2,349,000 going to Hiroshima and ¥1,173,000 to Nagasaki. The cities, however, required ¥325,800,000 to cover medical costs of hibakusha, such as surgery, as well as other living subsidies. Although the government allocated funds to Hiroshima and Nagasaki again in 1955 (¥8,303,100 and ¥4,138,900, respectively) and 1956 (¥16,750,000 and ¥8,932,000), its official position regarding the promulgation of a special law that would recognize hibakusha as different from other aerial bombing and war survivors remained the same. If the government "accorded special treat-ment" to the hibakusha, they thought, "then all casualties and their survivors must be given compensation."[8]

While the national government ignored the requests of the hibakusha, activist groups in Nagasaki became openly critical of municipal approaches to commem-oration of the bombing, which seemed, despite the city's best efforts, to make the health and well-being of survivors its last priority. When a major international peace conference was under way in Hiroshima in summer 1955, officials in Nagasaki installed an enormous statue in Peace Park, costing the city ¥30 mil-lion, more than seven times the amount of money received by the city from the national government for medical treatment of hibakusha the same year.[9] The hibakusha were livid, failing to see how it connected to the bomb at all.[10] The sculptor, Kitamura Seibō, intended his work to represent Nagasaki's atomic destruction as well as its rebirth as a city of international culture.[11] Yet many residents did not see the relation of the statue to either theme. The statue, which is of a large, shirtless "Olympic" man, "a human who transcends all mankind," stands today. His right hand points to the sky, representing the atomic bombing, while his other arm extends straight out to the left; visitors are told to interpret this position as the figure guiding humanity toward peace. His facial expression is supposed to convey "a prayer for the eternal happiness of those who died."[12] Kita-mura's statue, not the cenotaph at ground zero, became the center of the annual municipal commemoration ceremonies.[13] The design of Kitamura's statue echoes the early postwar saying, "Peace from Nagasaki," as well as the calls by city officials and the emperor to convert the tragedy into happiness.

Some hibakusha saw the statue not only as a confusing symbol of their trauma but also as a waste of municipal funds that could have been used to improve the lives of the survivors. In 1955, hibakusha poet Fukuda Sumako wrote an open letter to the city in the form of a poem published in the *Asahi shinbun*. She wrote, in part:

> I have become disgusted with it all.
> The giant peace statue towers over the atomic wasteland.
> That's fine. That's fine, but
> with that money, I wonder if something else couldn't have been done.
> "We cannot eat a stone statue; it will not alleviate our hunger."
> Please don't call us selfish.
> These are the honest feelings of the victims
> who have barely lived the ten years after the bomb.
>
> Sigh. I have no energy this year.
> Peace! Peace! I'm so tired of hearing [that word].

No matter how much one shouts or cries out,
there is a powerlessness, as if it disappears into the deep sky.
I am completely tired
of the unseen anxiety (shōsō) for whatever the reply.

Fukuda expressed the frustration and displeasure of the Nagasaki hibakusha, who felt that municipal funds were being wasted on meaningless projects and empty symbols of peace, instead of supporting their medical treatments and improving their living standards. "The more everyone gets excited [over the statue]," she lamented, "the emptier my heart is."[14]

Such legacies of the dark era echoed for decades. The statue reflected the city's approach to commemoration, which rarely took into consideration the voice of the hibakusha, as exemplified in the 1958 debate over the ruins of the Urakami Cathedral. Again in 1997, the hibakusha opposed the efforts of city architects who commissioned a bronze sculpture from Kitamura's protégé, Tominaga Naoki, that was supposed to replace the cenotaph column at ground zero. Tominaga created another "colossal statue" that failed to represent the horror of the bomb; his, which stands nine meters tall, is of a mother wearing a flowing dress adorned with golden roses and holding a baby. In response to hibakusha outcry against the statue, which culminated in a "human chain" of residents around the ground-zero cenotaph on August 9, 1997, the city abandoned plans to replace the cenotaph, but placed the statue just meters away, where it stands today.[15] Despite municipal policies of commemoration that seemingly ignored the plight of hibakusha, the local government did more than Tokyo in working to relieve the suffering. The Nagasaki Atomic Bomb Casualty Council built a therapeutic facility in 1965 at the natural hot springs in nearby Obama City and installed other clinics and medical facilities throughout Nagasaki City in the late 1960s and the 1970s. The facilities provided examinations, treatment, and aid for daily life, including counseling services.[16] Still, the relief efforts of the city and prefecture were limited without national funds.

During the dark era, survivors formed groups that put forth two primary purposes: to promote peace through activism that sought to educate posterity about the atomic bombing of the city and to ensure that such a bombing never happened again; and to fight for the implementation of a national system of relief that recognized the suffering of hibakusha and provided them with medical care. Thus the peace movement and the fight for relief—medical as well as psychological—were intertwined.[17] When the activist groups grew in prominence from 1954, their political voice began producing results, at least on the medical-care front, using the momentum of the mid-1950s national peace movement to draw attention to the causes. At the Second World Conference against Atomic and Hydrogen Bombs held in Nagasaki in August 1956, the Nagasaki genbaku hisaisha kyōgikai, or Nagasaki hisaikyō (Nagasaki Council of Atomic Bombing Victims), and the Nihon gensuibaku higaisha dantai kyōgikai, or Nihon hidankyō (Japan Confederation of Atomic-Bomb and Hydrogen-Bomb Sufferers Organizations), agreed that the national government had a responsibility to improve the conditions of survivors.[18] On August 9, the Socialist Party of Japan (JSP) took the first step in Tokyo to improve the situation of hibakusha by announcing that it would support a bill in the next National Diet meeting that demarcated ¥230 million yen in support.[19] Encouraged by the action of the JSP, the Nihon hidankyō submitted a request on behalf of all hibakusha to the Diet and to each political party, stating that the hibakusha "were the sacrifices of a war executed under the responsibility of the nation (*kuni*)," and therefore financial support of their "medical treatment and livelihood [should] be carried out under the responsibility of the nation." The Ministry of Health and Welfare drafted a law in response, requesting ¥267,493,000 from the Ministry of Finance. On March 31, 1957, the Diet passed the Genshi bakudan hibakusha no iryō nado ni kan suru hōritsu (Law Related to the Medical Treatment and Other Needs of Hibakusha; Hibakusha Relief Law), which included a fund of ¥174,589,000.[20]

Passage of the law was groundbreaking. First, it recognized the survivors of the atomic bombings as a distinct legal category of war survivor. The law also allowed that the term *hibakusha* could be applied to anyone exposed to the radiation from the bomb, not just those exposed directly to the blast. Second, *genbaku shō* (atomic-bombing illness) was recognized as a unique sickness resulting from the bomb. Combined with recognition of hibakusha as a special category of survivor, this implied the national government's acknowledgment that radiation from the bombs was indeed a factor in the suffering of the survivors. And third, the number of hibakusha who applied for national aid in response to the law, 200,984, revealed that the need for aid was myriad times more pressing than previously thought.[21]

In regard to how the national law affected the lives of the hibakusha, though, it did not correspond sufficiently to what the activists had been pursuing; it was seen as "woefully inadequate" and a "far cry" (*hodo tōkatta*) from the needs of the hibakusha.[22] The law did not mean recognition for all. Out of the 200,984 hibakusha who applied for relief, only 1,436—less than 1 percent—were legally recognized as atomic-bombing survivors and eligible for aid. Furthermore, it did not address support for the families of those who died in the bombing or who later died from injuries or radiation sickness. The law had turned the petition of the Nihon hidankyō on its head: it made the treatment of survivors the responsibility of the national government, but only survivors who were recognized by the government as hibakusha were eligible to receive aid.[23] The rest were left without recourse. As Ōda Takashi put it, "Those of us who are not recognized patients do not receive any kind of benefits (*onkei*)."[24] Additionally, some hibakusha, fearing social discrimination, did not apply for relief in order to avoid drawing attention to themselves.[25] In response to the inadequacy of the national relief law, prefectural and municipal governments in Hiroshima and Nagasaki supplemented relief efforts with their own funds and activities, as mentioned earlier.

The dark era was the first of three major periods of hibakusha activism for relief. The second began in 1956 with the Nihon hidankyō petition to the national government and ended in 1965 after activist groups split apart because of political partisanship between 1959 and 1964. Though the activists achieved some success in improving hibakusha relief in 1964, the political infighting and split stalled the groups' overall activism in the latter part of the second period. The third (and current) period began in 1966 with a renewed effort by the Nihon hidankyō to bring national attention to the hardships of the hibakusha. The group published a pamphlet entitled "Genbaku higai no tokushitsu to 'Hibakusha engo hō' no yōkyū" (Characteristics of damage by the atomic bombs and demands for the "Hibakusha Relief Law"), which stressed what they considered the realities of the atomic bombings and the suffering of the survivors. It asserted that adequate government relief in all aspects of the hibakusha's lives was a goal that would not be compromised. The "Crane Pamphlet," as it came to be known for the image of a paper crane on the cover, marked the "development of an epoch-making movement" (*kakkiteki na undō no tenkai*) from the spring of 1967.[26]

In 1973, the Nihon hidankyō released a revised Crane Pamphlet that set forth three demands to the national government regarding the past (compensation), present (relief), and future (peace pledge). The first demand, however, was addressed in part to the United States, requiring that it admit to concealing and "monopolizing" information about the damage of the atomic bombings during the occupation and that it assume responsibility for starting the nuclear arms race. In addition, the Japanese government had to accept responsibility for aggression during the Second World War and for neglecting the hibakusha after the war. The hibakusha sought compensation for damages suffered. The second demand called for comprehensive relief for atomic-bombing survivors to overcome health, living, and spiritual burdens. The third demand charged the national government to establish a commitment to the hibakusha and to the people of Japan that it would work to prevent another atomic bombing—that is, a commitment to peace and antinuclear activism. The Nihon hidankyō campaigned in 1973 to encourage national political parties to push their interests through the National Diet in the form of a bill. Supportive parties introduced a joint bill accordingly, but it was ultimately defeated.[27] Although the dark era ended in 1957 with the passage of the first medical relief law, the response of the national government to the needs of the hibakusha remained inadequate, and groups have continued their activism into the present along similar lines as discussed here.

Walls of Silence

Many social and political obstacles impeded the attempts of Nagasaki hibakusha to give voice to their experience in the decades following the bombings. Memory studies scholars have argued that trauma requires the passing of time, a "period of latency," to be properly addressed.[28] In the case of Nagasaki survivors, the period of latency was in part imposed from the outside, by occupation censorship, social discrimination, political interests, municipal policies of reconstruction, the Christian image of ground zero, and the persistent Hiroshima-centrism of discussions on the atomic bombings. The latter three obstructions to atomic-memory activism that existed in Nagasaki were never present in Hiroshima.[29]

First, occupation censorship created an atmosphere of apprehension around discussion of the bombings. Even after a change to censorship in late 1949 when the Civil Censorship Detachment was dissolved, media representations of the bomb continued to be suppressed if they appeared critical of the United States.[30] On June 9, 1950, the communist newspaper *Akahata* (Red flag) released a special issue on the Hiroshima bomb entitled "Heiwa sensen" (Peace front), which included six photographs. To coincide with distribution of the paper, *Akahata* members coordinated a photo exhibit in Hiroshima called *Genbaku no sanjō* (The brutality of the atomic bomb).[31] American occupation officials quickly suppressed the Hiroshima publication and targeted *Akahata* to be shut down. Of course, the communist position of the paper explained this reaction. On June 7, General MacArthur had already ordered the purge of the editorial board of *Akahata*; on June 26, the publication was ordered to halt activities for one month for printing unfavorable articles on the American situation in Korea; and on July 18, it was terminated.[32]

This form of censorship, however, also linked critical discussion of the bombings to communism, forming a kind of political wall of silence. Nagasaki hibakusha Akizuki Tatsuichirō once noted that, after 1949, to speak critically of the atomic bombing within the city suggested revolutionary ideas because it went against the status quo that the American occupation had created. Furthermore, the Nagasaki Communist Party did speak critically of the atomic bombing, thus further linking discussion of the bomb to communism.[33] That is, to speak openly and critically about the destruction of the atomic bombing marked one as a communist at a time when Japan sought to cultivate a foundation for political allegiance to the United States. Immediately after the occupation ended in April 1952, hibakusha and journalists were free to write on the bombings in whatever way they chose, and many journals and other print media soon published special issues on them. On August 6, *Asahi gurafu* published a special issue entitled "Genbaku higai no hatsu kōkai" (The first presentation of the damage of the atomic bombs), and on November 15, the journal *Kaizō* dedicated an issue to "Kono genbaku ka" (This calamity of the atomic bombs). Both publications included grotesque photos of human casualties of the bomb, which signaled the demolition of the first wall of silence for both cities. Yet there remained more walls to break down.

Second, survivors in both cities endured social discrimination that convinced many of them that silence was preferable to unwanted attention. The atomic bomb created a stigma that plagued survivors and affected their livelihood for decades.[34] The hibakusha had difficulty getting work if they did not conceal the fact, if possible, that they had experienced the bomb, and at work, discrimination continued. A 1975 survey conducted by the Ministry of Health and Welfare found that 2 percent of respondents reported "adverse discrimination" in the workplace.[35] Even some second-generation hibakusha were refused work.[36] The stigma of the bomb also affected social interactions. Although hibakusha frequently married other hibakusha, many others had difficulty finding marriage partners for reasons of health or the fear that the effects of radiation would be passed on to their children.[37] One hibakusha woman from Urakami with keloid scarring covering her entire body was lucky enough to find a partner, also a hibakusha, and they were married in 1947. The following year she gave birth to a boy, but nine days later his nose began bleeding and he died. Her mother-in-law asked her to give her son a divorce because she "didn't want a daughter-in-law who breeds abnormal babies."[38] Birth defects were common among babies born of hibakusha. Some common birth defects and other complications that resulted from radiation, whether the mother was exposed with child in utero or the baby was conceived later by one or both parents who were hibakusha, were premature birth, stillbirth, artificial abortion, early death (within the first year), microcephaly (small head), and growth and mental retardation, including autosomal trisomy 21 (Down syndrome).[39]

Many survivors, including those who moved to other parts of Japan, concealed the fact that they were hibakusha, or even related to one, to avoid discrimination. "I don't want my name to be public (*seken ni shiraretakunai*)," said both Ms. "U" and Ms. "A" to a reporter for the *Mainichi shinbun* in 1970 for a story about hibakusha discrimination. "I don't know what kind of discrimination will strike again. I don't want to cause trouble for my family and relatives who are healthy."[40] The hibakusha struggled to live with social discrimination as well as health complications due to the bomb, such as keloid scarring and cancers, including leukemia. The psychological hardships of survival in this context produced among the hibakusha what they called "keloid of the heart" and "leukemia of the spirit."[41]

Daily life was difficult under the eyes of neighbors who worried about contracting radiation sickness from the survivors or who otherwise doubted the ability of the hibakusha to function as members of society. In Nagasaki, Yamaguchi Senji, whose face was badly burned from the intense heat of the bomb, which caused keloid scarring, recalled in 1985 the difficulty of living as a hibakusha, especially in the early postwar years. He returned home to the Gotō Islands near Nagasaki in 1946, with his "face resembling that of a demon," after seven months of treatment for his burns. Going to the public bath in the evening was the hardest (*tsurai*) thing for him to do. He dreaded it.[42] "Not only would everyone stare at me, but I felt in their eyes the fear that they might catch the atomic-bombing illness (*genbaku shō*)," Yamaguchi recalled. To avoid this situation as much as possible, he went to the bath "around ten o'clock in the evening, right before the bathwater is thrown out, and bathed while enduring the looks of others." Two months later Yamaguchi returned to Nagasaki to finish high school. On graduating in 1951, he had difficulty finding a job because the thick scar tissue that covered much of his body had handicapped his movement, so he went home to Gotō. The pain of living overwhelmed him, so, determined to die, he returned to Nagasaki in 1952. He slit both wrists with a razor, but, he recalled, "fortunately or unfortunately" he survived.[43] Numbers of hibakusha in both Nagasaki and Hiroshima committed suicide because the trauma was too great. Hiroshima survivor and accomplished writer Hara Tamiki killed himself in 1951 by lying down on train tracks in Tokyo, a suicide some considered a delayed death related to the bombing.[44]

The experience of Yamaguchi Senji enduring the suspicious eyes of society was typical for many survivors in both cities, especially those with physical traces of the bomb on their bodies, such as keloid scarring. This discouraged many from drawing further attention to themselves by recounting their experience of the atomic bomb through public testimony and talks or otherwise speaking of their survival. Hibakusha who had no trace of the bomb on their bodies were disinclined to admit that they were exposed to the bomb for fear of stigma and to avoid reliving the trauma. Nagasaki survivor Gotō Minako explained the difficulty of writing: "For me writing means reopening the 'grave' I have tried to cover for good. To reach into what lies at the base of consciousness, to retrieve it and turn it into words, is painfully difficult to endure. Writing becomes distasteful, and I find myself wishing to begin living with these memories of the past interred." Nonetheless, hibakusha writers, poets, and activists, as Gotō put it, were "urged to go on by another voice" and relate their experiences to others.[45]

Lastly, the biggest wall facing the memory activists of Nagasaki emerged out of the legacy of Nagai Takashi. As memory activist (but not hibakusha) Kamata Sadao pointed out, the "Catholic myth of Urakami" permeated Nagasaki memory for decades because the books of Nagai Takashi were the only widely available source about the bombs during the occupation.[46] Several scholars have pointed out the disparity in occupation-period literature stemming from Hiroshima and Nagasaki. From 1946, Hiroshima hibakusha authors and poets, such as Kurihara Sadako, Hara Tamiki, Ōta Yōko, and Tōge Sankichi, produced literature that conveyed the horror and inhumanity of the atomic bomb, while Nagai Takashi published books that depicted the bombing as an act of Providence with relative freedom, reaching a national audience. Tanaka Toshihiro rightly argues that the disparate themes of occupation-period atomic-bomb literature in the two cities, especially Nagai's "deification" (shinkakuka) of the bombing, created, in part, the postwar image of a passive, praying Nagasaki.[47]

Kamata stressed how Nagai's books developed an image of Nagasaki through his religious interpretations of the tragedy that expressed gratitude for the bomb instead of horror at its destruction. The books, especially Nagasaki no kane, he argued, promoted the "uniquely Catholic, or Nagai-like (Nagaiteki), reception of the atomic bomb as aesthetic martyrdom," exemplified best in the inclusion of his November 1945 eulogy at the mass funeral for the atomic-bombing dead. Kamata noted how the atomic bombing appeared as a natural disaster because Nagai wrote that the bomb "fell" (rakka) on Nagasaki, it was not "dropped" (tōka).[48] Nagai's argument that the destruction of Urakami exemplified God's love for the Catholics was a "masochistic logic" that was not representative of the hibakusha. Nonetheless, Kamata claimed, it produced best-selling books under the occupation, which prevented the development of alternatives in logic, sentiment, and literature about the bombing of Nagasaki.[49]

Akizuki, despite being an Urakami Catholic, did not agree with Nagai that the atomic bombing exemplified Providence, nor did he attend the mass funeral in November 1945. "I don't think it unfortunate that I did not go to the memorial service for the dead where thousands of Urakami Christian believers gathered. I didn't even want to hear the memorial address that was to be read in front of thousands of people. I cannot go along with Nagai-sensei's way of thinking that 'Because the Lord loves the people of Urakami he dropped the atomic bomb on Urakami. Because the people of Urakami are loved most by God, they must suffer time and time again.'" Furthermore, Akizuki explained, Nagai's way of thinking about the bomb was "too horrible" to go along with.[50] Yet despite views like those of Akizuki and other Christians, not to mention the opposition of hibakusha to the passive image of the city, the Christian link to the bombing persisted.[51]

The issue in the decades following the war was not so much a struggle between Catholic versus non-Catholic survivor memory but rather the persistence of Nagai as a voice for all Nagasaki survivors within the official narrative, as well as the passive image of the city that his influence had helped create. Some Catholics disagreed with those who thought that God had sent Nagai to them, pointing out that the Christianization of the image of the city in the first five years after the bomb had forced the non-Catholic hibakusha into silence. Akizuki, who was once a colleague of Nagai, believed that three factors fostered the silence: first, Nagai's books; second, the Nagasaki residents' joyful welcome of the emperor in 1949; and, third, the Catholic festivities in 1949 to celebrate the 400th anniversary of the arrival of Francis Xavier in Japan. The warm reception of the emperor in May 1949, Akizuki thought, represented Nagasaki's contribution to the "construction of a country (*kokka*) of peace and culture" through the misfortune of its atomic bomb. The emperor had called on the people of Nagasaki to turn misfortune into happiness in order to achieve a successful revival of the city. The seemingly uncritical nature of how Nagasaki accepted the emperor's call to "construct a country of peace and culture" led to the phrase "Nagasaki Prays," in contrast to "Hiroshima Rages," because Nagasaki residents exchanged their rage against the brutality and oppression of the war for prayers for peace and culture at the urging of the emperor, in whose name the war had been waged. After the 1949 Xavier festival, Akizuki lamented, no one in Nagasaki except the Communist Party said anything negative about the atomic bombing because to do so implied anti-American and revolutionary elements. Akizuki pointed out, "Religious leaders, too, fell silent and offered up nothing but prayers."[52] The silence of Nagasaki residents left their postatomic image firmly in the hands of Nagai Takashi.

The walls of silence, including the effects of municipal policies of reconstruction that allocated few resources to atomic-bombing-related issues, did not fall at the close of the dark era in 1957. Rather, the battle to break down the walls had just begun. The Nagasaki hibakusha challenged the dominance of Nagai in their city's atomic-bombing literature only from 1956, when Fukuda Sumako published a collection of poetry and essays titled *Hitorigoto* (Soliloquy). This marked the Nagasaki hibakusha's arrival on the stage of atomic-bomb literature and their first major step toward reclaiming their atomic memory by asserting their narrative's place within local and national discourses on the bombings. However, in subsequent decades, though they published numerous poetry collections, testimonial accounts, and novels, two walls persisted: the legacy of Nagai as the voice of Nagasaki and the dominance of Hiroshima in discourse on the bombings.

By 1970, the memory activists of Nagasaki had formed a well-organized movement, seeking to write their hibakusha experience into popular memory as well as into the city's official narrative. That year, the Nagasaki genbaku hibaku kyōshi no kai (Nagasaki Association of Atomic Bombing Educators) published a collection of essays that addressed the state of Nagasaki's image as an atomic-bombed city in Japan. The book *Chinmoku no kabe o yabutte* (Breaking down the walls of silence) analyzed the historical situation and discussed the representative figures who contributed to the formation of Nagasaki's postatomic image of passivity and prayer rather than activism and memory. No longer could the hibakusha scholars, poets, and activists let the significance of their city's atomic bombing be represented by Nagai Takashi, ignored in popular memory, and effaced by Hiroshima. The time had come to break down the walls of silence and educate the nation about the "living witnesses," who, like their Hiroshima counterparts, had experienced atomic destruction and strove to preserve their memory within atomic narratives through peace activism and testimonial literature.[53]

Activisms of Memory

Memory activism grew gradually in Nagasaki over the decades following the bombing. Although the vocabulary of the goals of activists groups sometimes changed along with the times, the primary purpose was always to alleviate the suffering of the hibakusha and to draw people's attention to the city's atomic experience. The first group to form after the bombing did not call themselves hibakusha, and they did not take up peace activism, but rather revival activism. Eight survivors, including Sugimoto Kameyoshi and Takigawa Masaru, organized a group in December 1945 called the Nagasaki sensaisha renmei (Nagasaki Federation of War Victims), which distributed material relief to residents and raised funds to build houses for survivors. The organizers and many of the group members later became leaders of the peace movement that burgeoned across Japan in the 1950s.[54] The March 1954 Lucky Dragon No. 5 incident ignited the national peace and antinuclear weapons movement in Japan. The fact that the "ashes of death" rained on Japanese citizens for a third time enraged the general public and inspired action in many parts of society outside of Hiroshima and Nagasaki, including a women's reading group in the Suginami Ward of Tokyo. The group initiated a petition against atomic and hydrogen bombs in May 1954, which became known as the "Suginami Appeal," and by mid-1955, the National Council for an Antinuclear Signature Campaign (formed in August 1954) had collected 32 million signatures in Japan.[55] The worldwide concern with nuclear weapons benefited the memory activists in Hiroshima and Nagasaki because national and international attention focused on the two cities.

When the World Conference against Atomic and Hydrogen Bombs was held in Hiroshima in 1955 and again in Nagasaki one year later, the attention of the world seemed to be on both cities. A group of women hibakusha in Nagasaki created the Nagasaki genbaku otome no kai (Nagasaki Atomic Bombing Young Women's Association) and dispatched two representatives, Watanabe Chieko and Yamaguchi Misako, to the Hiroshima conference on August 6, 1955.[56] Yamaguchi and Hiroshima survivor Takahashi Akihiro spoke about their atomic-bombing experiences, which some commentators noted "deeply moved" the approximately thirty thousand people in attendance in Peace Memorial Park, who for the first time felt the "painful responsibility of living in the nuclear age." After the conference, a nationwide citizen group against nuclear weapons was formed as the Gensuibaku kinshi Nihon kyōgikai, or the Nihon gensuikyō (Japan Council against Atomic and Hydrogen Bombs).[57]

The future of Nagasaki memory activism seemed bright. Months after the Hiroshima conference, on October 1, 1955, Yamaguchi Senji and other hibakusha who had been calling themselves the Nagasaki genbaku seinen kai (Nagasaki Atomic Bombing Young Men's Association) hung a signboard with their name in front of the *manjū* (steamed bun) store where Yamaguchi was living, establishing their headquarters and their determination to become a recognized and influential group in the peace movement. On May 3, 1956, Yamaguchi's group joined, or as Watanabe Chieko put it, "married," the Nagasaki genbaku otome no kai, creating the Nagasaki genbaku seinen otome no kai (Nagasaki Atomic Bombing Association of Young Men and Women). Watanabe recalled how everyone was "bright and happy" about the merger and hoped that with the efforts of the group, "the darkness, distortion (*hinekure*), nihility (*kyomu*), and hopelessness [of surviving the bombing] would completely disappear."[58]

The Nagasaki activist groups, empowered by the peace movement, hosted the Second World Conference against Atomic and Hydrogen Bombs in August. For this occasion, Nagasaki hibakusha, including Yamaguchi Senji, Takigawa Minoru, Kino Fumio, Sugimoto Kameyoshi, and other members of the Nagasaki sensaisha renmei, formed the Nagasaki hisaikyō, with Sugimoto becoming the group's first president. The Nagasaki hisaikyō unified the city's hibakusha groups, declaring its stance against nuclear weapons and its goal to receive compensation from the national government for survivors, positions that were shared by all hibakusha groups. On August 10, eight hundred hibakusha representatives from all over Japan formed the national hibakusha organization Nihon hidankyō.[59] During the Nagasaki conference, the Nihon hidankyō, too, declared its "appeal to the world" against nuclear weapons and its mission to gain compensation from "the state" (*kokka*).[60] The Nagasaki hibakusha had organized the 1956 event with enthusiasm and high hopes—it seemed that Nagasaki was gaining equal importance to Hiroshima in popular memory. But the event had unfortunate timing.

Despite the efforts of activists in Nagasaki and in contrast to the success of the conference in Hiroshima one year earlier, the Nagasaki conference fell flat. The popular attitude in Japan toward nuclear science had changed since the 1955 conference, with more attention, and hope, being given to the peaceful uses of atomic energy. The change in conversation came in part because of the Atoms for Peace campaign. President Eisenhower initiated the campaign in 1953, but it did not pick up steam in Japan until the American-led exhibit, which the Yomiuri shinbun company cosponsored, traveled around Japan in winter 1955, including making a stop in Hiroshima. Atoms for Peace appealed to many people, and although the campaign did not replace the antinuclear weapons movement, it did present a challenge to its message.[61] Moreover, because Hiroshima had already declared the movement's stance against nuclear weapons at the 1955 conference, discussions within the movement turned to the other, so-called peaceful uses of nuclear energy. Yet activists in Nagasaki continued in their approach to establish their city as another center for the movement based on the call to abolish nuclear weapons. However, events such as the Atoms for Peace campaign weakened Nagasaki activists' ability to tap into the antinuclear weapons fervor that swept the nation from March 1954 and to stake out their place in the burgeoning national narrative in which the atomic bombings defined much of Japan's war experience and postwar mission to eliminate nuclear weapons.[62] As a result, Hiroshima continued in its role as leader of the antinuclear peace movement and as symbolic city in the memory of the bombings. When Nagasaki officials approved the removal of Urakami Cathedral ruins just two years later in 1958, the loss of the last visible atomic ruins from the city's urban landscape added insult to injury for the memory activists.

Although the Nagasaki hibakusha who worked as memory activists encountered walls of silence, including the apathy of a nation that relegated Nagasaki to the shadows of Hiroshima, many found meaning to their suffering through peace activism. As Yamada Hirotami notes, "The creation of the Nagasaki hisaikyō was the first step by the hibakusha in overcoming the 'era of darkness.'" Indeed, every activist group—and there were many—that put forth the mission to work for peace, seek government compensation, and relate the experience of the bombing through testimony provided a sense of "life mission" (shimei) for survivors struggling to overcome trauma. Yamaguchi Senji, who just years earlier had attempted suicide, became a leader of the Nagasaki peace movement for six decades, and many other survivors found catharsis and relief from their psychological and physical pain.

The case of Taniguchi Sumiteru is illuminating. Taniguchi was sixteen at the time of the bombing, delivering telegrams on his bike when the bomb exploded over Nagasaki. His entire back, left arm, upper left leg, and face were scorched so severely that he had to lie on his stomach in a hospital for one year and nine months, during which time he stopped breathing twice. Taniguchi developed bedsores as well, which permanently damaged his chest. "How many times did I cry out, 'Kill me!'?" Taniguchi wondered in 1970 when he recalled the "pain and hopelessness." "So many times did I think about wanting to die."[63] Even after leaving the hospital in March 1949, the pain and hopelessness continued, despite miraculous strides toward physical recovery. Taniguchi could not sleep a full, painless night because of the stiff keloid scarring that covered most of his torso, impairing his movement—his left elbow's range of motion was less than 100 degrees.[64] An additional source of anxiety was that he would be unable to continue working as a postman or be effective at any job because of the physical limits of his body.

Taniguchi's anxiety was justified. After returning to postal delivery in April 1950, he found it difficult to work, so he received surgery on his elbow, but it did not improve much. Life was unbearable until he encountered the peace movement. When Yamaguchi Misako and Takahashi Akihiro shared their testimonies at the 1955 world conference in Hiroshima, they inspired many hibakusha to get involved in peace activism. Taniguchi recalled that when the two stood one at a time on the stage in front of tens of thousands of people, he realized for the first time that he was not alone and that there was a battle being waged by the hibakusha who felt that "enough was enough" (mō iya da). Inspired to take action, "I chose the path to become a witness for peace. I already had partly given up on life, so I was determined to dedicate my new life to the 'battle with the atomic bomb' (genbaku to no tatakai)."[65] For the 1956 Nagasaki conference, he led a group of hibakusha in publishing a collection of survivor testimonies titled Mō iya da: Genbaku no ikite iru shōnintachi (Enough is enough: Living witnesses of the atomic bomb). Taniguchi became president of the Nagasaki Atomic Bombing Association of Young Men and Women in 1959.

Taniguchi (and his wounds) became an icon of the Nagasaki peace movement. In 1970, Kamata Sadao was editing a collection of Nagasaki hibakusha testimonies entitled Nagasaki no shōgen: 1970 (Testimonies of Nagasaki), to be published in August, when two films that the United States had confiscated twenty-five years earlier were broadcast on national television, one black-and-white and one color. Kamata noticed in the color film a young man lying on his stomach with his back reddened from severe burning by the bomb, and he realized that it was Taniguchi.[66] The film produced an outpouring of support for the hibakusha. Within days of the national broadcast in June, Taniguchi received thousands of letters of encouragement from viewers all over the country, as well as requests to publish his story.[67] The Asahi shinbun sent Taniguchi a color photo of the scene of his suffering, which he brought to Kamata, deciding together to put it on the cover of

Nagasaki no shōgen. The publication included more than eighty testimonial accounts and primary documents, becoming a "central reference" in the Nagasaki testimony and peace movement.[68]

Taniguchi, in his contribution to *Nagasaki no shōgen: 1970*, wrote that he did not want his suffering to become a spectacle, but the importance of the peace movement outweighed his potential embarrassment. He emphasized that the cover photo of his wounds represented the pain of all hibakusha and showed the reality of the bomb. Speaking directly to the reader, he pleaded, "Those of you who have looked at my image, try not to look away. I want you to look once more, carefully. I miraculously survived, but still our entire bodies bear the cursed scars of the atomic bomb. I want to believe in the intensity (*kibishisa*) and the warmth of your eyes that stare upon us."[69] The Nagasaki testimony movement began in

FIGURE 5.1. Business card of Taniguchi Sumiteru.

Source: Author's personal collection.

earnest in 1968, but the 1970 publication represented the renewed determination of Taniguchi, Kamata, and other memory activists to give meaning to the suffering of all atomic-bombing survivors, not to mention their refusal to let the memory of their experience be forgotten, no matter how painful it was for them to recall.[70] Taniguchi printed the color photo of his wounds on his business card (he carries the same one today), not in order to garner sympathy, but in the hope of relating the horror of the atomic bombings and nuclear weapons more broadly to everyone he met.

The Nagasaki atomic-bombing literature movement did not begin as early as in Hiroshima, but many hibakusha in Nagasaki expressed an interest in building one from early on. In 1952, the Nagasaki shinbun company coordinated efforts with the prefectural and municipal governments to reach out to the city's hibakusha to collect and publish their testimonies of the bombing. The response was surprising. In just nine days, more than three hundred hibakusha submitted "My Account of the Atomic Bombing," when only one hundred seventy were collected in Hiroshima two years earlier. The editorial staff in Nagasaki were overwhelmed, resolving in the end to publish only six of the accounts.[71] The overwhelming number of hibakusha who wished to share their experience suggested that many survivors wanted to confront their trauma and speak openly of their experience, which had been difficult to do during the occupation. It also reflected the hope of the Nagasaki hibakusha that they could find a collective voice for memory activism. Four years later, in 1956, Taniguchi Sumiteru spearheaded the testimonial movement to publish *Mō iya da*.

The work of memory activists in Nagasaki suffered a setback in 1958, when the city lost its main symbol of the atomic bombing. The removal of the ruins of the Urakami Cathedral solidified the dominance of the Urakami region in the city's official narrative and popular memory of its bombing. The Catholics' desire to "quickly forget the wounds of the atomic bomb," Kamata Sadao once wrote, was shortsighted and erased a symbol that had stood equal to Hiroshima's Atomic Dome. The single column of the ruins preserved near ground zero was to serve that purpose, but "its image as a symbol of the Nagasaki atomic bombing is weak."[72] However, the loss of the atomic symbol fueled the fire in the bellies of the Nagasaki activists. It was the duty of hibakusha, Kamata claimed, to challenge the dominance of Urakami in representation of Nagasaki's experience. From the late 1960s, Nagasaki activists, such as Taniguchi Sumiteru, Kamata Sadao, and Yamada Kan, among many others, attempted to do just that. In the face of the long Christian history of the city and Catholic interpretation of the bombing, they "could no longer keep silent" and watch their trauma continue to be "concealed" (*inpei*) and "forgotten" (*bōkyaku*).[73] After a brief lull in the mid-1960s, they renewed the testimony movement in 1968 by forming the Nagasaki no shōgen no

kai (Nagasaki Testimony Association), which publishes annual collections of survivor accounts (it continues today).

Their efforts intensified again two years later in response to what they saw as
a revival of ultranationalism, evidenced by the government's declaration of a "National Day" during the Osaka World Fair in 1970, which included singing of the
"national foundation myths" and a musical performance by a Self-Defense Forces
band. The celebrations of National Day represented for Kamata and others the
government's militaristic recidivism, which had seemingly forgotten the realities
of the victims of war, especially the hibakusha. The second edition of *Nagasaki
no shōgen*, as the editors saw it, "returned a blow" to the "amnesia" and the "base
ultranationalist thought" of the national government.[74] The hibakusha activists
realized that the nation needed to be educated on the history and memory of the
atomic bombings, a realization that resulted in the book *Chinmoku no kabe o
yabutte*. Also in 1970, Taniguchi and other activists published the second edition
of *Mō iya da*, which included the testimony of twenty-five hibakusha to commemorate the twenty-fifth anniversary of the bombing.[75]

Some hibakusha memory activists, empowered by the growing strength of
their collective voice, focused their efforts on specific walls of silence that remained
standing. The legacy of Nagai remained the biggest challenge, but few activists
challenged it directly, or at least not aggressively. The most vocal critic of Nagai
was the poet and hibakusha Yamada Kan. Yamada experienced the atomic
bombing at 2.7 kilometers from ground zero at fifteen years old, along with his
younger sister. Yamada began writing poetry in 1948, and he published his first
collection of poems in March 1954, two months after his sister committed suicide to escape the psychological hardships of being a hibakusha. Yamada published
the collection of poetry, *Inochi no hi* (Fire of life) because he wanted to commemorate her death, but more than that, it was for himself: it served as his atonement
for not fulfilling his duty as an elder brother to protect her and as a way for him
to deal with survivor guilt.

Before the 1970s, few hibakusha publicly criticized Nagai. Yamada Kan recalled
in 1999 that nobody in Nagasaki ever addressed the "Nagai Takashi problem,"
because, "once you touch that, you're on your own." Yamada claimed that even
in 1999, Nagai was "untouchable," and peace research institutes and other scholarly institutes avoided the topic altogether, although Yamada never understood
the reason for the taboo.[76] In 1972, he wrote a criticism of Nagai in the national
journal *Ushio*, in which he called Nagai the "uninvited representative" of Nagasaki hibakusha and pointed out that his interpretation of the bomb seethed with
"self-righteous Catholic egoism."[77] The same journal also included an article
written by Taniguchi Sumiteru. Shortly after Yamada's article was published, he
received a phone call from an influential Catholic scholar in Nagasaki, Kataoka

Yakichi, who was also a Catholic priest, had been Nagai's close friend, and was the author of the official biography of Nagai.[78] Kataoka apparently berated Yamada for the sacrilege of criticizing the saint of Urakami.[79]

Yamada was not attacking Nagai as a person but as *the* representative of Nagasaki atomic-bombing literature. As Yamada wrote to author Yasuda Mitsuru, "I am not aware if there is anyone who dislikes [Nagai]. To express my conviction and as part of my literary theory, I published criticism of Nagai Takashi, but there is no one continuing it." Yamada was not interested in the "extraliterary" (*bungakugai*) persona of Nagai, but rather in how his literature affected other hibakusha from Nagasaki and muffled the impact of their literary voice in comparison to that of Hiroshima. Yamada said, "I'm not saying he's bad," only that his literature needed to be interrogated from a literary perspective. He intended to point out how Nagai's books were simply not good literature and were not representative of Nagasaki writers. Yet, after the 1972 *Ushio* article, no one in Nagasaki would work with Yamada, not even authors in the broader literary world. Yamada had simply argued that Nagai "was obviously embroiled in the policies of the American occupation," but, he said, if you say that within Nagasaki, "everyone hates you."[80]

In his battle for Nagasaki hibakusha memory, Yamada's weapon of choice was poetry.[81] Avoiding lofty religious imagery or claims of beauty in death, Yamada depicted the grotesque realities of atomic destruction. He replaced Nagai's sacrificial lamb with ravens perching on the corpses in the atomic-bombed landscape. As Yamada walked with his younger sister through the Urakami valley the day after the bomb, he noticed some wooden poles on top of a pile of corpses; nearby, a soldier had died with his head in a tub of water and his boots off. All of a sudden, a raven flew down to the corpses and perched calmly on one of the poles. Yamada saw many ravens sitting on the corpses, poking at the bodies with their beaks—a scene that burned into his memory.[82] In March 1972, he evoked the raven he had seen with his sister in "The Dead Raven" (*Shinda karasu*):

> One raven walks along with its head hanging.
>
> Indeed, [the bombing] must have been around here.
> It's a wasteland of corpses.
> Burned pieces of wood had blown over the browned roof tiles.
> Corpses you can see. Corpses you can't see.
> Raise their hands. Tear their stomachs.
> Raise their scorched heads. Spread their crotches.
> Everything lies in the abyss of darkness. Smoke flows.
>
> One raven.
> Perches atop the head of a corpse.

> It (*soitsu*) [the corpse] never moves.
> We cried out loud and moved along.[83]
> The raven looks from above,
> walking along slowly with its head hanging.[84]

Yamada saw no salvation in the destruction. The motionless and charred corpses remained frozen in grotesque poses as ravens perched on their lifeless bodies that were powerless to shoo away the birds. The scene represented for Yamada the helplessness of human beings in the face of the destruction of the atomic bomb and its aftereffects, where the raven embodied the death that awaited even the so-called survivors.

Yamada considered his poetry a voice expressing the experience of all hibakusha. In 1999 he commented on how he used the presence of ravens in his work to do that: "I depicted the anxiety over the occurrence of blood cancer under the pretense of the raven swooping down."[85] For Yamada and many Nagasaki hibakusha, the representative image of the atomic bombing was no sacrificial lamb but death, human destruction, and the persistent anxiety of dying. His poetry presented a challenge to Nagai as the voice of Nagasaki, drawing attention to and contextualizing the issue of Nagasaki hibakusha memory and representation, but the resistance he encountered was indicative of the persistence of Nagai in the official narrative. Today, Nagai's memory is still venerated, his city-sponsored museum attracts numbers of tourists, and his books occupy a special shelf in local bookstores.

• • •

The place of the hibakusha in atomic narratives evolved over the course of three distinct but overlapping time periods. The first period, 1945–54, saw discussions surrounding the aftermath of both atomic bombings remain regional issues. At the end of the war, more than one hundred cities lay in ruins, and everyone in Japan struggled to recover from the devastation of war. Thus, few outside of Nagasaki and Hiroshima embraced the idea that the two cities somehow deserved special attention from the nation, let alone special treatment. In Nagasaki, a hyperlocal narrative of the bombing developed within and about the city, which centered on the northern Urakami valley and painted the image of ground zero as a site of Catholic destruction. Meanwhile, municipal officials implemented their vision for reconstruction and shaped the urban identity of the city as foremost an international cultural city, a vision in which recent memory was secondary to the historical memory of an international past. In other words, atomic narratives in Nagasaki initially did not present the bombing as a citywide tragedy to be commemorated, but rather as a hyperlocalized tragedy that was just one part of the city's long history.

The postwar lives of the survivors in both cities did not figure largely in narratives of the war during the first eight years. Survivors often lived their lives as social outcasts, enduring discrimination and a general lack of empathy for their suffering, an experience which became the subject of a 1953 film by Sekigawa Hideo called *Hiroshima*. The film, a cinematic masterpiece, illuminated the plight of the hibakusha, but it flopped in Japan for a variety of reasons, not least of which was because national audiences failed to care about the suffering of one city and its people when the destruction of war had affected the entire country. Hiroshima and the atomic bombings more generally had not yet become a symbolic event in the national narrative of the war and therefore the hibakusha's experience did not yet warrant national (or regional) sympathy. Although it is tempting to point to occupation-period censorship as a reason for the lack of national attention paid to the atomic-bombed cities from 1945 to 1952, the poor reception of Sekigawa's film in 1953, for example, indicates that politics of recovery and memory were more at play than censorship.

For more than a decade, the national and municipal governments avoided affording the hibakusha official recognition of their suffering as being different from other war survivors in Japan. Officials considered it dangerous politics to create a special relief law for the survivors of the atomic bombings because, they believed, it would cause a kind of survivor envy among other Japanese citizens who had lived through the war. Such thinking characterized the response of the government to the hibakusha's demands for decades.[86] The national government avoided, as much as possible, recognizing the atomic bombings as different from other catastrophic events of the war because it also ran the risk of accepting responsibility for the war and the atomic bombings. Paying for the medical costs of hibakusha was especially fraught with danger for the government because it implied responsibility for the bombings. The Socialists, though self-proclaimed advocates for hibakusha issues, only made things worse regarding the hope for full medical relief from the government during the first postwar decade because they insisted on linking the result of the war for Japan (i.e., the atomic bombings), to Japanese aggression more broadly, a link which ultimately worked against their cause.[87] And so until 1954, survivors, activists, and officials in Nagasaki and Hiroshima developed their postwar narratives amid local contexts and based them on local issues. Even though discussions of the Second World War abound during the first decade of the postwar era, Hiroshima, and to a lesser extent Nagasaki, as part of the national war narrative and as a center for the peace movement crystallized only after 1954.[88]

During the second period, 1954–58, discourse surrounding the bombings underwent dramatic changes. A confluence of events concerning nuclear weapons and energy ushered atomic-bombing-related issues from local to national concern, while allowing for Hiroshima to solidify as the iconic atomic-bombed city. When the 1954 Lucky Dragon No. 5 incident led to national outrage in Japan, it brought attention to the dangers of the nuclear age, leading to popular interest in the history of the atomic bombings and their aftermath, which had not yet received sufficient discussion or working-through in popular discourse. The antinuclear peace movement, which grew rapidly, turned to Hiroshima as the center of activism. City officials there had linked the memory of the bombing to peace activism during the city's reconstruction, and so, compared to Nagasaki, which had not done so to the same extent, Hiroshima seemed the natural leader for such a cause. When Nagasaki officials approved the removal of the ruins of Urakami Cathedral in 1958 against the wishes of hibakusha and other peace activists, they demonstrated their unwillingness to give priority to atomic memory in the city's urban identity, as well as their unwillingness or inability to develop Nagasaki as an equal center of antinuclear peace activism. As a result, from 1954 to 1958, Nagasaki became further relegated to the corners of the history and memory of the bombings. Thus this period could be termed the "rise of Hiroshima."[89]

The third period, 1959–68, saw the rise of the hibakusha, as well as their voice, as the focus of peace activism and discourse surrounding the bombings. In the mid-1950s, the hibakusha had not yet become the moral authorities regarding nuclear weapons that they are known as today. From 1954 to the early 1960s, political ideology of the activist groups served as the driving force of the antinuclear peace movement. From the mid-1960s, along with attention paid to the historical experience of the hibakusha, came recognition of their continued suffering. The collective experience and individual traumatic memories of the hibakusha also became central to the antinuclear weapons movement. After political infighting fractured the unity of the movement, the activists reconsidered their atomic narrative, which since 1954 had been centered in Hiroshima, focused on the destruction of the *city* instead of the human suffering, and spoke of that city's atomic experience as a warning for future generations. In other words, atomic-memory activism during the preceding period had reduced the story to statistics of death and physical destruction and tended to occlude discussion of the continued suffering and traumatic memory of the hibakusha.

The hibakusha slowly found their place in the atomic narratives of the national peace movement from the late 1950s and early 1960s, thanks primarily to their efforts as memory activists, but also to the work of activists and writers outside of the two cities. In 1955, Norman Cousins helped Hiroshima activists draw international attention to a group of young women survivors from Hiroshima, the "Hiroshima Maidens" as they came to be known, who traveled to the United States to receive surgery on their scarred faces. From the 1960s, intellectuals such as Ōe Kenzaburō and Robert Jay Lifton captivated their readers with explorations of the experience and suffering of the hibakusha in a way that few others had done: they made the survivors the subject of their inquiries, instead of the history of the war, the politics of remembering it, or the urban destruction. Of course, popular interest in the matters of the survivors at this time was located in Hiroshima, not Nagasaki. Even so, the moment when popular discussions of the atomic bombings shifted from a focus on the cities in general to the trauma and suffering of the survivors coincided with and contributed to a rise in the power of the political voice of the hibakusha. The survivors became "moralists," as Ōe referred to them, or sages of atomic and nuclear destruction. This third period can thus be termed the "rise of the moralists."

During this period, the hibakusha became the most vocal presence in postatomic Nagasaki. From the 1950s into the early 1960s, hibakusha from both Nagasaki and Hiroshima found strength in a unified front against government neglect of the survivors, which for them presented the last, unfinished work of reconstruction. They berated the national government for its neglect of their needs and insufficient care. And their criticism continued even after a national relief law finally passed in 1957 because of its inadequacies and its refusal to recognize large numbers of hibakusha. The determination of the hibakusha activists to redress these injustices never flagged, even after the political infighting that broke the unity between and within the two cities in the 1960s.

The Christian image of ground zero, which had distracted from the broader hibakusha story since 1945, however, remained one of the enduring challenges to memory activists in Nagasaki. The image intensified in the late 1950s, when Catholic leaders and municipal officials worked to fulfill their visions of reconstruction, altering the urban landscape at the expense of the city's image in the popular memory of the bombings, especially compared to Hiroshima. When the city council allowed the Urakami Catholics to remove the ruined walls of the cathedral, the walls of silence surrounding the official narrative grew stronger. However, the 1960s shift in focus of the peace movement to the suffering of the survivors also strengthened the presence of the hibakusha experience in local discussions of the bombing. Once they formed the Nagasaki Testimony Association in 1968, their work as memory activists began to successfully write their experience (personal trauma, memory, and suffering) into the official narrative, despite such symbolic losses as the cathedral ruins. The experience of the hibakusha remains an important part of the city's identity into the present.

RUINS OF MEMORY

The Urakami Cathedral and the Politics
of Urban Identity

Residents of a city who seek to reconstruct after a devastating, traumatic event face a difficult problem. In the process of removing the rubble and debris from destroyed parts of the city in order to revive the landscape and rebuild, they must decide what to do with the traumatic memory encoded in the ruins. To what degree should preservation of the ruins factor into the renewal process of the landscape? How do you realize a vision of reconstruction when relics of a tragic past appear as an obstacle to that progress, both psychologically and physically? How do you reconcile physical destruction, traumatic memory, and visions of reconstruction? In short, what do you do with the past when you move forward? Do you bring it with you, or do you erase its traces and leave it behind? For decades after the bombing, some groups in Nagasaki disagreed on how to treat the ruins of the atomic past. The Urakami Cathedral ruins in particular loomed large in discussions of reconstruction and urban identity through the late 1950s.

In 1958, the mayor of Nagasaki, Tagawa Tsutomu, approved a bid from the Urakami Catholics to remove the atomic ruins of their cathedral and build a brand new one in its place. This came as a shock to Nagasaki residents and to people all around Japan, especially considering the intensity of the antiwar and antinuclear weapons movements of the 1950s. Moreover, since 1945, the ruins had stood as a symbol of the tragedy of the atomic bombing of Nagasaki and as the center of its commemoration. The cathedral ruins usually appeared alongside the Hiroshima Atomic Dome in media discussions of the bombings. The removal of the ruins in 1958 represents what Pierre Nora, in his discussion of sites of memory, has termed a "disappearance of an intimate fund of memory."[1] A clash of visions led to the disappearance of the Urakami Cathedral ruins in 1958, elucidating a rift among politicians, residents, and peace activists in regard to the treatment of the memory of the bombing within the city.

Ruins link the past to the present, living on as remains of what once was, but, in the case of a destructive event, they also ensnare the present in a contested past. The ruins of a building or structure no longer serve any practical function, but they sometimes serve an important social one. People in the present look at the ruins, not for the building as it once stood, but rather as a record of the event that reduced it to such a state, the significance of which depends on the viewer. Ruins become mnemonic devices that convey in the simplest possible way a past that has gone but has some kind of relevance to the present, whether that be for politics, religious belief, or commemoration.[2] Indeed, the destructive past lives on in the ruins. Individuals and interest groups, such as the hibakusha, the Urakami Catholics, and municipal officials, loaded the ruins of the Urakami Cathedral with symbolism and meaning, depending on their vantage point. They never disputed the occurrence of the atomic bombings, but they did not always agree on the reading of ruins as a text in the present.

While residents renewed the cityscape of the Urakami valley, the cathedral ruins became Nagasaki's mnemonic device that recalled the tragedy of the Second World War and the horror of atomic weapons in ways that reflected the interests and concerns of individuals and groups. For activist groups, hibakusha, and other city residents, the ruins became the center of the commemoration of the bombing and a popular symbol within their atomic narrative, providing a shorthand reference for the human trauma of the bombing. When Nagasaki activists found themselves competing with Hiroshima for a voice and while municipal officials pursued reconstruction policies that downplayed the bombing as part of the city's identity, the cathedral ruins provided weight to the work of the activists, keeping them at least somewhat in the spotlight with Hiroshima. In other words, the presence of the ruins and their ability to convey the shorthand version of Nagasaki's atomic experience helped the hibakusha-focused atomic narrative survive the growing dominance of Hiroshima in popular memory. Hibakusha memory activism was highly invested in the cathedral ruins.

For Urakami Catholics, the ruined cathedral represented the destruction of their religious community. To move forward from the tragedy that befell them, the Catholics sought a complete renewal of the Urakami valley, and by the early 1950s, the cathedral ruins remained their last obstacle to achieving it. The cathedral was no longer a functioning building, and so it did not serve the religious purposes of the Catholic community. When municipal officials granted the Catholics permission to clear the ruins and build a brand-new cathedral on the same spot, they were not giving priority to the Urakami Catholics' desire to erase a physical trace of a traumatic past over the desire of city residents and memory activists to preserve it. Rather, clearing the landscape of the ruins simply fit into the municipal approach to shaping the urban identity of the city in the mid-1950s. Indeed, there was much disagreement, indecision, and apathy among city council members during the debates over the fate of the ruins, but the Catholics themselves led the drive to remove the ruins, providing the necessary, if controversial, rationale to convince officials of their desire to achieve their vision of reconstruction.

The approach of city officials to the presence of the ruins evolved over the first decade after the bombing and reflected the evolving interpretation of the identity of the city as a *kokusai bunka toshi*. From the start, there was no single definition of what the term meant. In the first five years or so after the bomb, emphases on the meaning of the first two words of *kokusai bunka toshi* manifested as a "city of international culture," as seen in the municipal drive to emphasize Nagasaki's famed history as an international port city in the reconstruction. City planners had cultivated that image by highlighting the city's past relations with the West and the rest of East Asia and by rebuilding and emphasizing related historic sites in its tourism. By the mid-1950s, after the city had physically rebuilt, emphases shifted to the first and last words of *kokusai bunka toshi*, which came to mean "international city of culture," as the mayor and other city officials sought to shape the urban landscape to reflect the modern layouts of what they considered international cities around the world. City officials did not abandon their vision to cultivate and maintain Nagasaki's international history; rather, by adding a layer of meaning to *kokusai bunka toshi*, they set out to strengthen the international identity of the city by placing it back (as they saw it) into the ranks of world cities that served as global crossroads. The mission, much to the dismay of most of the city residents, became one of creating a "modern" city, which in mid-1950s Nagasaki meant clearing the landscape of what city officials and especially the mayor considered the unsightly physical remains of the atomic bombing.

The desire to achieve complete renewal of decimated cityscapes was widespread in the 1950s. City officials and residents in Japan, Germany, England, and elsewhere shared a desire to modernize their urban landscapes, especially in cities that had been damaged by aerial bombing during the Second World War.[3] Modernizing the city during reconstruction meant leaving the past behind by clearing the physical traces of the war to make way for a modern and peaceful future.[4] Only in a few cases did reconstruction plans to clear cities of their ruins meet with opposition from the general public or memory activist groups who sought to preserve ruins of the war as physical lessons of history, such as in the case of the Gedächtnis Church in Berlin. Nagasaki's treatment of its ruins of memory in 1958 reflected a worldwide trend, but city officials failed to recognize, it seemed, that Nagasaki was not like every other city. The actions of Nagasaki officials appeared out of touch with reality to people all around Japan at a time when the current of memory was clearly flowing toward making the atomic bombings the central experience of Japan's war narrative. Nagasaki's approach to modernizing its landscape to move forward reflected the norm, whereas Hiroshima's approach, which sought to stay frozen in the traumatic, atomic moment, indeed to perpetuate that moment and define the city's entire existence by it, did not. In Hiroshima, preservation of its Atomic Dome (also known as the Peace Dome) and other ruins were key to remaining frozen in the atomic past in order to bolster its urban identity as a peace commemoration city (*heiwa kinen toshi*). In other words, in the first decades after the bombings, Hiroshima cultivated a *milieu de mémoire* (real environment of memory), to use the words of Pierre Nora, whereas Nagasaki failed to preserve its only *lieu de mémoire* (site of memory).

Conflicting Symbolism of the Ruins

When it was completed in 1925, the Urakami Cathedral stood as a symbol of the international nature of Nagasaki culture. Nagasaki residents and visitors admired the cathedral and enjoyed the ringing of its massive bells when they echoed throughout the city daily. Non-Christians, too, found aesthetic value in the cathedral. Novelist and Nagasaki native Kamohara Haruo, an understudy of Akutagawa Ryūnosuke, wrote in 1931 of the wondrous sites of his hometown, including among them the "red-bricked Urakami Cathedral, which greets us not with its religiousness but with its beauty." Writing six years after the bell towers were completed, Kamohara described a typical stroll through the Urakami valley as he listened to the sound of the Angelus bells from the Urakami Cathedral. He wrote that when the sound hits your ears, you should hurry and look closely to observe the "unusual custom" (*ifū*) of the Christians, who were "mostly peasants," gradually stopping their work in the fields to quietly bring their hands together.[5] The bells could be heard throughout much of the city, and the cathedral represented the exoticism that Nagasaki cultivated as part of its unusual international history. After the atomic bomb destroyed the Urakami Cathedral in August 1945, the rubble became the symbol of the decimation of the Catholic community, whose few survivors hoped to rebuild the cathedral. To non-Christian city residents, the ruins of the cathedral stood as a reminder of the tragedy of the atomic bombing and a symbol of the city's role in showing the folly of war and promoting "everlasting world peace." From the late 1940s through the 1950s, the cathedral ruins remained a central image of the city's experience in discussions of the bombings within and outside of the city.

The cathedral ruins became the symbol of Nagasaki's tragedy just one month after the bombing. On September 6 and 7, 1945, before the arrival of U.S. troops, two reporters for the *Yomiuri hōchi shinbun* traveled to Nagasaki and walked through ground zero to survey the damage.[6] As they endured the stench of rotting bodies (*shishū*) mixed with "pungent gas," the remains of the giant cathedral on the hill caught their eye amid the flattened wasteland. The horror of the bomb hit the reporters hard as they stood in the gruesome remains of what was once a vibrant community, where they estimated at least one-third of the presumed 30,000 dead from the bombing were Catholic. As they walked among the rubble of the cathedral, they were told of the two priests and forty parishioners who had died in the blast and whose bodies still remained buried under the bricks. For the reporters, the tragedy of the atomic bombing of Nagasaki was exemplified by the destruction of Urakami, where "10,000 Christians (*seikyōto*) had been sacrificed" and the historic cathedral that had represented the international nature of the city now lay silent in a pile of rubble and corpses. The reporters called for the cathedral's "preservation as a memento (*kinenbutsu*)."[7]

As time passed, the ruins became attached to Nagasaki's atomic experience in popular memory, both in and outside of the city. As the central site of commemoration for the bombing, an image of the ruined church would often appear alongside Hiroshima's symbolic Atomic Dome when the bombings were discussed in media, often in terms of a single event represented by Hiroshima. The cathedral walls served as shorthand in newspapers, magazines, and newsreels to convey the atomic experience of Nagasaki; like the dome in Hiroshima, the cathedral ruins carried the weight of a cultural memory that was at once local and national. Nagasaki's experience was thus boiled down to the ruins of a Catholic cathedral, reinforcing the Christian image of ground zero through much of the 1950s. Moreover, because the ruins were located in the Urakami valley, far to the north of the main part of the city, residents in Nagasaki proper who viewed the bombing as an "Urakami problem" benefited from the city's memento of the atomic experience being physically located in the north. They enjoyed Nagasaki's place in the peace movement yet maintained a safe distance from the social stigma of the bombing.

When the city council began regulating the selection of artifacts and relics of the bombing for preservation, the ruins of the cathedral seemed an obvious choice, as those were the most conspicuous and most visually symbolic of the city's experience. In 1949, the Nagasaki City Council inaugurated the Committee for the Preservation of Atomic Bombing Materials (Genbaku shiryō hozon i'in kai) and charged it with the task of designating and maintaining physical traces of the atomic bombing, including melted bottles, flash-burned wood, and the two cathedral walls that had remained standing. During its twenty-seven general meetings held between 1949 and 1958, the committee voted nine times in favor of preserving the Urakami Cathedral ruins, which reflected the general point of view in the city. Indeed, one reporter noted in 1958, the committee represented "the voice of the residents."[8] The primary goal of the city council and the committee in preserving physical traces of the bomb's destruction was to convey Nagasaki's atomic experience to visitors and to educate posterity, and so in their annual reports to the mayor, the committee recommended "the ruins should be preserved."[9]

Preservation of the ruins was a priority for Nagasaki politicians from the late 1940s through the mid-1950s because they thought the site could serve as both a site of memory (for locals) and of tourism (for visitors). In other words, for the first decade after the bombing, preservation of the ruins made political sense because it appeased the demands of both the peace activists and hibakusha, including those on the city council, and more business-oriented officials who saw economic value in cultivating the ruins as a tourist site. In the early 1950s, the Nagasaki City Tourism Association (Nagasaki-shi kankō kyōkai) and the Nagasaki Cultural Association formed a movement to ensure the preservation of the ruins as a memorial (kinenbutsu) to the atomic bombing and as "significant evidence (shiryō) that speaks of the tragedy of war." It was the primary "sightseeing relic of Atomic Nagasaki" (atomu Nagasaki kankō ibutsu), to which visitors looked to understand especially the horrific power of the atomic bomb.[10] The city council and the other groups had the full support of the non-Catholic hibakusha, who wanted neither the memory of their tragedy diluted nor the voice of their peace movement silenced.

The Urakami Catholics saw the ruins in a much different light. From the beginning, they considered the reconstruction of the Urakami Cathedral synonymous with the revival of their community. There could be no recovery, no healing, until the cathedral had been reconstructed on the same spot where their ancestors had labored for more than thirty years to build the original church. In the months following the bombing, approximately one thousand Urakami Catholics, still living in the dugout trenches, gathered for mass every Sunday in the "field of burned ruins," as one Nagasaki reporter referred to it, near the crumbled cathedral. In early October 1945, Sadata Hiroshi, an Urakami Catholic clergyman, declared the hope that the cathedral would be reconstructed as soon as possible because a church was central to a "speedy revival" (kyūsoku na fukkō). The greatest desire of the Catholics, he noted, was to "spread the teaching of 'love,'" which defines "our dogma," to the souls of people in order to "breathe a strong breath" into the reconstruction effort. A church would be central to realizing this aim. The voices of the thousand or so Catholics chanting amid the atomic ruins, as the reporter for the Nagasaki shinbun put it, prayed for a place of worship.[11] For the Catholics, the primary concern in the years after the bombing was not commemoration of the tragedy; rather, their primary objective was the survival, revival, and renewal of their community and the Urakami valley more generally.

The approach of the Urakami Catholic community to remembering and commemorating the atomic bombing was, in a word, complicated. They considered themselves firstly Catholic and only secondly hibakusha, if they identified as hibakusha at all. That is, being Catholic was a chosen and proud identity, whereas being a hibakusha was incidental, traumatic, and stigmatizing in postwar society. Moreover, the approximately fifteen hundred Catholics who survived the bombing had become a minority within their own community by the mid-1950s when their numbers had risen to about five thousand. Indeed, some of the new members were also hibakusha who converted to Catholicism or married into the community, but most came to Nagasaki after the bomb and were thus not hibakusha themselves. Even if the fifteen hundred or so hibakusha had given priority to their identity as hibakusha or demanded first and foremost recognition of their traumatic memory over the interests of their community, their voice would have been drowned out by the rest of the community who either wanted to forget the tragedy or who could not relate to the experience on a personal level. Some Catholic hibakusha, such as Akizuki Tatsuichirō, did become leaders in the Nagasaki peace movement, but they never represented the views of the Catholics. Moreover, the writings and voice of Nagai Takashi had presented the official Catholic narrative of the tragedy as "God's Providence," making it difficult for Catholic hibakusha to work through their trauma qua trauma, not to mention creating a wall that all Nagasaki hibakusha had to overcome to present their experience to the world outside of Nagasaki. As a result, even though the Urakami community as a whole believed in the ideals of the peace and antinuclear movements of the 1950s, they saw their needs as a religious community as outweighing the demands of local activists to preserve the ruins.

The leaders of the Urakami Catholic community had indeed experienced the trauma of the atomic bombing, but they sought to move past it to achieve their vision of a renewed Urakami. They envisioned the reconstruction of the valley purely in terms of restoration, not preservation, and they never wavered from that vision. Preservation of the ruins, they thought, would keep the community from moving forward. As Bishop Yamaguchi told a journalist in early 1958, not only did the remains of the atomic bombing not represent peace, they were also "too inextricable from the memory of a tragic past."[12] (Yamaguchi did not elaborate on what he meant by "tragic past," whether he meant the atomic bombing generally or his community's patriotic fervor in a war that decimated them.) The primary concern of the leaders of the Catholic community was to maintain the Catholic identity and religious character of the community. They also saw the destruction of the cathedral through the lens of their religion. Nagai, Yamaguchi, Urakawa Wasaburō, and other leaders framed the destruction of Urakami by the atomic bomb as one more instance in a history of "destructions" (*kuzure*) of their community; the atomic bombing was stripped of its world-war context and placed within a Catholic historical tradition peculiar to Urakami. The view of the destruction of Urakami as part of an Urakami Catholic history of martyrdom and destruction continued long after Nagai's death in 1951. Some Catholics in Nagasaki today continue to embrace this position.[13]

Catholic leaders promoted education about the folly of war and the importance of peace, but they also advocated the erasure of any physical evidence that could tie their community to the war. Nagai wrote, "Every time we see [the ruined cathedral] (*konna mono*), not only do our hearts ache, but we also do not want to show the children who will be born in the future traces of the crimes (*tsumi no ato*) of our generation that erred and committed a war that burned even the house of God. Rather, we want to build a peaceful and beautiful church, and make this place a hill of blossoming flowers to point the hearts of the children freely to heaven."[14] The "crimes of our generation" to Nagai meant those of all humanity, not just the Urakami believers. Future generations should not have to suffer for the crimes of the past generation, or so Nagai seemed to be arguing. The preservation of the cathedral ruins would both impede a revival of the community that survived the atomic bombing and threaten the spiritual freedom of future generations. Similar to Bishop Yamaguchi, however, Nagai promoted sacrificing the memory of the bombing in favor of the possibility that through a sort of utopian education, future generations would not repeat the same mistake. Though the goal here was the same as that of the hibakusha and other peace activists, the role of the cathedral ruins in achieving that goal was quite different.

In the early years after the bombing, Catholic leaders understood that rebuilding the cathedral similar to the original one would be "more difficult than one could dream," but they found strength in their faith. They first resolved to build a temporary wooden church.[15] By November 1945, construction of the provisional church next to the cathedral ruins was under way, as various groups in Nagasaki, including occupation forces, contributed materials and labor to the effort.[16] The small, wooden church, completed in December 1946, was the first public building erected after the bombing; it was also the first symbolic revival project undertaken by the Catholics.[17] "The cathedral was demolished," wrote Nagai in 1949, "but that does not injure the omnipotence of God even a little, because it was a building. It was a collection of stones and bricks built by the hands of humans. That it would crumble when receiving the pressure of a blast is a phenomenon that rightly abides with physics."[18] In his 1949 book *Hana saku oka* (Hill of blossoming flowers), Nagai wrote that the reconstruction of the cathedral was essential to revive the "society of love" of ten thousand Catholics that had existed before the atomic bomb and had centered on the largest cathedral in Asia. The destruction of the cathedral by the *pika-don* (flash-boom) and the departure of eight thousand believers from this world forced the villagers left behind to "think deeply about the Providence" of the tragedy, and now they "thank God who swells with love, praise [Him], quietly and brightly continue prayers and sacrifice day and night, and strive to build a village of blossoming flowers of love."[19] The wooden church alone could not fulfill this vision of renewal.

FIGURE 6.1.   A wedding among the ruins of the Urakami Cathedral, 1958.

Source: Photograph taken by and courtesy of Takahara Itaru.

FIGURE 6.2. Children playing among the ruins of the cathedral, 1950s.

Source: Photograph taken by and courtesy of Takahara Itaru.

Catholic leaders began campaigning for funds to rebuild the cathedral by raising awareness of the Catholic desire to clear the ruins, which they portrayed as the last remaining obstacle to the "new life" that breathed throughout the valley. Nagai and other Catholic leaders, such as Bishop Yamaguchi Aijirō and Vicar Francis-Xavier Nakada, put together booklets appealing to national and international audiences alike. One 1949 photo booklet entitled *Urakami tenshudō: The Church of Urakami, Nagasaki, Japan*, summed up the position of the Catholics. It included sixteen pages of photos with short captions in both Japanese and English, telling the story of the cathedral. Nagai described how just as Nagasaki's mushroom cloud represented a "beacon of peace" that ended the war (2), so too did the cathedral that "bursted [*sic*] into flames" (3). The booklet concluded with several photographs of the landscape of Urakami in 1949 that shows "no vestige of ruins." Nagai boasted, "Many houses are already rebuilt, fields have been cleanly tilled, every human figure on the road is moving actively. If you look [at] this bright view, you shall feel the Will which comes from the Love of Lord [*sic*]" (15).[20] Vicar Nakada noted in a separate English booklet the "generous effort in manual labor and use of their own money" of the "few faithfuls [*sic*] who survived—some 2000, with the benediction of the Lord," built a "temporary chapel in six months," which was blessed by American Bishop O'Hara in June 1946. Still, he continued, "there will be no rest in this parish till the Catholic parishioners by their own efforts and the assistance of every sympathiser have erected a new and larger Church over the ruins of the old one."[21]

By 1949, Urakami residents had made strides in recovery. The only thing left to achieve complete physical reconstruction, from the Catholics' point of view, was the removal of the two remaining walls of the old cathedral and the construction of a new one. In the early 1950s, however, the atmosphere within Nagasaki was still one of preservation. Meanwhile, the ruins and the provisional church built next to it served as the center of Catholic worship. Celebrations of religious holidays, funerals, prayer vigils, and mass were held as regularly as could be managed in the first decade after the bombing. In 1950, weddings averaged twenty-five per month, sometimes with two or three ceremonies per day.[22] The Catholic desire to rebuild the cathedral grew with each of these religious ceremonies amid the ruins.

The Debate to Preserve or to Remove the Ruins

Discussion over the fate of the ruins, including in newspapers and journals, was often phrased as "preserve or remove?" (*hozon ka tekkyo ka*). The cathedral ruins became the primary site of memory over which various groups vied for a stake, leading to a debate that lasted for a decade between the Urakami Catholics and the non-Christian residents, including members of the city council. In 1951, the Catholics explained their side of the issue in the bimonthly parish bulletin, *Katorikkukyō hō*. Removal of the ruins was necessary, they argued, because the remaining walls of the old Urakami Cathedral were a "significant obstacle" to building a new cathedral on the same spot. Furthermore, "rather than leave behind a relic (*ibutsu*) of war," it would be more appropriate to remove the ruins and cultivate the "hill of blossoming peaceful flowers" in order to "plant hearts of peace."[23] Construction of a new cathedral was also a physical necessity. In the years since the bombing, the numbers of parishioners increased to such a degree that the makeshift wooden church built in 1946 could not serve the needs of the growing community. In late 1948, the community in Urakami had grown to 4,319 adherents, including 285 newly baptized Catholics in the same year.[24]

Catholic leaders recognized the "high honor" of Urakami's popular image as an "atomic-bombing tourism site," but they also felt that the impediments represented by the ruins of the cathedral could not be left unaddressed. It would be an unconscionable act against the "guardian of Urakami, the Immaculate Mother Mary, and to our ancestors in heaven" if a new cathedral were not built. In February 1953, community leaders decided that reconstruction of the cathedral could only take place on the same spot as the old one.[25] In July of the following year, the Catholics formed the Association for the Reconstruction of Urakami Cathedral (Urakami tenshudō saiken i'in kai) to raise money for the project. In May 1955, Bishop Yamaguchi left for a ten-month trip to the United States to seek funding for the project, visiting St. Paul; Chicago; New York; Washington, D.C.; New Orleans; Los Angeles; San Francisco; and Honolulu, among other cities.[26] On his return in 1956, Catholic leaders submitted a request to the city to remove the ruins of the cathedral.

The Catholic rationale for removal and reconstruction evolved to include other justifications: Catholics could not fulfill their worldly mission, they felt like spectacles among the ruins for the enjoyment of tourists, and they thought that they had historical rights to the land. Bishop Yamaguchi told a journalist in 1958 that the mission of the Catholics was the "salvation of souls" and a new cathedral was absolutely necessary to this end. The ruins were also an impediment to the daily life of Urakami Catholics. One parishioner told the same journalist that it was "bothersome" (komaru) that the ruined cathedral was considered a sightseeing destination. "Many people point their cameras at believers who are holding mass" and take their photograph, "snap" (pachi pachi). Day after day, "busloads of tourists pulled up to the chapel and the adjoining ruins, and near the devout prayers being offered they oohed and aahed (abekku no kyōsei) as if looking in a zoo."[27] Moreover, since the Catholics wanted to build a new church with their own labor and money "on our own land," "it doesn't make any sense when people shout, 'Come now, leave the ruins! They're a symbol of peace.'"[28]

The Catholics viewed Urakami as a holy land that was rich in Catholic history and martyrdom, and so the city officials' approach to maintaining the ruins as a tourist site irked the Urakami leaders. In early 1958, the head of the Nagasaki City Tourism Office pointed out the loss of revenue for the city that would result from removing the cathedral walls. "The ruins of the cathedral are the most important tourism resource of atomic-bombed-city Nagasaki," he declared. "Removing them will be a fatal minus of financial resources for the city." The Catholics were appalled at the city's insistence on "using the sacred cathedral as a tool for tourism." Kataoka Yakichi responded to the city official that "[we] want to rebuild (saiken) as quickly as possible with the strength of Catholic believers. To ignore this wish of ours and insist on using the present state [of the cathedral] as a billboard for tourism is religious sacrilege."[29] The arguments of Urakami leaders for the construction of a new cathedral picked up steam, forcing municipal officials to act.

Realizing the need to respect the religious concerns of the Catholics, the Committee for the Preservation of Atomic Bombing Materials proposed several compromises: (1) reinforcing the ruins so that they would not pose a physical threat as time went on; (2) building a new cathedral out of the bricks and two walls of the ruins, thus incorporating the old cathedral into the new design while maintaining the ruins as mementos; (3) building a new cathedral next to the present ruins (the architect Egon Eiermann took a similar approach to rebuilding Berlin's Gedächtnis Church in 1959); and (4) building a new cathedral in an entirely new location. Father Nakashima Banri, who represented the Urakami Catholics in the meeting with the city committee, responded that (1) the present site was entirely too small, so it is impossible to leave the ruins as they were; (2) the ruins were weathering and would present a danger in the future; and (3) refining the tragic appearance of the cathedral, from a religious standpoint, was not acceptable (*omoshirokunai*).[30] In short, the Catholics would not budge.

Some city council members and hibakusha also refused to budge as they fought to protect the ruins known as *akuma no tsumeato* (scar of the devil), but others became apathetic over the years.[31] At city council meetings since the late 1940s, officials had been unanimously in favor of preserving the ruins, but the persistence of the Catholics challenged their resolve. On January 21, 1958, at a meeting of the Committee for the Preservation of Atomic Bombing Materials over the fate of the two church walls, Father Nakashima declared, matter-of-factly, that the Catholics would begin removal of the ruins in February and construct a new cathedral on the same site.[32] The city council responded by holding an emergency meeting on February 17 to produce a resolution of the city's official approach to the issue. Iwaguchi Natsuo, a former reporter for the *Nagasaki nichinichi shinbun* and, at thirty, the youngest member of the city council, stood out in the meeting. Iwaguchi pleaded to the mayor and the rest of the council that the ruins held value in conveying the experience of a generation and educating others about the history of the city, not to mention standing as a relic of the bombing to warn future generations of the dangers of war and atomic weapons. He pointed out that only the residents of Nagasaki and Hiroshima knew the realities of the atomic bomb, something that not even President Truman or the politicians who waged the war or anyone else in the world could ever know. The two cities were the only ones in the world where boys and girls walked around with keloid scars. Furthermore, Iwaguchi argued, it was the right and, indeed, the duty of the citizens of Nagasaki and Hiroshima to prevent future atomic tragedies (*hisan*) and to cry out (*sakebu*) for peace. He asked for the opinion of Mayor Tagawa and for an explanation of the political negotiations (*seiji kōshō*), as well as the process of negotiation (*sesshō*) with the Catholics, that "invited the most regrettable result," namely, the removal of the ruins.[33]

Tagawa, instead of offering an explanation of the negotiations, disagreed with Iwaguchi on three grounds. "It is true that [the ruins] serve as a resource of tourism for Nagasaki City today," but it was not easily discernable "whether or not [the ruins] are essential to protect peace." In regard to the debate over the role of the ruined cathedral as "an adequate resource (*shiryō*) to relate the tragedy (*hisan*) of the atomic bomb," Tagawa declared, "I will speak frankly. As a resource to convey the tragedy of the atomic bomb, it is not appropriate. In my view, there is no need to maintain [the ruined cathedral] to protect peace." Tagawa continued, "I whole-heartedly (*zenpuku*) support the hope that the Urakami Cathedral will be quickly restored (*fukkō*) to its former appearance and reconstructed as a future anchor for the hearts of the believers. I pray that such a church be built as soon as possible."[34] Tagawa was not Catholic.

The apathy of the majority of the city council members shone through at this meeting. The meeting had officially begun at 11:04 a.m., but after the statements by and brief discussion between Iwaguchi and Tagawa, the council broke for lunch at 11:33 a.m. When it resumed at 2:40 p.m., only twenty of the original forty-one attending council members returned, leaving the matter unresolved. Iwaguchi was furious and demanded that the absence of his twenty-one colleagues go on record. The few remaining council members, among whom not everyone felt as passionately as Iwaguchi about preserving the ruins, agreed to leave the final decision to the city council chairman, Wakiyama Hiroshi, who had not shown up to the meeting at all.[35]

Iwaguchi tried another avenue to fight for preserving the ruins. Shortly after the February meeting, he formed the group Satsuki kai, which nicknamed themselves the Justice League (*Seigiha*) and declared their role as "proprietors of 'passion.'" The league promoted the same arguments to preserve the ruins that Iwaguchi had put forth in the February meeting.[36] They joined with the hibakusha group Nagasaki Atomic Bombing Association of Young Men and Women and submitted a petition to Mayor Tagawa with ten thousand signatures in support of their cause. The groups realized, however, that mere signatures would change little and that more concrete action had to be taken. The hibakusha group became the "earnest voice of city residents," joining with another survivor group headed by Fukahori Katsuichi (himself a Catholic), and together submitted three concrete proposals to the Nagasaki City Council to prevent the removal of the ruins.[37] They proposed (1) to hold surveys all over the country and publish the results in the media to develop the issue as one of "national public opinion"; (2) to invite the National Commission for Protection of Cultural Properties (Bunkazai hogo i'inkai) to Nagasaki and "request its opinion" (the commission had already made Ōura Cathedral in southern Nagasaki a national treasure in March 1953); and (3) to provide financial backing to gain control of the reconstruction project. At one point, Iwaguchi even suggested petitioning the Pope, but he realized that he could not compete with the influence of Bishop Yamaguchi.[38]

The appeals of Iwaguchi and his Justice League, the hibakusha organizations, and city residents, fell on deaf ears and their efforts were to no avail. Unlike Councilman Iwaguchi, many of the other members of the city council were apathetic, and the movement of the residents came too late to inspire any action in the council. In a final meeting on the matter of the ruins in mid-March, the city council voted to leave the final decision in the hands of Mayor Tagawa.[39] The mayor decided to allow the Catholics to remove the ruins and build a new cathedral. In the end, a single column from the old cathedral was placed in Peace Park near ground zero to continue as a memorial to the tragedy of the atomic bombing, but for Iwaguchi and the hibakusha, it stood as a memento of the loss of the city's main symbol of the atomic tragedy. The column, measuring ten meters by three meters, cost the city ¥1 million to move.[40]

Kokusai bunka toshi and Ruins of Memory

Mayor Tagawa's decision left many Nagasaki residents furious, and some people around the country confused. One resident attributed the loss of the ruins to the apathetic and uncaring attitude of the city council and general public in Nagasaki. Survivor groups in Hiroshima and Tokyo, such as the Nihon gensuikyō and the Fujin dantai, struggled to comprehend Nagasaki's self-destruction of their peace symbol.[41] Another resident noted that the "heartless echoes of hammers" could be heard tearing down the ruined walls of the Urakami Cathedral.[42] Nagasaki non-Catholic hibakusha considered the loss of the symbol as a product of "religious egoism" because the Catholics wanted to forget their own suffering at the expense of the memory of other survivors. Hibakusha blamed city officials, too, because their approach to commemorating the bomb seemed incongruous with their stated mission as an atomic-bombed city to stay active in the peace movement. Survivor and activist Watanabe Chieko asked why the city had spent ¥30 million on the Peace Statue in 1955 but refused to leave the ruins of the cathedral at no cost. She declared that leaving at least the "burned Maria statue" would "have given us courage," but more important, the ruins "were no longer just the possession of the [Catholics]." For her and the other hibakusha, the cathedral ruins stood as a symbol of the tragedy that they would never forget and did not want to be forgotten by others.[43]

The Catholics, on the other hand, were delighted. The clergy boasted to the community that the new cathedral would be the same design as the old one, but bigger, and instead of bricks it would be built of reinforced concrete. The cost of the initial construction stage would be ¥50 million, but, whereas the first cathedral had taken thirty years to build, planners estimated less than one year for the new one.[44] The new Urakami Cathedral was completed by October 1959.[45] While the Catholics gained a new place of worship that symbolized the recovery of their community, Nagasaki lost its most recognizable symbol as an atomic-bombed city.

Although Mayor Tagawa had supported preservation of the ruins through the mid-1950s, a visit to cities in the United States changed his mind. In 1956, the mayor and a delegation of city officials traveled to the United States and visited the same cities as Bishop Yamaguchi had in 1955, in the same order, and the met with the same people. The primary purpose of Yamaguchi's trip was to raise funds for the reconstruction of the cathedral, which, plausibly, came up in discussion between American officials and Mayor Tagawa during his visit. During his political tour from August 23, the layout and infrastructure of American cities impressed Mayor Tagawa and his delegation, informing their vision of Nagasaki's future as a modern, international city. On their return to Nagasaki in September, Tagawa addressed the city council, presenting his impressions and reflections from meetings and tours with mayors and other city officials in St. Paul; Chicago; New York; Washington, D.C.; New Orleans; Los Angeles; San Francisco; and Honolulu. Tagawa was impressed mostly with the warm perceptions of and trust in Japanese people that Americans had in the mid-1950s, which he attributed to the cultural interaction with the occupation forces until 1952. The Americans who had resided in Japan, Tagawa claimed, returned to the United States and told other Americans how the Japanese were an "extremely good" and "extremely kind" people and that Japan was "an extremely beautiful place." Having realized this during his trip, Tagawa said, "I was delighted as I returned to Japan."[46]

Most of the cities that he and his colleagues visited, Tagawa thought, were well organized and maintained. In Chicago, "we learned much about the infrastructure of large cities," parts of which could become a "reference" for Nagasaki. In New Orleans, the "second largest trade port in America" that was on the verge of surpassing New York, they received a tour of the harbor from the mayor, who also gave them "detailed materials" regarding the infrastructure of the port. The mayor of San Francisco presented Tagawa with a key to the city. Two cities that did not particularly impress Tagawa were New York and Los Angeles. New York's streets were narrower than even Tokyo's and, "indeed, it is a congested city." Tagawa declared that "it is perhaps the most inconvenient city," and city officials failed to impress him with their explanations of building construction. The biggest issue for Los Angeles was its smog and pollution, which made the city "extremely unpleasant." It was the Nagasaki group's first stop in St. Paul for six days that left the greatest impression regarding American cities and the potential for Nagasaki to become an equally modern city. St. Paul, Tagawa later told the council members, was "one of the top ten most cultural and prettiest cities in America." He continued that it would not be an exaggeration to say that the fact that Nagasaki and St. Paul made the first ever sister-city relationship between Japan and the United States meant that they were representative cities of their countries, noting that other cities were following Nagasaki and St. Paul's lead by creating sister-city alliances as well. Tagawa was honored to present such a positive report regarding Nagasaki's sister city.[47]

Some Nagasaki residents who were baffled at Tagawa's turnabout on the ruins suspected that he had been bribed during his tour of the United States. His visit to St. Paul especially "stinks," the rumor went, as if he had promised something to officials there, such as erasing the symbol of the American bombing. Other rumors posed the possibility that half of the reconstruction fund had come from overseas and therefore the Christians had stronger influence over the situation.[48] At the very least, however, it was clear that influential Christian groups and politicians with whom Mayor Tagawa met during his trip to the United States had indeed changed his mind. Perhaps they had managed to persuade Tagawa that the preservation of an atomic relic of the American destruction of Japan's Christian center would complicate the cultivation of relations between Nagasaki—not to mention Japan—and the United States.[49] The characterization of the atomic bombing of Nagasaki as retribution for Japanese military acts during the war, especially for the attack on Pearl Harbor, surfaced again when the city officials of St. Paul considered making Nagasaki a sister city. St. Paul officials had drafted an agreement between the two cities to be signed by Mayor Tagawa on his scheduled (but postponed) trip to the city on December 7, 1955, the fourteenth anniversary of Pearl Harbor and tenth year since the atomic bombings.[50] Even though Mayor Tagawa did not make his visit to the United States until August 1956, the purpose of his trip was to improve relations between Nagasaki and the United States, and the Pearl Harbor connection could perhaps be seen as a gesture of reconciliation on the part of St. Paul officials.

The trip to American cities had a profound impact on the mayor and his delegation: it showed them that Nagasaki's reconstruction was not yet complete because its cityscape had remnants of the past that kept it from moving forward. In other words, one requirement of becoming an "international city" in the mid-1950s, according to Tagawa and a growing number of city council members, urban planners, and local politicians, was having clean, orderly urban landscapes. The cities that Tagawa and the Nagasaki group had visited (minus New York and Los Angeles, of course) gave them the feeling that American cities were well organized and "pretty." They were not, however, "beautiful," Tagawa claimed. Even so, the visit presented Nagasaki city officials with a direction of city construction for which to aim. Tagawa explained to the council that there were areas of Nagasaki that could not even be called "pretty," let alone "beautiful," and the desire to make the city "beautiful" should drive construction and tourism projects.[51] In 1958, Nagasaki had the potential to be an international city on par with St. Paul, Chicago, and New Orleans, and some city officials saw the cathedral ruins as the last remaining physical obstacle to realizing this new vision.

From the standpoint of constructing Nagasaki as a modern, "beautiful" city as Tagawa came to hope after his visit, the preservation of the cathedral ruins would only impede such a plan. Specifically, Tagawa thought that city funds could be put to better use in achieving the construction of a "beautiful" Nagasaki, rather than wasted on maintaining a destroyed cathedral, which he claimed had no role in "protecting peace." He explained to Iwaguchi Natsuo during their debate in 1958, "I have no intention (*kangae*) to throw large amounts of city funds into preserving (*nokosu*)" the cathedral ruins.[52] The ruins, Tagawa thought, presented an obstacle to progress. In short, the Urakami Cathedral ruins had run their course in the eyes of city officials who saw value in commemoration of the atomic experience only as it complemented the city's image of international culture. The ruins now prevented the completion of Nagasaki's reconstruction, which had become a mission of modernizing the landscape a la St. Paul, Minnesota. The custodian of the municipal vision of reconstruction, the mayor, was also the custodian of Nagasaki's urban identity. For Mayor Tagawa, reconstruction was not yet complete in the mid-1950s and traces of the recent war presented a burden to be overcome in the name of reconstruction, revival, progress, and modernity.

The approach of municipal officials to cultivating the city's urban identity always sought to place Nagasaki among the cities of the world in some way. In the first decade of reconstruction, Nagasaki officials rejected the immediate, dark past and looked *inward* to the city's distant, bright past. In this way, rebuilding as an international cultural city presented a way for the city to reengage with the international world, including China (until 1949) and the West in a peaceful way. In the mid-1950s, Nagasaki officials then looked *outward*, to the cities of the West, for a model of what it meant to be a modern, international city. For the mayor and others in 1950s Nagasaki, removal of the ruins meant the achievement of a modernized city; a modernized city meant better international relations with cities in the United States and, for the Catholics, with the Vatican. Indeed, the removal of the ruins seemed like a victory for the Catholics that went beyond physical reconstruction as it raised Nagasaki's status among international Catholic cities. On May 25, 1959, midway through the construction of the new Urakami Cathedral, the Vatican raised the status of Nagasaki from diocese to archdiocese.[53] The elevation of Nagasaki complemented the evolving interpretations of *kokusai bunka toshi* as both "international culture" and "international city." But Nagasaki had gained status among international Catholic cities at the expense of the city's atomic memory.

FIGURE 6.3. Cathedral ruins being torn down for removal in 1958. This photograph captures the moment this wall crumbled.

Source: Photograph taken by and courtesy of Takahara Itaru.

FIGURE 6.4. The rebuilt Urakami Cathedral in 1960.

Source: Photograph taken by and courtesy of Takahara Itaru.

The gain for the Catholics proved to be a loss for the memory activists of Nagasaki. The repercussions of the events of 1958 extended far beyond the physical landscape of the city, as the "intimate fund of [atomic] memory" encased in the atomic ruins of the Urakami Cathedral was lost forever. For thirteen years the ruins of the Urakami Cathedral had stood as the city's symbol of the experience of the atomic bombing.[54] When the antinuclear peace movement burgeoned from the mid-1950s, Hiroshima became a powerful force in the movement, while Nagasaki removed its only remaining ruins of atomic memory. The failure of Nagasaki residents to protect their atomic symbol harmed the city's national image. Hiroshima became the center of the peace movement, fulfilling its mission as put forth in the reconstruction laws of 1949 to become the peace commemoration city. Nagasaki, in contrast, had been growing farther away from its distinctiveness as an atomic-bombed city in its mission to rebuild as an international city and as a city where the Catholic community had considerable influence. Some commentators acknowledged—and many Nagasaki residents agreed—that without the cathedral ruins, the city was left with only "empty symbols" (kyozō), such as the 1955 Peace Statue.[55] The popular statement that emerged in the 1950s describing the presence of Hiroshima and Nagasaki in the peace movement— "Hiroshima Rages, Nagasaki Prays"—captured the moment when the Catholic influence on the cityscape and the Christian image of ground zero were arguably at their strongest.

When Hiroshima faced the same dilemma as Nagasaki in the 1960s—preserve or remove atomic relics from the landscape—the city chose to preserve its ruins of memory. In the mid-1960s, hibakusha and city officials in Hiroshima began a movement to ensure the preservation of the Atomic Dome. They reached out to the nation for donations, hoping to raise ¥100 million, but the overwhelming response they received brought in ¥409 million, enough to maintain the dome for at least several decades. Approximately thirty-five hundred letters of support poured in to the city from all over Japan along with donations.[56] Unlike Nagasaki, preservation of atomic ruins such as the dome bolstered the urban identity of Hiroshima as envisioned by reconstruction planners since the late 1940s. In other words, Nagasaki's interpretation of their urban identity had evolved and thus shaped the landscape accordingly; Hiroshima's did not.

If Nagasaki's goal in the 1950s and 1960s was modernized urban reconstruction, then Hiroshima's goal was preservation and cultivation of its relevance as the atomic-bombed city. The Urakami Cathedral ruins impeded the completion of Nagasaki's goal, but the Atomic Dome in Hiroshima bolstered that city's goal. Mayor Tagawa's decision to remove the cathedral ruins took place outside of the context of atomic memory; as he saw it, the maintenance of atomic relics no longer fit into the urban identity of Nagasaki. In this sense, his approach to reconstruction was the same as the early reconstruction planners who had made commemoration of the bombing a secondary concern in the revival process, instead holding a "trade revival festival" on the 1947 anniversary of the bombing. Hiroshima's decision to preserve the ruins, on the other hand, reflected the goals of city officials, who were bent on shaping atomic narratives in ways that supported their vision of reconstruction as a peace city. Both cities worked from the standpoint of maintaining their urban identities that had been developing since the early postwar years. Early reconstruction had already set Nagasaki down a disparate path from Hiroshima as an atomic-bombed city, but the 1958 removal of the cathedral ruins made the city appear to outsiders as though it had little interest in maintaining the atomic experience as part of the urban identity. In other words, although activist groups in Nagasaki had opposed the removal of the ruins and worked to promote the antinuclear peace movement, the actions of municipal officials made it appear that apathy represented the city's general attitude amid the antinuclear mood of the mid-1950s. In the end, the removal of the *lieu de mémoire* in Nagasaki presented a defeat for memory activists in the face of Hiroshima dominance in popular memory of the bombings, adding insult to injury. After that, Nagasaki's only remaining intimate fund of memory were the hibakusha, who continued to fight for their place in the official atomic narrative of the city.

· · ·

The reasons for the disappearance of the intimate fund of atomic memory were not cultural, nor were they religious. Although it appeared as though the Catholic community wielded tremendous power, it was, rather, the mayor, supported by like-minded city officials, who determined the fate of the ruins. By the mid-1950s, the atomic relic no longer served their understanding of *kokusai bunka toshi*. Indeed, when the reconstruction law passed in 1949, few agreed on exactly what *kokusai bunka toshi* meant, leaving Nagasaki's urban identity project open to interpretation. In other words, although the law recalled the past in order to rebuild, Nagasaki was never imprisoned by its past. This was different in Hiroshima, where that city's reconstruction law forever linked it to the atomic experience. Municipal officials in both cities had approached atomic relics from their respective approaches to reconstruction and urban identity. The hibakusha groups and other memory activists working to cultivate a place for their atomic narrative within Nagasaki's urban identity failed to preserve the ruins because their political voice carried little weight in municipal politics for decades following the bombing. Furthermore, the municipal vision(s) of Nagasaki's urban identity seemed rigidly opposed to including their voice. As municipal and national officials saw it, to afford too much power to the memory activists was rife with danger because their experiences of the war unsettled the waters of war memory, so to speak, because they led to discussions of responsibility for the war. That is, the politics of atomic narratives depended on the politics of war memory more generally.

Relics, as material vessels of memory, can be emptied of their original meaning and filled with new meaning to fit the needs of the present. Or, they last as mementos, never letting a memory be forgotten. When relics and ruins are erased, then the memento simply vanishes, thus endangering the survival of the memory that had existed within it. Ruins serve no purpose unless they contain meaning and become part of a narrative. For Mayor Tagawa, the ruins lost their meaning as a symbol of the bombing and of peace and therefore they lost their purpose, making them an obstruction to an otherwise "clean" (*kirei*) urban landscape. Despite the motivations of Mayor Tagawa and others in Nagasaki who supported the removal of the ruins, few people in Nagasaki or around Japan saw it as a benefit to the city. Rather, most people saw it as a direct attack on the memory of the bombing of Nagasaki. Even today, residents, including some Urakami Catholics, lament the events of 1958.

By the end of the 1950s, the Catholics had achieved their vision of reconstruction. They had rebuilt the landscape of Urakami, increased their numbers, built a children's library and other educational facilities, planted a hill of cherry trees, and received recognition from the Vatican. Most importantly, they had fought against formidable political forces to win the right to rebuild the spiritual center of their community. Many accused the Catholics of wanting to forget the atomic bombing, but community leaders such as Nagai Takashi never encouraged such forgetting. Forgetting the experience of wartime, however, was a different matter. During the war, the Catholics dedicated themselves to the war effort as much as their neighbors, but in the postwar years they took advantage of the view of the international Christian community that the Japanese Christians had been victims of the state. With the removal of the cathedral ruins in 1958, the last remaining physical trace of Urakami's "tragic past," as Bishop Yamaguchi had called it, vanished.

The atomic past also faded further from municipal representations of Nagasaki's urban identity. Tourism guidebooks, for example, reduced mention of the bombing to a few scant references and gave only a token nod to its atomic tourism. In one guidebook from 1959, *Nagasaki e no shōtai* (Invitation to Nagasaki), the atomic bombing, referred to simply as *pika-don*, receives just three pages of mention out of 243 pages in the book. Topics emphasizing the city's history or bolstering the city's image as an international city, such as discussions of the Nagasaki dialect, major festivals throughout the year, or local versions of "international" food, all receive lengthy discussions. In particular, Nagasaki's Christian history figures largely in the book's discussion of the city's international urban identity.[57] The atomic-bombing sites figure relatively little among the recommended tourist spots. The main course for a tourist to take when visiting the city, called the Preferred Course, does not include a single site related to the bombing. Among the courses that do include atomic-bombing related sites, the book recommends Nagai Takashi's former house, Nyokodō, and the Peace Statue installed in 1955, the latter of which hibakusha had voiced their opposition to as an empty symbol of their atomic experience. The Preferred Deluxe Course includes only a single atomic site: the one-legged *torii* (Shinto shrine gate) of the Sanno Jinja (144). Mayor Tagawa, in his preface to the guidebook, makes no mention of the atomic bombing, but, rather, celebrates the seventieth anniversary of the formation of the Nagasaki City government during the early Meiji period.[58] Meanwhile, in Hiroshima guidebooks throughout the 1950s and 1960s, city officials portrayed Hiroshima as the "city of death," describing the many atomic sites to visit and including numerous photos of survivors and of course the Atomic Dome, to emphasize the city's atomic history.[59] If guidebooks are any measure of a city's urban identity, Hiroshima was *the* city of atomic memory but, in Nagasaki—less than a year after the fall of the cathedral ruins—the bombing had become a distant memory.

Conclusion

VALLEY OF MEMORIES

In 1997, former Nagasaki mayor Motoshima Hitoshi published an article in response to Hiroshima City's successful bid to the United Nations Educational, Scientific and Cultural Organization (UNESCO) the previous year to have the Atomic Dome designated a World Heritage site. The title—"Hiroshima yo, ogoru nakare" (Hiroshima, be not proud!)—set the tone of the article, which Motoshima intended to bring attention to what he saw as Hiroshima's perpetuation of Japan's sense of victimhood and inability to confront its wartime aggression. He did not pull any punches. Hiroshima's campaign on behalf of the dome was shameful, he said, especially since the two countries that dissented in the vote, the United States and China, had been the primary enemies of Japan in the Second World War. Their nonsupport "piled on the shame" (*haji no uwanuri*). If there had been any "reflection on the great war" by Hiroshima officials, Motoshima thought, they certainly would not have focused so much on their own victimization by pressing to have the dome made a World Heritage site.[1]

Motoshima thought that Hiroshima's memory of the war—or rather, its amnesia—reflected the general attitude of Japanese society. As an imperial military command center for decades, "Hiroshima was a victimizer in war," only later becoming a victim. In order to move forward from the nation's wartime past, Motoshima challenged Hiroshima (and Japan) to confront that past through reflection and to practice self-restraint, rather than display self-indulgence. "What we must do now," he asserted, "is to apologize to the peoples of China, Asia, and the Pacific nations. Beg from the heart for forgiveness. For the sake of the past and the future of Japan." The present was crucial. He recommended that Japan "apologize for Pearl Harbor, and that Hiroshima and Nagasaki forgive the atomic bombings. Rage and hatred are not good for individuals, nor for the state (*kokka*)." He pleaded that Japan adopt the "mindset of forgiving that which is unforgiveable." Accordingly, "Hiroshima and Nagasaki should stand as the vanguard of the 'world of reconciliation' (*wakai no sekai*). The twenty-first century must be a 'world of reconciliation.' "[2] As the only Nagasaki voice among ten Hiroshima scholars writing in that 1997 issue of the journal *Heiwa kyōiku kenkyū* (Peace education research), Motoshima had turned the criticism of passive Nagasaki on its head, pointing to Hiroshima's self-indulgence in its postatomic demeanor.[3] Hiroshima had a history problem, he suggested, unlike Nagasaki, which had looked beyond the atomic bombings toward a longer history as the basis for its reconstruction.

Motoshima's way of thinking was not uncommon in Nagasaki. Oka Masaharu was an ordained minister, three-term city council member, and peace activist who worked to gain the Korean hibakusha of Nagasaki recognition and compensation from the government. After his death in 1994, supporters built the Nagasaki heiwa shiryōkan (Nagasaki Peace Museum) entirely through citizen donations to continue Oka's activism.[4] The first floor of the museum presents the forced labor of Koreans in wartime Japan, and the second floor displays Japanese military atrocities in Asia, focusing on events such as the Nanjing Massacre and the sexual enslavement of the "comfort women." Like Motoshima, Oka viewed (and the private museum continues to display) the atomic bombings as a result of Japan's war of aggression, quite different from the way the publicly funded museums have presented the bombing. Since the mid-1990s, however, even the city museum Nagasaki genbaku shiryōkan (Nagasaki Atomic Bombing Museum) has provided visitors with an enlarged context of the war. At the insistence of local scholars, the museum installed a permanent exhibition on the non-Japanese hibakusha, including Korean and Chinese forced laborers as well as Allied POWs. Several Nagasaki-based scholars, including some hibakusha, have now made a point of placing the atomic bombings in the larger context of the war.[5]

Some Nagasaki intellectuals have proposed to confront the past by accepting Japan's war responsibility. During his career as a politician, Motoshima made a name for himself through his outspokenness on such issues, most famously when he demanded in late 1988, as Hirohito lay on his deathbed, that the emperor accept responsibility for the war. Motoshima was one of the first to do so publicly. During a city council meeting on December 7 of that year, Motoshima responded to a question from a Communist Party member, "I think that the emperor does bear responsibility for the war." He then explained to reporters:

> It is clear from historical records that if the emperor, in response to the reports of his senior statesmen, had resolved to end the war earlier, there

would have been no Battle of Okinawa, no nuclear attacks on Hiroshima and Nagasaki. I myself belonged to the education unit in the western division of the army, and I instructed the troops to die for the emperor. I have friends who died shouting "banzai" to the emperor. I am a Christian, and I had difficult moments as a child when I was pressed to answer the question, "Who do you think is greater, the emperor or Christ?"[6]

Motoshima did not think that the emperor was a god, though he could not admit it during his childhood because of the social discrimination against Christians.[7] In response to the statement about the emperor's war responsibility, he received more than seven thousand letters from around the country, some in support (many from hibakusha), but also some that derided him as an "idiot" (baka) or told him to "die!"[8] Conservatives demanded that Motoshima retract his statement, but he never backed down. A member of the fanatic right shot Motoshima in front of Nagasaki City Hall on January 18, 1990, an attack he survived.[9]

Although he was not a hibakusha, Motoshima in many ways exemplified Nagasaki's convergence of atomic narratives. He was a descendant of the hidden Christians (kakure Kirishitan), a fervent Catholic, and an admirer of Nagai Takashi. He wrote about the bomb, often sympathizing with the Urakami community and commenting on Nagai, whose work he placed in the context of Catholic dogma and the history of Urakami as a site of martyrdom. Although he linked the bombing to the regional history of Christian martyrdom, his insistence on confronting the past for the purpose of the present reflected the city's emphasis on its long history of contact with international (Western) culture. For Motoshima and others, postwar Germany served as a model for accepting war responsibility and working toward reconciliation.[10] His time as mayor bolstered his role in the Nagasaki peace movement. While in office he was a strong supporter of the hibakusha, and he championed Nagasaki's international cultural approach to its atomic memory in contrast to the self-centered approach of Hiroshima. His memories of fighting in China during the war impelled him to call attention to the aporia of memory, including the black hole surrounding the atomic bombings that had resulted from popular remembrance of the bombs but not of the war preceding them. In this way, the narratives of postatomic Nagasaki that had emerged from diverse sources—Allied occupation forces, city officials, Catholics, and hibakusha—coalesced under Motoshima, revealing their postwar traces reaching across the decades.

The tension among competing narratives may have made Motoshima's public utterances more controversial. His view of the atomic bombings as an unavoidable end to Japan's war of aggression was sometimes misunderstood as a moral justification of the bombings, or even senility, especially when he played so prominent a role in Nagasaki's peace movement during his time as mayor

(1979–95). A comment he made much later, in 2007, that the atomic bombings "couldn't be helped," drew criticism from all sides, including in Nagasaki. His comment echoed a statement made by Kyūma Fumio months earlier that the bombs "couldn't be helped" because they were necessary to end the war. Kyūma was a member of the Nagasaki Prefectural Assembly in the 1970s, later becoming a National Diet representative and defense minister in the conservative Koizumi administration, but national backlash against the comment led to his resignation in summer 2007. "It couldn't be helped" is different from "it was morally justified," but there are many who will not accept any historical justification for the atomic bombings. In Nagasaki, Hiroshima, and indeed much of Japan, the inhumanity of the atomic bombings, which the hibakusha have striven to convey for seven decades, remains inviolable common sense. Motoshima never set out to denigrate the work of the hibakusha, only to promote peace and reconciliation through mutual forgiveness. For him, as for others, Nagasaki's reconstruction as an international cultural city implied a move toward forgiveness.

The character of postatomic Hiroshima with which Motoshima took issue in the mid-1990s had taken shape decades earlier, as did that of Nagasaki. An article in *Time* magazine captured the mood in 1962: "Hiroshima today is grimly obsessed by that long-ago mushroom cloud; Nagasaki lives resolutely in the present. . . . Hiroshima has made an industry of its fate." In contrast, "Nagasaki is a monument to forgiveness." Former chairman of Nagasaki City Council, Wakiyama Hiroshi, who had overseen the council debates over the Urakami Cathedral ruins in 1958, told the *Time* correspondent, "We don't want to go around bragging about being victims of the atomic bomb. It is not compatible with the character of Nagasaki."[11] Whether or not Wakiyama was qualified to speak for all of Nagasaki, his statement revealed that the city's self-image from the early postwar era persisted, just as Motoshima's views showed more than three decades later. The fact that Hiroshima and Nagasaki developed in such disparate ways after the bombing should not be surprising—the only major historical similarity between the cities is the atomic bombings. It is perhaps more surprising that Hiroshima has made an industry out of its trauma. It should be said, however, that Nagasaki has also made an industry of its history.

Today Nagasaki is a vibrant city that both champions its international past and commemorates its atomic tragedy. With a population of more than 400,000, the city thrives with a tourism industry that displays both characteristics of the city— just as the early city planners had envisioned—attracting 6,108,300 visitors in 2010, which was 500,000 more than the previous year. The spike in 2010 may have been partly due to a popular television drama about Sakamoto Ryōma, who had aided in the "opening" of Japan to the West in the nineteenth century through his relationship with Thomas Glover, a British merchant and arms dealer who lived in Nagasaki. Glover Mansion, still a popular tourist destination, had 1,015,415 visitors in 2010, a 15 percent increase from the previous year's number of 882,810. The former site of the Dutch encampment on Dejima attracted 404,078 visitors in 2010, the city having restored its buildings a few years earlier. Atomic-bombing tourism has also continued strongly: the Atomic Bombing Museum (Genbaku shiryōkan) saw 693,391 visitors in 2010, about the same as in 2009.[12] In January 2011 alone, 28,871 people visited the museum. Many of the tourist sites in Nagasaki related to both its international history and the atomic bombing do not require entrance fees but see equal numbers of visitors, among them Chinatown, numbers of Buddhist temples and Shinto shrines, Nagasaki Peace Hall, and the Nagasaki National Peace Memorial Hall for the Atomic Bomb Victims (Kokuritsu Nagasaki genbaku shibotsusha tsuitō heiwa kinen kan).[13]

If tourism boosts Nagasaki's economy, Mitsubishi Heavy Industries (MHI) fuels much of the rest of it. Rebuilt after its destruction in the bombing, the Nagasaki shipyard was building ships again by 1947 and still manufactures a variety of sea vessels. Other Mitsubishi factories in Nagasaki produce weapons, such as the MK41 Vertical Launch System (VLS) (licensed through Lockheed Martin) and the Type 97 Torpedo, developed by Japan.[14] MHI has become the Japanese equivalent of the Lockheed Martin Corporation, and it also maintains license agreements with the American manufacturer.[15] The production of weapons at the Nagasaki Mitsubishi plants is one manifestation, if somewhat contradictory, of the city's postatomic reconstruction. Nagasaki was the original site of Mitsubishi Shipbuilding in the latter part of the nineteenth century, playing a major role in the economic history of the city through the end of the Second World War. The city's vision to recreate the international cultural city included the restoration of Mitsubishi as a central industry. That Mitsubishi produces materials for war suggests the selective memories in this city dedicated to peace and international exchange. Postwar Mitsubishi built its first battleship in 1956 in Nagasaki Bay, proving that even the international cultural city could not entirely escape its wartime past.

Municipal rivalries with Hiroshima have recently been renewed. In summer 2010, Nagasaki announced plans to build a research center similar to the Hiroshima Peace Institute at Hiroshima City University, which would invite scholars from around the world to study in Nagasaki and address a wide range of issues relevant to the "construction of peace," including the abolition of nuclear weapons. The tentative name of the institute, the Nagasaki University Research Center for the Construction of Peace (Nagasaki daigaku heiwa kōchiku kenkyū sentaa), echoes the rhetoric of the immediate postwar period pledging to construct peace.[16] In 2012, the university did create the Research Center for Nuclear Weapons Abolition (RECNA), a think tank involving local scholars and researchers in developing policy toward abolishing nuclear weapons, seeking to make its mark as the first research center in Japan dedicated to such a goal.[17] The formation of research institutes and other activities and projects related to the city's atomic history demonstrates Nagasaki's unending competition with Hiroshima over its stature as an atomic-bombed city and clarion voice in the peace movement, but it also reflects the continuing challenge of scholars, municipal officials, and other residents to define the city's role and urban identity as an atomic-bombed city.

The construction of the Nagasaki National Peace Memorial Hall for the Atomic Bomb Victims and its counterpart in Hiroshima shows that the government approach to the hibakusha has not changed. The two museums, completed in 2003, were built as a result of Article 41 of the Hibakusha Relief Law of 1994, which provides for construction of "facilities for the sake of commemorating everlasting peace." The Nagasaki museum cost ¥4.4 billion ($40 million) in national funds.[18] The museum spaces are largely underground, conveying the atmosphere of a mausoleum, and in them are preserved testimonial accounts of the bomb, including videos, as well as the books that record the names of all the people who have died to date as a result of the atomic bombing. In 2011, the shelves in a massive glass pillar in the Nagasaki museum housed 153 books containing the names of 152,276 persons.[19] New names are added at each annual commemoration ceremony on August 9 for those who died during the previous year. As of August 2015, on the seventieth anniversary of the bombing, the pillar contained 170 books including 168,767 names.[20] Not all of the names included in the books have been legally recognized as hibakusha by the government, but their inclusion grants them a kind of acknowledgment that they may have been unable to win when they were alive. For, despite the grandiose museum, built with national funds, the hibakusha continue to fight for recognition, compensation, and relief in the face of municipal and national peace projects that have persistently ignored their plight. Nonetheless, Nagasaki continues its role as a center of peace activism. The city holds annual commemoration ceremonies of the bombing on August 9 at Peace Park, in front of the "Olympian" statue, drawing thousands of participants, although the crowds are always smaller than those at Hiroshima's annual commemoration. The city sends its mayor and several hibakusha to the Nuclear Non-Proliferation Treaty meetings that take place at the United Nations. At Nagasaki University, students can major in Peace Studies, which for years has been the self-classification of the work that many scholars undertake in the city and around Japan.

Municipal officials have renewed their efforts to maintain an atomic narrative that places the bombing within the longer history of international culture. In spring of 2014, Mayor Taue Tomihisa visited the United States and presented on Nagasaki's "character" at so-called town meetings in cities including New York.

The theme, "Peace from Nagasaki," echoed the catchphrase of the city that had taken shape in the years after the bombing. The mayor's talk placed the bombing and subsequent reconstruction in the context of the city's "unique" international history, including events such as a Portuguese ship arriving in 1571, or Commander Victor E. Delnore dedicating his life to Nagasaki's revival during the Allied occupation.[21] In other words, the city's approach to cultivating and maintaining its urban identity that began as early as September 1945 continues in the present: the atomic bombing and peace activism continue to represent parts of the city's official narrative but they do not define it.

A recent development in the official commemoration of the bombing suggests an attempt by municipal officials to reimagine the critical voice of the hibakusha and activist groups in the city's image. Since 1970, the memory activists have chosen one representative, always a hibakusha, to give the *heiwa e no chikai* (peace pledge) at the annual ceremony on August 9. The speech, in addition to conveying the human tragedy of the bombing through a survivor's eyes, has at times provided an opportunity for the hibakusha to publicly voice their criticism of the policies of the national government. Recent hibakusha speakers Jōdai Miyako (2014), Taniguchi Sumiteru (2015), and Ihara Toyokazu (2016) have accused the Abe administration of trampling on the constitution in order to remilitarize Japan. In early 2016, city officials proposed creating a selection review committee (*sentei shinsakai*), nominally in order to expand the pool of potential speakers, but the activist groups have interpreted the move as an attempt to control the content of the speech given by the hibakusha representative.[22] Put another way, the creation of the committee could point to an attempt by city officials to regain control of the official atomic narrative.

Should the selection review committee become a permanent fixture, the hibakusha would become the minority voice in selecting their own representative to speak about the legacies of collective atomic trauma. The committee, still in its early stages, would consist of five members, including three specialists (*gakushoku keikensha*) chosen by the city and two people recommended by the activist groups. The city council approved creation of the committee in March 2016, but relentless opposition from the activist groups prevented the committee from selecting a speaker in time for the ceremony that year. Yet city officials have continued to push forward. At their first meeting on January 17, 2017, the committee decided that they would select the hibakusha speaker exclusively from among applications from the public. They stated they would not consider the recommendation of the activist groups, nor the recommendation of the municipal government; the hibakusha had protested against such direct municipal involvement in the selection process from the beginning.[23] Even if municipal officials would not be directly involved or have a final say in the selection, the function of the review committee the city council has put in place limits the ability of the hibakusha and activist groups to maintain their atomic narrative within public discourse on the history and memory of the bombings within the city, around Japan, and around the world.

Reconstruction after disaster almost always links a city's past with visions of its future. The past presented Nagasaki city planners and citizens with historical templates they immediately grasped, not least because memories of a storied past shone bright in the catastrophic days of 1945. The visions of the revival of Nagasaki that so many groups articulated in the early decades after the bombing generated atomic narratives that remind us of how the past lives on in the present, sometimes in trickling streams, often in grand rivers that carry us forward into the future.

Notes

LIST OF ABBREVIATIONS

I have relied on many primary-source materials that are preserved at the Archival Materials Room of the Nagasaki City Nagai Takashi Memorial Museum, and so I have used the abbreviation NTMM when citing these sources in the notes.

Because the book draws heavily on Japanese newspapers from the 1940s and 1950s, I have abbreviated the titles of the most frequently cited newspapers in the notes.

AS: *Asahi shinbun*
KH: *Katorikukyō hō*, also *Katorikkukyō hō*
MS: *Mainichi shinbun*
NM: *Nagasaki minyū*
NN: *Nishi Nippon shinbun*
NNN: *Nagasaki nichinichi*
NS: *Nagasaki shinbun*

INTRODUCTION

1. See, for example, statement by Mayor Ōhashi, *NM*, August 9, 1947; statement by Emperor Hirohito, *NNN*, May 25, 1949.

2. Carol Gluck, "Operations of Memory: 'Comfort Women' and the World," in *Ruptured Histories: War, Memory, and the Post–Cold War in Asia*, ed. Sheila Miyoshi Jager and Rana Mitter (Boston: Harvard University Press, 2007), 57.

3. Literally, "Hiroshima of Rage, Nagasaki of Prayer." I borrow the translation given in the text from John Whittier Treat, *Writing Ground Zero: Japanese Literature and the Atomic Bomb* (Chicago: University of Chicago Press, 1995), 301.

4. Bishop Yamaguchi, as quote in Op-Ed, "Kieru tsume ato: Urakami tenshudō tekkyo no shinsō," *Shūkan shinchō*, May 19, 1958, 29.

5. Treat, *Writing Ground Zero*, 301.

6. Takahashi Shinji, ed., *Appeals from Nagasaki* (Nagasaki: Nagasaki Association for Research and Dissemination of Atomic Bomb Survivors' Problems, 1991), 4.

7. Committee for the Compilation of Materials on Damage Caused by the Atomic Bombs in Hiroshima and Nagasaki, *Hiroshima and Nagasaki: The Physical, Medical, and Social Effects of the Atomic Bombings*, trans. by Eisei Ishikawa and David L. Swain (New York: Basic Books, 1981), 353–54, 359, 369. This book, originally published in Japanese in 1979 by Iwanami Shoten, is the most comprehensive study of the atomic bombings. Three editors and thirty-four scientists compiled decades of scientific data and social research, presenting it in a format accessible to the nonspecialist reader. It is still the best overall reference work on the bombings and their aftermath.

8. Takahashi Shinji discusses this in *Nagasaki ni atte tetsugaku suru: Kakujidai no shi to sei* (Tokyo: Hokuju shuppan, 1994), 193.

9. "Nō moa Hiroshimazu" [No More Hiroshimas], special issue, *Shūkan asahi*, August 7, 1949.

10. Iwada Yukio, quoted in *Yūkan Nagasaki*, May 13, 1950.

11. Iwada, quoted in newspaper clipping, n.d., Kokusai bunka toshi folder, NTMM.

12. Funakoe Kōichi discusses the Christianization of the atomic bombing in relation to this phrase in "Jū roku seiki made sakanobotte genbaku o kangaeru," in *Nagasaki kara heiwagaku suru!*, ed. Takahashi Shinji and Funakoe Kōichi (Kyoto: Hōritsu bunka sha, 2009), 29–36. The exact phrase as it appears in Funakoe (30) is the "atomic bomb fell on Urakami." My addition of "not Nagasaki" is based on conversations with Nagasaki-based scholars, including Abe Shinji, who have used the phrase as I have written it. For more examples, see Tomu Sakon, "Fire Sent from Above: Reading Lamentations in the Shadow of Hiroshima/Nagasaki" (PhD diss., Princeton University, 2010), 42.

13. A Nagasaki resident to writer Hotta Yoshie, quoted in Sakon, "Fire Sent from Above," 41.

14. Discussed in Takahashi, *Nagasaki ni atte tetsugaku suru*, 201.

15. The version of the article that is referenced here is from *NS*, September 15, 1945. At the time, the *Nagasaki shinbun* ran stories in cooperation with the *Asahi shinbun*, *Mainichi shinbun*, and the *Yomiuri hōchi*. Only the surnames of the reporters are given: Miyamoto and Oshikawa.

16. *NS*, September 16, 1945.

17. Prefectural Governor Sugiyama Sōjirō, quoted in *NM*, August 9, 1947.

18. Mayor Ōhashi Hiroshi, quoted in Nagasaki bunka renmei hen, *Nagasaki: Ni jū ni nin no genbaku taiken kiroku* (Tokyo: Jiji tsūshin sha, 1949).

19. See, e.g., Motoshima Hitoshi, "Urakami no kirishitan no junnan: Kinkyōrei, yon-ban kuzure, genbaku," *Seibo no kishi*, October 2000. For a recent study of the Christian origins of Nagasaki City, see Reinier H. Hesselink, *The Dream of Christian Nagasaki: World Trade and the Clash of Cultures, 1560–1640* (Jefferson, NC: McFarland, 2015). For an additional study of representations of the atomic experience in Nagasaki and especially as they relate to discussions of Urakami memory, see Araki Takashi, "Nagasaki ni okeru genbaku no hyōshō to 'Urakami' no kioku," *Rekishi hyōron* 639 (July 2003): 64–80.

20. Karl D. Qualls, *From Ruins to Reconstruction: Urban Identity in Soviet Sevastopol after World War II* (Ithaca: Cornell University Press, 2009), 2.

21. There have been several journalistic books on the Nagasaki bombing and aftermath. See, e.g. Frank W. Chinnock, *Nagasaki: The Forgotten Bomb* (New York: New American Library, 1969); Craig Collie, *Nagasaki: The Massacre of the Innocent and Unknowing* (Sydney, Australia: Allen and Unwin, 2011); Susan Southard, *Nagasaki: Life after Nuclear War* (New York: Viking, 2015).

22. For example, Robert Jay Lifton's *Death in Life: Survivors of Hiroshima* (New York: Random House, 1967) builds on his decades-long work on trauma survivors by exploring the psychological experience of the Hiroshima survivors in the 1960s. Lisa Yoneyama's *Hiroshima Traces: Time, Space, and the Dialectics of Memory* (Berkeley: University of California Press, 1999) looks at postatomic Hiroshima from an anthropological perspective, including forgotten survivors such as Korean hibakusha in her analysis. John Treat's seminal work *Writing Ground Zero* puts literary theory to use to understand the atomic experience, exploring the prose, testimony, and poetry of Hiroshima survivors over nine out of ten lengthy chapters. Treat notes, too, that "there exists in the historiography of the nuclear age a hierarchy—Hiroshima and then, only sometimes, Nagasaki" (301). Here, Treat acknowledges the dominance of Hiroshima even as he, too, restricts Nagasaki's literary experience of its atomic bombing to one chapter, giving voice to the Hiroshima-based literature over Nagasaki's. The hibakusha of Nagasaki did write less about their experience than their counterparts in Hiroshima, in part because they encountered obstructions to their memory that did not exist in Hiroshima.

23. For example, Ōe Kenzaburō's award-winning dispatches from Hiroshima in the early 1960s, later compiled and published as *Hiroshima nōto* (Hiroshima Notes), illumi-

nated the continuing trauma of the hibakusha in that city. The artist couple Maruki Toshi and Iri produced a set of murals termed the *Genbaku-zu*, beginning in 1950 and spending more than three decades on the project. The conventional English translation of this body of work is the "Hiroshima Panels" because all except the last mural depict Hiroshima's experience. The Nagasaki panel, which was the fifteenth and last panel, completed in 1982, locates the experience of the city within the atomic narrative that depicts the bombing as a Christian event, complete with the cathedral ruins and an image of a crucifix. In fact, the Nagasaki mural seems like an afterthought among the works of the Marukis when considering that the artists produced murals for the Nanking Massacre and the Okinawan experience of the war before turning their attention to Nagasaki as a subject.

1. ENVISIONING NAGASAKI

1. *NM*, May 17, 1949. Rep. Tsubouchi Hachirō's op-ed article, "Nagasaki wa Hiroshima ni maketa" [Nagasaki lost to Hiroshima], outlines the behind-the-scenes politics that resulted in the two cities' laws. He wrote it on May 11, the day after the laws were passed in the Diet.

2. This plan was the "Sensai fukkō keikaku kihon hōshin"; see Nagasaki shiyakusho, ed., *Nagasaki genbaku sensai shi* (Nagasaki: Nagasaki kokusai bunka kaikan, 1977; revised edition, Nagasaki: Fujiki hakuei sha, 2006), 1:665. Nagasaki City has recently published an English translation of the 2006 edition as *The Nagasaki Atomic Bomb Damage Records: General Analysis Version, Vol. 1 (Revised Ver.)* (Nagasaki: Fujiki Hakueisha, 2016).

3. *NM*, May 12, 1949.

4. For "Kyoto of Kyushu" and "Naples of Japan," see Saitō Tetsurō, "Dai Tōa no kyōyō moji toshite no Nihonji," *Nagasaki dansō* 30 (October 1942): 84. Also see Lane R. Earns, "Italian Influence in the 'Naples of Japan,' 1859–1941," *Crossroads* 6 (1998): 71–88. http://www.uwosh.edu/home_pages/faculty_staff/earns/italian.html.

5. See, e.g., Colonel Delnore's New Year's address to Nagasaki residents in *NNN*, January 1, 1947.

6. Committee for the Compilation of Materials on Damage Caused by the Atomic Bombs in Hiroshima and Nagasaki, *Hiroshima and Nagasaki: The Physical, Medical, and Social Effects of the Atomic Bombings*, trans. by Eisei Ishikawa and David L. Swain (New York: Basic Books, 1981), 57, 64, 62. There have been different calculations of the exact time the bomb detonated, but 11:02 a.m. has become the iconic time (27).

7. Ibid., 62, 66.

8. See Araki Masato, ed., *Genbaku hibaku kiroku shashinshū* (Nagasaki: Nagasaki kokusai bunka kaikan, 1996), esp. 101–11.

9. For one of the best discussions of the effects of the atomic bombs on the human body, including the numerous illnesses resulting from them, see Committee for the Compilation of Materials, *Hiroshima and Nagasaki*, esp. 105–332.

10. Ibid., 615.

11. Ibid., esp. 67–79. For statistics on radiation-induced cancers and other illnesses related to the atomics bombs, see esp. pt. 2, 105–332.

12. W. McRaney and J. McGahan, "Radiation Dose Reconstruction U.S. Occupation Forces in Hiroshima and Nagasaki, Japan, 1945–1946," Defense Nuclear Agency, Report Number DNA 5512F, August 6, 1980, 62.

13. Masayoshi Yamamoto, Kazuhisa Komura, and Masanobu Sakanoue, "Discrimination of the Plutonium due to Atomic Explosion in 1945 from Global Fallout Plutonium in Nagasaki Soil," *Journal of Radiation Research* 24, no. 3 (1983): 250–58, "highly contaminated" on 250.

14. Committee for the Compilation of Materials, *Hiroshima and Nagasaki*, 357–59. Later, when Hibakusha Relief Laws were written, this became a category of people who were considered "survivors" of the atomic bombing of Nagasaki (and Hiroshima).

15. Nagasaki shiyakusho sōmubu chōsa tōkeika, *Nagasaki-shi sei roku jū go nen shi* (Nagasaki: Nagasaki shiyakusho sōmubu chōsa tōkeika, 1959), 3:482.

16. Committee for the Compilation of Materials, *Hiroshima and Nagasaki*, 478–79, 359, 363.

17. For a study of the medical relief activities immediately following the bombing, see Nobuko Margaret Kosuge, "Prompt and Utter Destruction: The Nagasaki Disaster and the Initial Medical Relief," *International Review of the Red Cross* 89, no. 866 (June 2007): 279–303.

18. Atomic-bombing survivor Kawasaki Sakue, quoted in Nagasaki shiyakusho, *Nagasaki genbaku sensai shi*, 1:649.

19. The translation of Nagai is from William Johnston; Nagai Takashi, *The Bells of Nagasaki*, trans. William Johnston (Tokyo: Kodansha International, 1984), 113. Johnston incorrectly translates *ni tsubo* as "three meters square." For "six meters squared" huts, see Nagai Takashi, *Nagasaki no kane* (Tokyo: Hibiya shuppan, 1949), 182. The term Nagai uses is *ni tstubo naigai*, or "approximately two-*tsubo*." One *tsubo* is an area measurement equal to about 3.306 meters squared. Two *tsubo* would be about 6.612 meters squared. Nagai's own hut, Nyokodō, was approximately one-*tsubo*.

20. Nagasaki shiyakusho, *Nagasaki genbaku sensai shi*, 1:651.

21. Nagai Takashi, *Nagasaki no kane* (Tokyo: Hibiya shuppan, 1949), 183–84.

22. Harold Jacobson, quoted in Nagasaki shiyakusho, *Nagasaki genbaku sensai shi*, 1:654–56. The U.S. War Department denied the claims published by Jacobson. For a short but good discussion of this and related issues, see, e.g., William Wallis, "The Atomic Bomb," *Fourth International* 6, no. 9 (September 1945): 277–78.

23. Nagasaki shiyakusho, *Nagasaki genbaku sensai shi*, 1:655–56. An August 10, 1945, article in the Australian newspaper *The Argus* mentioned that "published reports" had quoted Jacobson's claim that the bombed-out area would cause death for seventy years.

24. Kataoka Yakichi, *Nagai Takashi no shōgai* (Tokyo: San Paolo, 1961; 17th Edition, 2002), 234–35, 361. Observations of plants and animals near ground zero: Nagai, *Nagasaki no kane*, 180–81.

25. Nagasaki shiyakusho, *Nagasaki genbaku sensai shi*, 1:663–64.

26. *NS*, September 1, 1945.

27. Itō Hisa'aki, "Nagasaki saiken no kōsō," *NS*, September 14, 1945.

28. The parishioner leader of the Urakami Catholics, Nagai Takashi, echoed this sentiment by declaring that even though the community was decimated and their beloved cathedral lay in ruins, the atomic bomb did not destroy their faith.

29. Itō, "Nagasaki saiken no kōsō." Itō writes *tenshudō* (cathedral) with an unconventional character (*kanji*) for *shu*. Instead of 主, he uses 守.

30. *NS*, September 16, 1945.

31. *NS*, October 7, 1945. The article points out that the name of the company is a tentative name (*kashō*). Also, see Nagai, *Nagasaki no kane*, 181, among others.

32. *NS*, October 7, 1945.

33. *NS*, August 13, 1946.

34. Prime Minister Higashikuni Naruhiko, quoted in *NS*, September 18, 1945. Prince Higashikuni, who was a member of the imperial family, expressed the hope that Japan and the United States could work together for peace, but made a special request of the victors: "American citizens, won't you please forget about Pearl Harbor? Let us Japanese also forget the ravages (*sangai*) of the atomic bomb. Then let us set out as a completely new, peaceful nation. America won. Japan lost. The war is over. Together, we will sweep away hatred. This is the position of my cabinet from the beginning." As Higashikuni's statement reveals, it appears that Americans were not the only ones who saw the atomic bombings as retribution for Pearl Harbor. Higashikuni resigned a month later in October after he

disagreed with the American occupation government's decision to repeal the 1925 Peace Preservation Law (*Chian iji hō*), which had essentially served the purpose of quashing political dissent against the Japanese government for two decades. The word "peace" of the law, *chian*, actually means "public order." See John W. Dower, *Embracing Defeat: Japan in the Wake of World War II* (New York: W. W. Norton, 1999), 81.

35. Dower, *Embracing Defeat*, 176–77. Romanization of the slogans is intentionally so written (sic).

36. *NS*, August 4, 1946.

37. "Bōeki ya kankō no saiken e: Atomu shimin no kibō wa fukuramu" [Toward the reconstruction of (foreign) trade and tourism: The hope of atomic citizens grows stronger], *NN*, August 8, 1948.

38. *NS*, October 8, 1945. The article does not list Kunitomo's first name, but this is probably Kunitomo Kanae, who was once a professor of anatomy at Nagasaki Medical School.

39. Ibid.

40. See, e.g., *NN*, August 8, 1948.

41. *NS*, August 24, 1946.

42. *NS*, August 4, 1946.

43. *NS*, August 24, 1946.

44. *Bōeki* can be literally translated as "trade," but in the case of Nagasaki it implies "foreign trade." I have translated *fukkō* here as "revival," whereas elsewhere I translate it as "reconstruction."

45. For *kadode*, see *NNN*, August 8, 1947.

46. *NM*, August 9, 1947. The Foreign Trade Revival Festival was sponsored by Nagasaki Nichinichi shinbunsha (newspaper company), Nagasaki City (government), Nagasaki Assembly of Commerce and Industry (Nagasaki shōkō kaigisho), Nagasaki Prefectural Trade Association (Nagasaki-ken bōeki kai), and the Association for the Promotion of Foreign Trade at Nagasaki Harbor (Nagasaki-kō bōeki shinkō kai).

47. The Urakami Catholic community held a large commemorative mass on August 9, 1947.

48. Notice that it is "those who died in the *war*" (*sensaisha*), not specifically those who died in the atomic bombing. *Sensaisha* can also be translated as "war victims."

49. Notice that Sakamoto said the atomic bomb "fell" (*ochita*); it was not "dropped," thus removing the actor (United States) from the narrative of the bombing.

50. The exchange between Mayor Ōhashi and reporter Sakamoto appears in *NM*, August 9, 1947.

51. Mayor Ōhashi, quoted in *NM*, August 9, 1947.

52. Governor Sugiyama, quoted in ibid.

53. For culture festival, see *NNN*, August 10, 1948; for reconstruction festival and Atom Park, see *NNN*, August 9, 1948.

54. Mayor Ōhashi, quoted in *NNN*, August 10, 1948.

55. See Brian Burke-Gaffney, *Starcrossed: A Biography of Madame Butterfly* (Norwalk, CT: EastBridge, 2004), esp. 172-84.

56. For these and other details, including an intriguing analysis of the role of the legacy of *Madame Butterfly* in postwar Nagasaki reconstruction, see ibid. The legacy of *Madame Butterfly* was often used as shorthand for Nagasaki's international past in promotions intended to boost the city's tourism industry through the 1950s. Considering the early postwar presence of the Americans and the push by municipal officials to cultivate Nagasaki's international past in its urban identity, it is little surprise that, as Burke-Gaffney puts it, "The Madame Butterfly craze came in the same parcel with hamburgers, Mickey Mouse, professional wrestling, Westerns, striptease, and all the other Americana flooding Japan in the wake of defeat" (184).

57. *NNN*, August 10, 1948. From 1949, the mayor read the annual Peace Declaration, although there was no declaration in 1950. Nagasaki City's webpage, accessed August 4, 2010, http://www1.city.nagasaki.nagasaki.jp/peace/japanese/appeal/history/1948.html, contains a version of the 1948 Peace Declaration that contains disparities with the 1948 newspaper version, but I have relied on the 1948 newspaper for my translation here. For example, the 1948 version that appears in the newspaper has in the first sentence *seiki* (century), but the present version online has *sekai* (world). The newspaper version also omits a vital character, indicated in brackets, in the sentence, "Atomu Nagasaki o futatabi kurikaesu [na]" (Never repeat Atomic Nagasaki!).

58. For comments of city officials made at an ad hoc Nagasaki City Council meeting on May 9, 1949, see *NNN*, May 10, 1949.

59. See Kadoya Seiichi's preface to Teramitsu Tadashi, *Chūkai: Nagasaki kokusai bunka toshi kensetsu hō* (Sasebo: Sasebo jiji shinbun sha, 1949), 9–10.

60. *NNN*, May 10, 1949.

61. *NM*, May 17, 1949.

62. On the reconstruction laws of Kyoto and Nara, see *Shintoshi* 4, no. 10 (1950): 5–6. Yokohama and Kobe were each designated as *kokusai kōto* (international port city; 6–7). On the reconstruction laws of Beppu, Itō, and Tokyo (*shuto*), see *Shintoshi* 4, no. 6 (1950): 7–11. It would make an interesting study to see whether the focal point of the word "culture" became blurred as a result of the numerous "cultural cities" in postwar Japan.

63. Tsubouchi, quoted in *NM*, May 17, 1949. I have translated *aran* (v. *aru*) as "sustain."

64. See, e.g., *NNN*, May 11, 1949; ibid., May 12, 1949.

65. Wakamatsu Torao, quoted in Teramitsu, *Nagasaki kokusai bunka toshi kensetsu hō*, 5. Wakamatsu translates the motto *Heiwa wa Nagasaki yori* as "Peace from Nagasaki."

66. Emperor Hirohito, quoted in *NNN*, May 25, 1949.

67. Kino Fumio, "Kokusai bunka no yokogao," *Nagasaki bunka* 3 (1950): 6–7.

68. For a brief summary of his office's activities, see Naruse Kaoru, "Nagasaki-shi sensai fukkō jigyō o kaerimite," *Shintoshi: Nagasaki-ken tokushūgō* 15, no. 11 (1961): 61–62.

69. Naruse's quotation in Japanese: "Dai ichi kokusai bunka toshi to wa ittai donna mono de aru ka sae mada tsukamenai."

70. Naruse Kaoru, "Nagasaki kokusai bunka toshi kensetsu no kōsō," *Nagasaki bunka* 4 (1950): 10. *Ikasu* as used here can also mean "revive."

71. Nagasaki shiyakusho, *Nagasaki genbaku sensai shi*, 1:667. By comparison, residents of Tokyo voted on the Capitol Construction Law (Shuto kensetsu hō) as follows: out of 1,840,312 ballots cast, 1,025,790 (55.7%) voted in favor and 676,550 (36.8%) voted against, with 137,972 (7.5%) invalid votes (*mukō tōhyō*); ibid., 1:11.

72. *NNN*, August 9, 1949.

73. The word *nioi* usually carries a negative connotation and is generally translated as "smell," but in the context of the article by Shimauchi Hachirō, the word suggests a positive nuance, so I have translated it here as "aroma."

74. Shimauchi Hachirō, "Nagasaki-shi kōgai," *Shintoshi: Nagasaki kokusai bunka toshi tokushū gō* 5, no. 8 (1951): 44–46.

75. Shimauchi Hachirō, "Risō no naihatsu," *Nagasaki bunka* 3 (1950): 5.

76. That is, "heiwa yokkyū e no jissen undō."

77. Envisioned (*shidōteki kōsō*).

78. Editorial, *NN*, August 21, 1949. There was a similar article in the *NNN*, August 22, 1949, that contemplated the course of action to take to build Nagasaki as an "international cultural city" and "model world city." One of the main goals, it argued, should be to "first promote (*shinkō*) education" in order to "advance the level of the residents (*shimin*)."

79. Nagasaki shiyakusho, *Nagasaki genbaku sensai shi*, 1:666.

80. For "a beautiful icon of Nagasaki," see *Yūkan Nagasaki*, February 26, 1950.

81. For more on this event, see *Nagasaki taimuzu* [The Nagasaki Times], November 22, 1949; *Yūkan Nagasaki*, November 25, 1949.

82. For an article discussing Kadoki Hisako and Nagai Takashi as the two representatives of Nagasaki, see *NNN*, February 26, 1950.

83. See, e.g., Kino, "Kokusai bunka no yokogao," 7.

84. *NM*, August 9, 1947.

85. Step in unison (*ashinami ga sokkuri sono mama*).

86. *NNN*, June 26, 1949.

87. Soon after the law emerged, Nagai began sketching with excitement the possible emblems he envisioned to represent the city in English translation. Every sketch included the word "peace": the phrase "Mother of Peace Nagasaki" encircles a drawing of Mother Mary (halo included); "Message of Peace Nagasaki" flies in the air with a dove carrying an olive branch in its mouth; "Bell of Peace Nagasaki" appears on a bell that includes a protruding crucifix on its surface; "Harbinger of Peace Nagasaki" surrounds a mushroom cloud; "Pray for Peace Nagasaki" shares a shining light with a praying female Christian, presumably Mother Mary. Nagai also considered possible English translations of the city's title: The International Culture City, The International Cultural City, The Open City of Culture, The Open Cultural City, and A City of International Culture. See "Scrapbook: *Kokusai bunka toshi*," Archival Materials Room, NTMM.

88. Nagai Takashi, *Nagasaki no hana*, in *Nagai Takashi zenshū*, ed. Nagai Tokusaburō (Tokyo: San Paolo, 2003), 2:434–35.

89. *NNN*, May 30, 1949.

90. Irie Shigeki, "Toshi keikaku," *Shintoshi: Nagasaki kokusai bunka toshi tokushū gō* 5, no. 8 (1951): 9.

91. Tagawa Tsutomu, "Nagasaki-shi tokushū gō no hakkan ni yosete," *Shintoshi: Nagasaki kokusai bunka toshi tokushū gō* 5, no. 8 (1951): 1. Photos are on the opposite page in the journal.

92. See pamphlet, "Mitsubishi jūkōgyō kabushiki gaisha, Nagasaki zōsenjo: Shiryōkan" (Nagasaki: Mitsubishi jūkōgyō Nagasaki zōsenjo shiryōkan, 2007).

93. Nagasaki hibaku kyōshi no kai hen, *Chinmoku no kabe o yabutte* (Tokyo: Rōdō shunhō sha, 1970), 17.

94. Committee for the Compilation of Materials, *Hiroshima and Nagasaki*, 604–5.

95. *MS*, August 1, 1969.

96. *NNN*, May 28, 1949.

97. Emperor Hirohito, quoted in *NM*, May 28, 1949.

2. COEXISTING IN THE VALLEY OF DEATH

1. John W. Dower, *Embracing Defeat: Japan in the Wake of World War II* (New York: W.W. Norton, 1999), 87.

2. See, e.g., Gar Alperovitz, *The Decision to Use the Atomic Bomb and the Architecture of an American Myth* (New York: Alfred A. Knopf, 1995), 515.

3. The term "exhaustion and despair" is Dower's. For more on this topic, see Dower, *Embracing Defeat*, esp. chap. 3, "*Kyodatsu*: Exhaustion and Despair."

4. See, e.g., Pfc. Leo L. Wright and Pfc. Herman E. Erke, eds., "Pictorial Arrowhead: Occupation of Japan by Second Marine Division" (Headquarters, Second Pioneer Battalion, Pictorial Arrowhead, Second Marine Division, C Company, 1st Platoon, Team 7, Nagasaki, Kyushu, Japan, 1946). This was a photo booklet issued to the Second Marine Division to commemorate their occupation of Nagasaki. See also Brian Burke-Gaffney, *Starcrossed: A Biography of Madame Butterfly* (Norwalk, CT: EastBridge, 2004), 162–63.

5. *Hiroshima shinshi: gyōsei hen* (Hiroshima: Hiroshima City, 1983), 25.

6. George Weller, *First into Nagasaki: The Censored Eyewitness Dispatches on Post-Atomic Japan and Its Prisoners of War* (New York: Crown, 2006), 25, 29–31. Of course, there had been American POWs in Nagasaki before the atomic bombing, who witnessed the bomb's destructive force or were killed by it. By "first" into Nagasaki, I mean (as does the title of the collection of Weller's dispatches) the first postsurrender entrant. Weller himself writes that he entered Nagasaki "as the first free westerner to do so after the end of the war" (3). Weller was surprisingly accurate in describing the height of the explosion at fifteen hundred feet.

7. W. McRaney and J. McGahan, "Radiation Dose Reconstruction: U.S. Occupation Forces in Hiroshima and Nagasaki, Japan, 1945–1946," Defense Nuclear Agency, Report Number DNA 5512F, August 6, 1980, 16.

8. Major Arthur, quoted in *NS*, September 14, 1945. On September 25, George Weller wrote that the *Haven* "bore homeward the last load of liberated POWs from Japan"; Weller, *First into Nagasaki*, 144.

9. The government relied heavily on the local newspaper, the *Nagasaki shinbun*, much as it had throughout the war, as a vehicle to communicate essential information to its citizens. The bombing had wiped out virtually all other lines of communication, and the central disseminator of information became the newspaper. Even though the central office of the Nagasaki Shinbun Company had been destroyed in the bombing, reporting never ceased and after the bombing the paper was for a time printed outside the city.

10. *NS*, September 14, 1945. Another notable warning, Number 8, stated, "Absolutely refrain from words such as 'captive' (*furyo*) in reference to the captives (*furyora*) who have been released." This would have been especially important during the first weeks when the American ships were still aiding Allied POWs.

11. *NS*, September 24, 1945. One article mistakenly put "two ships" as the number of vessels in which the soldiers arrived on the twenty-third.

12. SCAPIN 33 (Press Code for Japan), September 18, 1945, as quoted in Monica Braw, *The Atomic Bomb Suppressed: American Censorship in Occupied Japan* (Armonk, NY: M. E. Sharpe, 1991), 41.

13. Dower, *Embracing Defeat*, 406–8.

14. *NN*, September 25, 1945.

15. McRaney and McGahan, "Occupation Forces in Hiroshima and Nagasaki," 21.

16. Takemae Eiji, *Inside GHQ: The Allied Occupation of Japan and Its Legacy*, trans. Robert Ricketts and Sebastian Swann (London: Continuum, 2002), 126, 131.

17. McRaney and McGahan, "Occupation Forces in Hiroshima and Nagasaki," 16, 18, 22–26.

18. Takemae, *Inside GHQ*, 126; McRaney and McGahan, "Occupation Forces in Hiroshima and Nagasaki," 21.

19. Takemae, *Inside GHQ*, 126.

20. John D. Bankston, *Invisible Enemies of Atomic Veterans* (Victoria, Canada: Trafford, 2003), 59. See also Wright and Erke, "Pictorial Arrowhead."

21. Takemae, *Inside GHQ*, 108. SCAP specifically meant General Douglas MacArthur (hence "commander"), but the acronym was also used to refer to the offices of the occupation as a whole, as was GHQ (General Headquarters).

22. McRaney and McGahan, "Occupation Forces in Hiroshima and Nagasaki," 24–25.

23. See Wright and Erke, "Pictorial Arrowhead"; Bankston, *Invisible Enemies*, 59; McRaney and McGahan, "Occupation Forces in Hiroshima and Nagasaki," 24.

24. See Wright and Erke, "Pictorial Arrowhead"; Bankston, *Invisible Enemies*, 59.

25. The English term "Atomic Field" inspired Urakami residents to call the flattened landscape of the valley by the same name: see Kataoka Yakichi, *Nagai Takashi no shōgai* (Tokyo: San Paolo, 1961; 17th Edition, 2002), 205. Nagai Takashi decided to translate the term literally

as "*genshino*," which for residents meant the entire bombed-out area of Urakami (206). It is this word, *genshino*, which is translated back into English today as "atomic wasteland."

26. McRaney and McGahan, "Occupation Forces in Hiroshima and Nagasaki," 23–26. For more on the occupation's use of DDT to prevent disease, see Takemae, *Inside GHQ*, esp. 405–12.

27. Takemae, *Inside GHQ*, 117.

28. David C. Milam, *The Last Bomb: A Marine Remembers Nagasaki* (Austin: Eakin Press, 2001), 35. "Valley of Death" was the name given to the Urakami valley by the Second Marine Division. See Wright and Erke, "Pictorial Arrowhead," photo of the Urakami valley taken from the north and labeled "VALLEY OF DEATH."

29. Bankston, *Invisible Enemies*, 63, 59. Chapter 12 is entitled "Valley of Death."

30. Milam, *The Last Bomb*, 28.

31. See various pages in Wright and Erke, "Pictorial Arrowhead."

32. Milam, *The Last Bomb*, 23. Milam mentions that "an organization called the National Association of Atomic Veterans was later to fight the U.S. government for years to help men who suffered from the effects of radiation poisoning."

33. Bankston, *Invisible Enemies*, 61, 156–59, 168–79.

34. John D. Lukacs, "Nagasaki, 1946: Football Amid the Ruins," *New York Times*, December 25, 2005. Also see John A. Gunn, *The Old Core* (Costa Mesa, CA: J & J Publishing, 1992). The game did not appear in the *Nagasaki shinbun* in January 1946, probably because of censorship. For a photo of the game and the pep band, see Wright and Erke, "Pictorial Arrowhead," which has the name of the bowl game as the "Atomic Bowl," not the "Atom Bowl."

35. *NS*, October 6, 1945.

36. For a cultural history of how the United States repaired its perception of the Japanese people, see Naoko Shibusawa, *America's Geisha Ally: Reimagining the Japanese Enemy* (Cambridge, MA: Harvard University Press, 2006).

37. For an example, see *NS*, October 4, 1945.

38. See Wright and Erke, "Pictorial Arrowhead."

39. *NS*, October 4, 1945.

40. *NS*, October 15,1945. All *katakana* spelling, word spacing ("niwa"; "gozai masu"), and translation as it appears here is from original article, including the *hiragana* "*ko*" in Japanese "*gozaimasu*." This first Japanese-English lesson concluded, naturally, with arguably one of the most useful phrases one can learn: "Thank you very much. (サンク　ユ　ー　ベリ　マツ　チ) Arigato. (ありがだう)." My number count of fourteen phrases includes the topic title: "Asking the way. (アスキング　ザ　ウエイ) Michi wo tanunete (道を尋ねて)." The mis-Romanized "tanunete" is the original.

41. "Shinchūgun shōheisan naka yoku shimaseu."

42. The emphasis I refer to is a series of double dots (*dakuten*) on each character, which is common in newspapers and other writings in Japanese.

43. *NS*, October 17, 1945.

44. Ibid., esp. "Part 3. Greetings."

45. See, e.g., *NNN*, February 3, 1947.

46. *NS*, October 30, 1945.

47. Lukacs, "Nagasaki, 1946." Lukacs's article does not identify the children's choir as being from the Kassui school for girls. This is from a photo in Wright and Erke, "Pictorial Arrowhead," of a Christmas concert with girl students from Kassui school: "Christmas carols sung in English by girls from the Methodist Kassui School."

48. The exchange between the reporter and the U.S. Marine chaplain appears in *NS*, October 8, 1945. The article prints "Nagasaki" in katakana occasionally when the chaplain speaks, but only that word. It appears in kanji when the reporter is speaking.

49. American soldiers, quoted in *NS*, October 7, 1945.

50. Clement S. McSwanson, "Christianity Survives Persecution, A-Bomb At Nagasaki," *Pacific Stars and Stripes*, March 31, 1946, 3, photo caption on 4. The author includes discussion of seventeen non-Japanese Franciscans helping to rebuild the community.

51. Lane R. Earns, "'Dancing People are Happy People': Square Dancing and Democracy in Occupied Japan," *Crossroads* 2 (1994): 91–102. http://www.uwosh.edu/home_pages /faculty_staff/earns/niblo.html

52. *NS*, October 7, 1945.

53. *NS*, April 28, 1946, as translated and cited in Nakamura Masako, "'Miss Atom Bomb' Contests in Nagasaki and Nevada: The Politics of Beauty, Memory, and the Cold War," *U.S.-Japan Women's Journal* 37 (2009), 121, 138n10. For an excellent and more complete analysis of the 1946 Miss Nagasaki contest, see Nakamura's entire article (117–43). Nakamura suggests that the contest was also "meant to distract the attention of the Nagasaki people from their anger and frustration" to avoid "any explosive demonstration" on the first "May Day" after the war, at a time when the people were suffering from food shortages and, of course, daily struggles as a result of the war and the bombings (123).

54. *MS*, April 17, 1946. Historian John Dower argues that "responses to the victors," such as the pageant, "seemed exceptionally naive, accommodating, or superficial." "Even in nuclear-bombed Nagasaki, residents welcomed the first Americans with gifts . . . and shortly afterward joined local U.S. military personnel in sponsoring a 'Miss Atomic Bomb' [*sic*] beauty contest"; Dower, *Embracing Defeat*, 241. Many gestures may have been intended by Japanese to curry favor with the occupiers, but this was not the case of the pageant in Nagasaki; it was never a Miss Atom Bomb contest in the eyes of the residents. Also, Dower does not include the date of the pageant and claims that the Miss Ginza pageant on January 15, 1947, was the "first Western-style beauty contest to be held" (151). If the Miss Nagasaki pageant can be considered an official Western-style beauty contest, then it might very well have been the first.

55. Occupation document with photo and comments by public relations office, May 1, 1946, courtesy of Takahara Itaru. Comments by Melvin C. Dodson. Photographs of the event can be found in some publications, such as—and as cited in Nakamura, "'Miss Atom Bomb' Contests in Nagasaki and Nevada," 137n1—*Ichiokunin no Shōwa-shi, Nihon senryō* (Tokyo: Mainichi Shinbun-sha, 1980), 2:90; *Ketteihan: Shōwa-shi, haikyo to ketsubō, Shōwa 21–25 nen* (Tokyo: Mainichi Shinbun-sha, 1983), 13:198.

56. Pfc. Philip R. Wax, "Nagasaki School Girl Crowned 'Miss Atom Bomb,'" *Pacific Stars and Stripes* [*PSS*], May 16, 1946. In her article, "'Miss Atom Bomb' Contests in Nagasaki and Nevada," Nakamura argues that the contest was never known in Nagasaki as the "Miss Atom Bomb" contest, not even by the Marines there; furthermore, she says that discussions of it as "Miss Atom Bomb," as well as the residents' shock years later at the realization of such an insensitive name for the pageant, can be traced back to the Wax article in *PSS*. It is possible that Wax may have invented the name of the pageant based on his knowledge of Nagasaki; it is also possible that the event was indeed referred to by the Marines stationed in Nagasaki with a colloquial name referencing the atomic bombing; at any rate, Nakamura does not make this clear (128, 130). Nakamura is right, of course, that Wax misled his readers because the event was never officially called "Miss Atom Bomb of 1946." Nakamura is also right to point out that the article in *PSS* misled readers in other ways because "it gave the impression that many local women had willingly entered the beauty competition for the title of Miss Atom Bomb" (128).

57. See Sakamoto Hideaki, "'Misu genbaku' to sengo," *Sankei shinbun*, August 4, 2005, and August 5, 2005.

58. The jinrikisha contest held by the U.S. Marines in Nagasaki in late 1945 (Fig. 2.1) also demonstrated the victor-defeated relationship. Referencing another photograph of

Japanese men pulling American soldiers in jinrikisha during the occupation, John Dower writes in *Embracing Defeat* that such interactions illustrated "hierarchies of race and privilege . . . between victor and vanquished" (210).

59. For a good analysis of the gender politics of this and other beauty contests in Japan during the occupation, especially on how they relate to politics of class and ethnicity, see Nakamura, "'Miss Atom Bomb' Contests in Nagasaki and Nevada," 123–28.

60. Burke-Gaffney, *Starcrossed*, 163.

61. Shibusawa, *America's Geisha Ally*, 40–41.

62. Burke-Gaffney, *Starcrossed*, 164–65, 215n8.

63. There was one more Miss Nagasaki contest held in 1948; from 1949, it was called the "Miss International" contest.

64. *NS*, August 4, 1946. I have yet to find evidence of anyone being shot.

65. Discussed in Nakamura, "'Miss Atom Bomb' Contests in Nagasaki and Nevada," 139n23.

66. Lane R. Earns, "Victor's Justice: Colonel Victor Delnore and the U.S. Occupation of Nagasaki," *Crossroads* 3 (1995): 75-98. http://www.uwosh.edu/home_pages/faculty_staff /earns/delnore.html

67. Uchida Tsukasa, quoted in Braw, *Suppressed*, 6. Braw conducted the interview with Uchida Tsukasa in Nagasaki on June 21, 1978, 157n3.

68. Committee for the Compilation of Materials on Damage Caused by the Atomic Bombs in Hiroshima and Nagasaki, *Hiroshima and Nagasaki: The Physical, Medical, and Social Effects of the Atomic Bombings*, trans. by Eisei Ishikawa and David L. Swain (New York: Basic Books, 1981), 511.

69. Takemae, *Inside GHQ*, 430.

70. Committee for the Compilation of Materials, *Hiroshima and Nagasaki*, 511–12.

71. Takemae, *Inside GHQ*, 430–31.

72. Grant Taylor, quoted in M. Susan Lindee, *Suffering Made Real: American Science and the Survivors at Hiroshima* (Chicago: University of Chicago Press, 1994), 123.

73. Lindee, *Suffering Made Real*, chap. 7, "The No-Treatment Policy."

74. Bankston, *Invisible Enemies*, 59.

75. Colonel Delnore's quotations are from the English version of the address that appeared with the Japanese version in the *NNN*, January 1, 1947. For a good biographical essay on Delnore and his time in Nagasaki, see Earns, "Victor's Justice."

76. See *NNN*, August 9, 1948. I have relied on the Japanese version of Delnore's address. Many other prominent officials sent messages in 1948 as well, including Prime Minister Yoshida Shigeru.

77. Colonel Delnore, quoted in *NM*, August 9, 1947, and *NNN*, August 9, 1947. The two newspapers have slightly different Japanese translations of the address, and I have used the former here.

78. General MacArthur, quoted in *NNN*, August 10, 1948. I have relied on the Japanese newspaper version of MacArthur's address here as well.

79. Letter from Delnore to American occupation censors in Fukuoka, March 1947, Victor E. Delnore Papers, Gordon W. Prange Collection, University of Maryland Libraries.

80. The scrapbook that Nagasaki residents gave to Delnore on his departure is preserved within the Victor E. Delnore Papers, Gordon W. Prange Collection, University of Maryland Libraries. The Delnore Papers in general contain a rich collection of materials from Delnore's time in Nagasaki, including correspondence with city officials and community leaders, such as Bishop Yamaguchi, which continued long after he left the city.

81. Kino Fumio, "Kokusai bunka no yokogao," *Nagasaki bunka* 3 (1950): 7.

82. See, e.g., Kadoya Seiichi, preface to Teramitsu Tadashi, *Chūkai: Nagasaki kokusai bunka toshi kensetsu hō* (Sasebo: Sasebo jiji shinbun sha, 1949), esp. 7.

3. THE "SAINT" OF URAKAMI

1. In Mark 8:34, Jesus encourages believers to bear their cross and follow in his footsteps.

2. Takahashi Shinji, *Nagasaki ni atte tetsugaku suru: Kakujidai no shi to sei* (Tokyo: Hokuju shuppan, 1994), 201.

3. See, e.g., William Johnston's translation; Nagai Takashi, *The Bells of Nagasaki*, trans. William Johnston (Tokyo: Kodansha International, 1984). In his translation of the eulogy of November 1945, Johnston replaces "Urakami" with "Nagasaki" (106–109).

4. Kataoka Yakichi, *Nagai Takashi no shōgai* (Tokyo: San Paolo, 1961), 12.

5. Takahashi, *Nagasaki ni atte tetsugaku suru*, 195.

6. Kataoka, *Nagai Takashi no shōgai*, 39–44. See also Paul Glynn, *A Song for Nagasaki* (Hunters Hill, Australia: Marist Fathers Books, 1988; repr., Reconciliation Edition, 1995), 31–35.

7. The *chōgata* bore the responsibility of informing the parishioners of religious dates, such as the Assumption of the Virgin Mary on August 15, and passing on the essence of Catholicism from generation to generation.

8. See Nagai Takashi, *Horobinu mono o* (Nagasaki: Nagasaki nichinichi shinbun sha, 1948), 91–93. Page 92 of the original is mistakenly printed as 29.

9. Ibid., 93.

10. Takahashi, *Nagasaki ni atte tetsugaku suru*, 231. A different date of June 9 is found in Nagai Tokusaburō, ed., *Nagai Takashi zenshū* (Tokyo: San Paolo, 2003), 1:783, but I have relied on Takahashi's date. For a detailed account of Nagai's conversion to Christianity and his Catholic baptism, see Nagai, *Horobinu mono o*, 97–110. Nagai was named after St. Paul.

11. Kataoka, *Nagai Takashi no shōgai*, 360.

12. In Japanese, "*Minakerya hanashi ni naranu.*"

13. *KH*, September 15, 1937.

14. For witnessing "crimes" in China, see Nagai Takashi, "Shi ni chokumen shite," special issue (Bessatsu), *Shinchō*, January 15, 1951, 20. In the postwar years, Nagai did not often discuss his military service in China. The article cited here was written less than four months before he died, when, as the title points out, he was "facing death."

15. Nagai, quoted in *KH*, January 15, 1938. In the letter, Nagai makes no mention of the manner in which Nanjing fell to the Japanese military.

16. This passage is from the Bible, Romans 8:36. In Japanese, the verse as it appears in Nagai, *Horobinu mono o*, is "Warera hinemosu shu no tame ni shi no kiken ni ai, hōraru beki hitsuji no gotoku seraruru nari" (189). I have translated the Japanese verse into English instead of relying on conventional English translations of Romans 8:36.

17. Nagai, *Horobinu mono o*, "Providence" on 188; Raguet, "sacrificial lamb" (*hōraru beki kohitsuji*) on 189–190. Father Emil Raguet was once the rector of the Urakami Parish (*Urakami kyōkai no shunin shisai*; 189).

18. See Kataoka, *Nagai Takashi no shōgai*, 360; Nagai Tokusaburō, *Nagai Takashi zenshū*, 3:772; Glynn, *A Song for Nagasaki*, 82. See also Takahashi, *Nagasaki ni atte tetsugaku suru*, 211. Takahashi argues that Nagai, having seen the destruction wrought by Japanese forces in China, became militaristic (*gunkokushugi*) and his behavior back home in Nagasaki reflected the change. Takahashi discusses an instance where Nagai thought a certain young woman was "slacking" (*tarundeiru*) and threw her into ice water to teach her a lesson. However, Takahashi does not provide a reference.

19. *NS*, February 11, 1946.

20. Kataoka, *Nagai Takashi no shōgai*, 82.

21. Discussed in Glynn, *A Song for Nagasaki*, 92.

22. Josef Schilliger, *The Saint of the Atom Bomb*, trans. David Heimann (Westminster, MD: Newman Press, 1955), 92.

23. Indeed, Christians lived throughout the city, and the Ōura Cathedral, built by French missionaries in the 1860s, is located in the far southern part of the city. The Ōura Cathedral survived the atomic bombing completely unharmed, and the National Commission for the Protection of Cultural Properties declared it a national treasure in 1953.

24. Nagai, *Horobinu mono o*, 97.

25. In Japanese, the phrase is *"Onore no gotoku hito o ai seyo,"* or the simplified four-character equivalent, *"Nyoko aijin."* *Nyoko* is the abbreviated form of *onore no gotoku*, or "as thyself," and *dō* means "temple" or "church."

26. Nagai Takashi, *Hana saku oka* [Hill of blossoming flowers], in Nagai Tokusaburō, *Nagai Takashi zenshū*, 1:201.

27. Nagai Takashi, *Nagasaki no kane* (Tokyo: Hibiya shuppan sha, 1949), 171–79.

28. The English term "parishioner representative" (*shinto daihyō*) is from "Chronology of the Life and Work of Nagai Takashi," in the pamphlet, "The Life of Dr. Nagai Takashi" (Nagasaki: Nagasaki City Nagai Takashi Memorial Museum, n.d.). Nagai writes *"shinja daihyō"* at the end of the eulogy manuscript, which has the same meaning.

29. As Max Weber noted, one "can explain suffering and injustice by referring to individual sin committed in a former life (the migration of souls), to the guilt of ancestors . . . or—the most principled—to the wickedness of all creatures *per se.*" The pain and suffering of an individual or group, then, represents a martyr complex characterized by the "missionary prophecy" in which "the devout have not experienced themselves as vessels of the divine but rather as instruments of a god"; H. H. Gerth and C. Wright Mills, eds., *From Max Weber: Essays in Sociology* (Oxford University Press, 1946), 275, 285. For an analysis of Nagai's interpretation of the bombing from the perspective of religious studies, see Yuki Miyamoto, "Rebirth in the Pure Land or God's Sacrificial Lambs? Religious Interpretations of the Atomic Bombings in Hiroshima and Nagasaki," *Japanese Journal of Religious Studies* 32, no. 1 (2005): 131–59.

30. Nagai Takashi, *Genshi bakudan shisha gōdō sō chōji*, MS, eulogy delivered on November 23, 1945, NTMM.

31. The word *hansai*, which I translate as "holocaust," means "a burnt offering to God."

32. Nishida Hideo and Nagaoka Some, quoted in *Kami to genbaku: Urakami katorikku hibakusha no 55 nen*, television special, produced by NBC Nagasaki hōsō (aired May 31, 2000).

33. Rainer Maria Rilke, "Die Erste Elegie," [The First Elegy] in *Duino Elegies and The Sonnets to Orpheus—Rainer Maria Rilke*, ed. and trans. Stephen Mitchell (New York: Vintage International, 2009), 7.

34. *NS*, February 11, 1946. The article claimed that Nagai was building a "barrack" hut, but he had just moved out of that makeshift hut into a provisional house weeks earlier.

35. The correspondence between Nagai and Giblin is discussed in an article, "Kokkyō koeru shūkyō ai," *NNN*, August 9, 1947.

36. Ibid.

37. For a list of Nagai's publications, see Nagai Tokusaburō, *Nagai Takashi zenshū*, 1:785–89.

38. Tanaka Shinjirō, review of *Seimei no kawa*, by Nagai Takashi, *Asahi hyōron* 4, no. 1 (1949): 90–93.

39. Ono Tomoaki, review of *Rozario no kusari*, by Nagai Takashi, *Katorikku shisō* 28, no. 4 (1948): 104–5.

40. "Shuppanbutsu wa kanarazu ken'etsu o," *NS*, February 28, 1946.

41. Advertisement poster of Hasumi Shoten in Kanda, Tokyo, for *Horobinu mono o* (1948), Kōkoku folder, NTMM.

42. In *Pasadena Star-News*, "Doomed by Bombing: Leading Japanese Author Calmly Awaiting Death," June 5, 1949. Article written in Tokyo by AP staff, June 4, 1949.

43. *MS*, June 10, 1949.

44. Nagai Takashi, *Kono ko o nokoshite* (Tokyo: San Paulo, 2000), 27–30.

45. Inoue Hisashi, *Besuto seraa no sengoshi* (Tokyo: Bungei shunshū, 1995), 55.

46. *NS*, June 25, 1948. From 1948, Nagai was widely known as the "saint of Urakami" (*Urakami no seija*; *"seijin"* was also used). The newspaper cited here is the first public expression of Nagai as the "saint of Urakami," as far as I have seen. Most likely, there is an earlier instance, but I have yet to find it. An ad for the same book in the May 22, 1949, issue of the *Mainichi shinbun* referred to Nagai as an "apostle of Urakami" (*Urakami no shito*).

47. Advertisement clipping, Kōkoku folder, NTMM.

48. T S, " 'Kono ko o nokoshite' dokugo kan (sono ni)," *Koe*, no. 862 (July 1949): 40–41. This article was part 2 of two. Part 1 has "T K" listed as the author.

49. Notes of the National Diet of Japan, *Shūgiin, Kōsei i'in kai*, March 31, 1949, no. 3, p. 8.

50. Among them were Anzai Keimei, Hino Ashihei, Suzuki Shintarō, and many others. See Shokan file 1, NTMM.

51. The play was performed by the Bara za (Rose [theater] group) at the Mitsukoshi Theater (*gekijō*) in Tokyo in March 1949; see *Tokyo Times*, March 3 and 19, 1949. The group performed it in Nagasaki as well on March 6 and 7, 1949: see *NM*, May 2, 1949. The play version was arranged by Sasaki Takamaru, Chiaki Minoru's father-in-law. Sasaki and Chiaki starred together in the 1956 Inagaki Hiroshi film, *Kettō Ganryūjima*, about Miyamoto Musashi. Sasaki Takamaru also starred in the 1953 film *Senkan Yamato* [Battleship Yamato]. Sasaki's grandson, Chiaki's son, is the actor Sasaki Katsuhiko (b. 1944). The director Ōniwa Hideo made a film version of *Nagasaki no kane* in 1949, and it, too, became a hit. The film was produced by the Shochiku Company. See Eiga "Nagasaki no kane" shashin shū [Movie, "The Bell of Nagasaki" photo album] folder, NTMM.

52. Chiaki Minoru to Nagai Takashi, March 14, 1949, Shokan file 1, NTMM.

53. Although the 1984 English translation of *Nagasaki no kane* translates "*kane*" as "bells" (plural), the title in Japanese refers to a single cathedral bell unearthed by the Catholics in December 1945. This one bell held significant meaning for Nagai and the Catholics after the bombing, and so I maintain the nonplural translation of *kane*. For more on the significance of the bell, see, e.g., Hori Noriaki, ed., *Nagasaki yūgaku mappu 1: Genbaku hisaichi ato ni heiwa o manabu* (Nagasaki: Nagasaki bunken sha, 2004), 23.

54. Results published in *MS*, October 26, 1949. The poll also surveyed bookstores: "Name the book that had the best standing at your store in the past year." *Kono ko o nokoshite* secured the number-one spot with a 43% margin of votes over the number-two book, *Kyōsan shugi hihan no jōshiki* [Common knowledge of the criticism of communism]. Clearly, the publishing year of 1948–49 was defined by Nagai's *Kono ko o nokoshite*. According to a Yomiuri Shinbun Company poll, *Kono ko o nokoshite* was the number-one book in 1948 as well; see T K, " 'Kono ko o nokoshite' dokugo kan (sono ichi)," *Koe*, no. 861 (June 1949): 34.

55. *MS*, October 26, 1949.

56. Nagai gifted a copy each to the emperor and the crown prince. The Imperial Palace acknowledged receipt of the two copies of *Nagasaki no kane* on February 10, 1949, in a document sent to Nagai's publisher, Shikiba Ryūsaburō. See document of receipt in Shokan file 1, NTMM.

57. Emperor Hirohito, quoted in *NM*, May 28, 1949. Notice that Hirohito did not say he "read" it. He also called the book a *shōsetsu* (novel), which implies fiction.

58. Emperor Hirohito, quoted in Nagai Takashi, *Itoshigo yo* (Tokyo: San Paulo, 1995), 313. Originally published in October 1949 by Kodansha.

59. Notice that the newspaper reporter wrote, "human emperor." Hirohito was an amateur biologist, hence "scientist emperor." Nagai felt a deep connection to Hirohito

because they were both scientists. For reference to Hirohito's interests in science, see Herbert P. Bix, *Hirohito and the Making of Modern Japan* (New York: Perennial, 2001), esp. 60–62.

60. Emperor Hirohito, quoted in *NM*, May 28, 1949.

61. Nagai, *Itoshigo yo*, 313, "wished that the visit could have been under better circumstances" (*mottai nai shidai de atta*).

62. *NM*, May 23, 1949. Nagai Takashi was a prolific poet and painter, in addition to book author, scientist, and theological philosopher.

63. Bix, *Hirohito and the Making of Modern Japan*, 637.

64. Recorded, among other places, in Nagai, *Itoshigo yo*, 279–88.

65. *Nippon Times*, December 1, 1950.

66. One letter had an address in Italian: "Illustre Signor, Prof. TAKASHI NAGAI, Professore della Facolta di Medicina, Università di, NAGASAKI (Giappone)." For both letters, see Shokan file 2, NTMM. Another letter was addressed to "Dr. Nagi" in "Nagisaki": W. H. Deal to Professor T. Nagi [*sic*], August 23, 1947, Shohyō folder, NTMM. Incidentally, Nagai's actual mailing address was Nagasaki-shi, Ueno-machi, 373.

67. El Secretario of Editorial Marfil, S. A. to Nagai Takashi, February 9, 1950, Shokan file 2, NTMM.

68. Amino Isao to Nagai Takashi Sensei, September 7, 1949, Shokan file 2, NTMM. Amino Isao wrote on behalf of the Shuppan Kyoku (Publishing Bureau) of DaiNippon Yubenkai Kodansha in Tokyo. The letter to Nagai outlined three issues about which Duell, Sloane and Pearce inquired regarding *Kono ko o nokoshite*: (1) the possibility of obtaining translation rights; (2) the existence of anybody in Japan suitable to translate the book for them; and (3) permission to intensify the Catholic aspects of the book (*Katorikku no nioi o yori koku sakaritai*), as well as the "feelings" of "Nagai the scientist" regarding the atomic bomb. Ray Falk, a reporter for the North American Newspaper Alliance dispatched to Japan, approached Kodansha for Duell, Sloan and Pearce and acted as liaison.

69. Charles A. Pearce to Shinnosuke Owari [*sic*], February 24, 1950, Shokan file 2, NTMM. *Genshiun senjo shinri* more literally means "battlefield psychology beneath the atomic mushroom cloud."

70. "Fall 1950: Books: Duell Sloan & Pearce," press release, 1950, Shokan file 2, NTMM.

71. Charles A. Pearce to Shinnosuke Owari [*sic*], February 24, 1950, Shokan file 2, NTMM.

72. Ruth Giblin to Dr. Nagai, January 28, 1951, Shohyō folder, NTMM.

73. Mary Rutherford to Dr. Nagai, February 13, 1951, Shohyō folder, NTMM.

74. Sister Mary Ambrose, BVM, to Doctor Takashi Nagai, January 25, 1951, Shohyō folder, NTMM. "BVM" stands for "Blessed Virgin Mary" and means the Sisters of Charity of the Blessed Virgin Mary, a charitable organization established in the United States in the 1800s.

75. *Nagasaki no kane* was not published in English translation as *The Bells of Nagasaki* until 1984. As of this writing, *The Bells of Nagasaki* and *We of Nagasaki* are the only two books by Nagai available in English.

76. From August 1946, Nagai published short writings of his own as series in newspapers and journals. He also gave several lectures and presentations on conditions in post-atomic Nagasaki from the latter part of 1946. The early writings were "Kagakusha no shinkō: Gakutō ni okuru" [The faith of a Scientist: A gift to students], *Katorikku shinbun* [Catholic newspaper], August 18 to September 2, 1946; "Genshino rokuon" [A (sound-) recording of the atomic wasteland], *Seibo no kishi* [Knights of the Blessed Mother (Mary)], January 1947; "Shi no shinri tankyū" [Investigation into the truth of death], *Dokusho tenbō* [Reading outlook], April 1947; "Kuro yuri" [Black lily], *Nagasaki bungaku* [Nagasaki

literature], September 1947. However, the 1947 cotranslation of Bruce Marshall's book, discussed later, was the first publication to produce substantial royalties for Nagai.

77. Kataoka, *Nagai Takashi no shōgai*, 233–34; Kataoka Chizuko and Kataoka Rumiko, *Hibakuchi Nagasaki no saiken* (Nagasaki: Nagasaki junshin daigaku hakubutsukan, 1996), 83. See also "Inzei o byōin saiken ni: Nagai hakase shōsetsu o kyōdō honyaku," newspaper clipping, n.d., Kiji kirinuki folder, NTMM. The Japanese edition of Marshall's book is *Sekai to nikutai to Sumisu shinpu*, trans. Nagai Takashi and Monfette Proudhon (Tokyo: Shufu no tomo sha, [December 20,] 1947); originally published as Bruce Marshall, *The World, the Flesh, and Father Smith* (Boston: Houghton Mifflin, 1945). Nagai's cotranslator was Father Monfette Proudhon, who was working in the Saint Francis Hospital in Nagasaki. Bruce Marshall lost an arm in the First World War, converted to Catholicism, and became a writer and priest. Nagai's trajectory was similar to that of Marshall's: he converted to Catholicism, was injured (leukemia), and became a writer and Catholic leader. Nagai and Proudhon cotranslated another book in 1949, Francis Clement Kelley's 1942 book, *Pack Rat* [*Nonezumi*, lit. "field mouse"]: see Nagai Tokusaburō, *Nagai Takashi zenshū*, 1:787. Kelley was the bishop of Oklahoma City and had died in 1948, one year before the Japanese translation of his book; see "Bishop Francis Clement Kelley," accessed July 6, 2010, http://www.catholic-hierarchy.org/bishop/bkelley.html.

78. See "Inzei o byōin saiken ni: Nagai hakase shōsetsu o kyōdō honyaku," newspaper clipping, n.d., Kiji kirinuki folder, NTMM.

79. *AS*, June 14, 1949.

80. *MS*, June 10, 1949.

81. *MS*, March 29, 1949.

82. *AS*, June 14, 1949. Individual high earners like Nagai paid extremely progressive tax rates from 1947. From September 1946 to March 1947, Japan underwent innovations to its tax system that expanded the nation's tax base as a way to begin relieving the wartime debt, funding reconstruction, and rebuilding the economy. For more on these innovations, see Henry Shavell, "Postwar Taxation in Japan," *Journal of Political Economy*, 56, no. 2 (April 1948): 124–37. The progressive tax rates that resulted from the early postwar innovations were also intended as a "key anti-inflation weapon" to subdue the economic chaos of the early postwar period; see Henry Shavell, "Taxation Reform in Occupied Japan," *National Tax Journal* 1, no. 2 (June 1948): 127–43.

83. *MS*, June 10, 1949.

84. Kataoka Yakichi, "Nagai hakase to chosaku," *NNN*, May 15, 1951. The article is reproduced in Kataoka C. and Kataoka R., *Hibakuchi Nagasaki no saiken*, 83–86.

85. A *sen* was the smallest unit of monetary measurement at the time. The saying is akin to "not a single cent."

86. Nagai, quoted in Kataoka, *Nagai Takashi no shōgai*, 218–19.

87. Nagai, quoted in Kataoka, "Nagai hakase to chosaku."

88. Nagai Takashi, *Nagasaki no hana* [Flowers of Nagasaki], in Nagai Tokusaburō, *Nagai Takashi zenshū*, 2:422.

89. *AS*, May 26, 1949.

90. "Zei de ikinayamu: Nagai hakase no inzei kifu" [Deadlocked over taxes: The royalty donations of Dr. Nagai], newspaper clipping, n.d., Kankei kiji folder 5, NTMM. *Zōyozei* can also be translated as "capital transfer tax." As the head of the Inheritance Tax Department of the National Tax Agency (Kokuzeichō sōzokuzei kachō) pointed out, the donation would not be taxed if it was simply to Nagasaki Prefecture or to the city, but only in the case that the companies (contractors) performing the various projects of the "cultural city construction" were "incorporated foundations" (*zaidan hōjin*), which most likely would be true in many cases. This particular case of taxation, when Nagai paid more than

¥4 million in taxes on ¥5 million in royalties, led to a discussion among policymakers in the National Diet about the need to revise tax law; see Notes of the National Diet of Japan, *Sangi'in, Ōkura i'inkai*, June 9, 1949, 14.

91. Nagai, quoted in Kataoka, *Nagai Takashi no shōgai*, 217.

92. Kataoka, "Nagai hakase to chosaku."

93. *NN*, December 26, 1948.

94. See, e.g., *NNN*, March 26, 1950.

95. See *Kyūshū taimuzu*, November 15, 1948.

96. *AS*, December 4, 1949.

97. *MS*, December 4, 1949.

98. Kataoka, *Nagai Takashi no shōgai*, 259. For "No qualifications," see *AS*, September 13, 1949.

99. *MS*, September 13, 1949. The vote was held the day before, on September 12.

100. The committee's report was titled "Nagai hakase hyōshō ni kan suru ken kiso chōsa." The version quoted here is from Kamiyama Shigeo, "Kami no mono wa kami no te ni," *Nihon hyōron*, November 1949. For excerpts, see also *MS*, September 13, 1949.

101. Kamiyama, "Kami no mono wa kami no te ni," 77. For discussion of 1949-50 awards, see also Takahashi, *Nagasaki ni atte tetsugaku suru*, 225.

102. Although Kamiyama Shigeo wrote the article on September 20, the version I use here is from the November 1949 issue of *Nihon hyōron*. At the end of the article, however, Kamiyama has included the date September 20, 1949.

103. Kamiyama, "Kami no mono wa kami no te ni," 73. Hereafter, page numbers are cited in the text. Most of the article originally appeared in the Communist journal *Akahata* in September 1949. The Communists' critiques of Nagai appeared in many newspapers and journals; see, e.g., *MS*, September 13, 1949.

104. Here, Kamiyama references Nagai's November 23, 1945, eulogy, which he also singled out for criticism.

105. Nagai's open criticism and dislike of communism was not atypical of Catholics. Even a cursory look at the Nagasaki-based *Katorikukyō hō* (also, *Katorikkukyō hō*) reveals numerous articles on the dangers of communism from as early as the 1920s, if not earlier.

106. This particular criticism of Nagai was not new, and Kamiyama referenced Uramatsu Samitarō's article in the *Shūkan asahi*, June 12, 1949, quoting it at length.

107. Nagai Takashi, quoted in *Katorikku shinbun*, October 9, 1949. Nagai opposed the nomination on similar grounds in other newspapers as well; see, e.g., *NNN*, September 14, 1949.

108. Konno Setsuzo, "Letters to the Editor: In the Japanese Press—(To the Mainichi)," n.d., newspaper clipping, unmarked, Kankei kiji folder, NTMM.

109. Shimokawa Ōten, "Ore ni wa mienai," *Tōkyō taimuzu*, September 15, 1949, newspaper clipping, Kankei kiji folder, NTMM.

110. See various sources, e.g., Takahashi, *Nagasaki ni atte tetsugaku suru*, 225; Mashima Kazuhiro, dir., *Nagasaki no kane: tsukurareta besuto seraa* (NBC Nagasaki Hōseisaku, 2000). The award certificate and silver cups are preserved and on display at NTMM.

111. Nagai Tokusaburō, *Nagai Takashi zenshū*, 3:777. Nagai was buried next to his wife, Midori.

112. The orations quoted here can be found in Tomita Kunihiko, ed., *Nagai Takashi hakase: Genshino no seija* [Dr. Nagai Takashi: The saint of the atomic wasteland] (Tokyo: Myōgi shuppansha, 1951), Yoshida on 11; Tagawa on 12–15; Pope Pius XII on 16. See also p. 311 for details on the pope's gifts to Nagai. For the pope's portrait with note, see also the 1951 film *Nagai hakase no omoide*, produced by Nihon nyūsu and Nagasaki shiyakusho.

113. Nagai Tokusaburō, *Nagai Takashi zenshū*, 3:777.

4. WRITING NAGASAKI

1. Takemae Eiji, *Inside GHQ: The Allied Occupation of Japan and Its Legacy*, trans. Robert Ricketts and Sebastian Swann (London: Continuum, 2002), 634n98.

2. The edition quoted here is Reorientation Branch, Office for Occupied Areas, Office of the Secretary of the Army, *Semi-Annual Report of Stateside Activities Supporting the Reorientation Program in Japan and the Ryukyu Islands*, January 1951, RG 331 (Allied Operational and Occupation Headquarters, World War II), Supreme Commander for the Allied Powers, Civil Information and Education Section, Religion and Cultural Resources Division, Special Projects Branch, Religious Research Data, 1945–1951, Religions Research to Christianity, box 5774, National Archives, College Park, MD. These reports cover the stateside programs that worked to send materials to Japan, such as "democratic" books to be translated and published in Tokyo. Some editions of these reports can be found on the Internet.

3. Takemae, *Inside GHQ*, 384.

4. This approach is similar to the point made by many scholars that censorship has a productive value; in one sense of the idea of its productive value, censorship forces authors or others to create works that they might not have otherwise created. See, e.g., Kirsten Cather, *Art of Censorship in Postwar Japan* (Honolulu: University of Hawai'i Press, 2012).

5. Head of PW Division, HQ, SACSEA, to Distribution as usual, "P.W. Division Propsig Letter No. 32," September 17, 1945, RG 208, Records of the Office of War Information, Overseas Branch, Bureau of Overseas Intelligence, Regional Analysis Division–All Regions (Entry 366A), box 230, National Archives. The July number, in "Leaflet Equivalent," is an astonishing 30,664,250.

6. For paper shortages in Japan during wartime, see SCAP, *History of the Nonmilitary Activities of the Occupation of Japan*, vol. 5: Civil Liberties, pt. 4: Freedom of the Press, 1945 to January 1951, 1–4, 31.

7. John W. Dower, *Embracing Defeat: Japan in the Wake of World War II* (New York: W. W. Norton, 1999), 180.

8. Ibid., 168, 186.

9. For the case of the Allies making use of the European people's hunger for books to disseminate propaganda, see, e.g., John B. Hench, *Books as Weapons: Propaganda, Publishing, and the Battle for Global Markets in the Era of World War II* (Ithaca: Cornell University Press, 2010).

10. SCAP, *Nonmilitary Activities*, "seeds of democracy" on 22, numbers of published books in app. 8, p. 16, Publishers' Code in app. 15, p. 31.

11. SCAP, *Nonmilitary Activities*, printing establishments on 4, rise of publishing companies on 187, "seller's market" on 188, precensorship on 22–28.

12. Dower, *Embracing Defeat*, 436, 432.

13. Nagai Takashi, *Horobinu mono o* (Nagasaki: Nagasaki nichinichi shinbun sha, 1948), 278, 283. The ink-redacted "Manchurian Incident" appears on p. 158; in fact, only "Manchuria" is redacted, and "Incident" was left readable. Personal collection.

14. Dower, *Embracing Defeat*, 436–37. Paper allotment fell under the purview of a group of Japanese men selected from various levels of the publishing world; see SCAP, *Nonmilitary Activities*, 37–38.

15. Dower, *Embracing Defeat*, 437.

16. See, e.g., Sebald to Secretary of State, RG 84, Records of the Foreign Service Posts of the Department of State, Japan, Tokyo, Office of U.S. Political Advisor, Classified General Records, 1945–52, box 49, National Archives. Many memos from 1948 to 1949 in the aforementioned document collection discuss concerns over the growing power of the communists in Japan more generally, especially anxiety over the potential for violence.

17. Inoue Hisashi, *Besuto seraa no sengoshi* (Tokyo: Bungei shunshū, 1995), 63.

18. Takahashi Shinji also discusses how Nagai viewed the cold war as a struggle between communism and Christianity; Takahashi, *Nagasaki ni atte tetsugaku suru: Kakujidai no shi to sei* (Tokyo: Hokuju shuppan, 1994), 217.

19. Nagai, *Kono ko o nokoshite* (Kodansha, 1948), 205–6; also Nagai, *Kono ko o nokoshite* (repr., San Paulo, 2000), 234–35.

20. Nagai Takashi, *Heiwa-tō* (Chūo shuppan sha, 1979), 100. Also quoted in Takahashi Shinji, *Nagasaki ni atte tetsugaku suru* (Tokyo: Hokuju shuppan, 1994), 217.

21. For correspondence between Deal and Nagai, see W. F. Deal to Professor T. Nagi [*sic*], August 23, 1947, Shohyō folder, NTMM.

22. Nagai Takashi, *Rozario no kusari* (Tokyo: Romansu sha, 1948), 182–84. In *Itoshigo yo* (Tokyo: San Paolo, 1995), Nagai uses the color white to refer to an ally and red to refer to an enemy (271). Catholic distaste for communism was nothing new. The Nagasaki Catholic publication *Katorikkukyō hō* made its disdain for communism quite clear for decades, from the 1930s into the 1950s.

23. Nagai, *Itoshigo yo*, 209.

24. For a monograph-length study on this topic, see James J. Orr, *The Victim as Hero: Ideologies of Peace and National Identity in Postwar Japan* (Honolulu: University of Hawai'i Press, 2001).

25. *MS*, October 26, 1949.

26. Nagai Takashi, *Nagasaki no kane* (Tokyo: Hibiya shuppan sha, 1949), eulogy, 174, 177, Yamada's visit on 171–72.

27. See also Nagai, *Itoshigo yo*, 303, where Nagai discusses the atomic bombing as attributable to the grace of God.

28. PPB Routing [*sic*] Slip, RRZ, March 24, 1947, folder 200.11 Book Censorship 1947, box 8655, SCAP. Unless otherwise noted, all SCAP documents cited in this chapter that relate specifically to *Nagasaki no kane* are through the courtesy of Nagasaki-based scholar Takahashi Shinji. The following narrative is based on the SCAP documents and Monica Braw, *The Atomic Bomb Suppressed: American Censorship in Occupied Japan* (Armonk, NY: M. E. Sharpe, 1991), where cited.

29. Check Sheet, ESS to PHW, "Transmittal of manuscript from CCD for recommendation; subj: Bell Tolls for Nagasaki by Dr. Takashi Nagai," March 31, 1947, folder 200.11 Book Censorship 1947, box 8655, SCAP.

30. PHW to ESS, "Manuscript, subj: Bell Tolls for Nagasaki," April 10, 1947, folder 200.11 Book Censorship 1947, box 8655, SCAP.

31. Mashima Kazuhiro, dir., *Nagasaki no kane: Tsukurareta besuto seraa* (NBC Nagasaki Hōseisaku, 2000).

32. For new title, see PPB Routing [*sic*] Slip, RRZ, March 24, 1947, folder 200.11 Book Censorship 1947, box 8655, SCAP. Braw, *Suppressed*, incorrectly copies the original English title as *The Bells Toll for Nagasaki*. For the name of the submitting publisher, see also Civil Censorship Detachment (CCD) to Civil Intelligence Section (CIS), April 29, 1947, folder 200.11 Book Censorship 1947, box 8655, SCAP. For an account of the journey of *Nagasaki no kane* through the censorship bureaucracy of SCAP, see Braw, *Suppressed*, 94–99.

33. CCD to CIS, April 29, 1947, folder 200.11 Book Censorship 1947, box 8655, SCAP.

34. Ibid.

35. JJC [Costello] to CCO, May 5, 1947, folder 200.11 Book Censorship 1947, box 8655, SCAP.

36. CCD to RK [Kunzman], May 5, 1947, folder 200.11 Book Censorship 1947, box 8655, SCAP. Kunzman retired soon after, and some attributed the "famous 5 May 1947 blast from Costello" to "the principal immediate causes for Kunzman's decision to resign"; Unnamed document, TJH to RMS (initials), handwritten date of February 10, 1949.

37. PPB, CCD to CCO, May 5, 1947, folder 200.11 Book Censorship 1947, box 8655, SCAP.

38. CCD to CIS, G-2, May 15, 1947, interoffice memo, folder 200.11 Book Censorship 1947, box 8655, SCAP.

39. General Willoughby, quoted in Braw, *Suppressed*, 95.

40. Handwritten note by Colonel Putnam (WBP) in CCD to CIS, G-2, May 15, 1947, interoffice memo, folder 200.11 Book Censorship 1947, box 8655, SCAP.

41. Press and Publications Subsection, Routing Slip, May 16, 1947, folder 200.11 Book Censorship 1947, box 8655, SCAP. "RMS" meant Captain Shaw. Colonel Putnam's note to Costello was originally scribbled at the bottom of Costello's memo from the previous day.

42. Costello, quoted in *Kami to genbaku: Urakami katorikku hibakusha no 55 nen* (NBC Nagasaki hōsō, 2000), at 18:22.

43. From early on, censors doubted the genuineness of Nagai's illness, and one noted, "I wish we could check"; Braw, *Suppressed*, 95.

44. TJH to RMS, "On Book 'NAGASAKI NO KANE' by NAGAI TAKASHI," June 3, 1948, SCAP; document courtesy of Takahashi Shinji.

45. See Braw, *Suppressed*, 98. .

46. Even though Hersey's account contained graphic scenes, the CCD could not censor the publication of a translation of *Hiroshima* in Japan because it lay outside SCAP's jurisdiction. They did, however, manage to stall its publication until 1949; Braw, *Suppressed*, 105–6.

47. PPB, CCD to CCO, May 5, 1947, folder 200.11 Book Censorship 1947, box 8655, SCAP. The part, "resembling Hersey's article in New Yorker," was crossed out by hand and not included in Costello's IOM to G-2 on May 15, but otherwise the IOM is nearly identical to the detachment. Costello's detachment appears to have been edited, most likely by Colonel W. B. Putnam, who attached a handwritten note addressed to Costello, saying, "Jack, write an IOM from Bratton to Gen. W., including the remarks in the attached notes, recommending suppression. Don't send any inclosures or the book, just the IOM." That Colonel Putnam suggested not to include a copy of the book could be for one of two (if not more) reasons: he did not want to bog down General Willoughby with unnecessary details and papers; or, since he concurred with Costello, he may have wanted to avoid any ambiguity about the content of the book that may have resulted from Willoughby's own reading of it (i.e., the heavily Christian message or the exemption of U.S. responsibility for dropping the atomic bomb inherent in Nagai's interpretation of the bombing as being the work of God).

48. AGH to RMS, April 26, 1949, SCAP; document courtesy of Takahashi Shinji. For the Shikiba request, see Shikiba Ryūsaburō, preface to Nagai, *Nagasaki no kane*, 2.

49. CCD, RMS to TJH, February 10, 1949, SCAP; document courtesy of Takahashi Shinji. The documents here refer to the book as "Bell of Nagasaki," "The Bell of Nagasaki," and "The Bells of Nagasaki."

50. Shikiba, preface to Nagai, *Nagasaki no kane*, 3–4.

51. See TJH to RMS, "On Book 'NAGASAKI NO KANE' by NAGAI TAKASHI," June 3, 1948, SCAP; document courtesy of Takahashi Shinji.

52. Braw, *Suppressed*, 98. Braw notes that General Willoughby in the beginning "ordered the book held for six months" and promised the publisher, Hibiya shuppan sha, an answer at the end of that time (95) . The manuscript had passed through the hands of two other publishers before reaching Hibiya shuppan sha: Tokyo Times Company and Showa shobo. The person in charge of Nagai's manuscript at Hibiya shuppan sha, Shikiba Shunzō, thought it strange that SCAP did not outright suppress *Nagasaki no kane* because of its graphic descriptions of the destruction and human suffering, but instead merely *suspended* its publication; see Mashima, *Tsukurareta besuto seraa*.

53. Braw, *Suppressed*, 98–99. For Shikiba Shunzō as editor, see Mashima, *Tsukurareta besuto seraa*. Nagai and the Shikiba brothers were put on the censorship watch list. Indeed, letters sent to and from Nagai Takashi in Nagasaki were subject to censorship. Correspondence that was censored is preserved at NTMM. The letters have stamps showing that they have been "Released by Censorship" (*Ken'etsu sumi*). To avoid such censorship, some delivered their letters to Nagai by entrusting them to visitors who could hand them directly to him. For example, actor Chiaki Minoru entrusted a letter to Shikiba Ryūsaburō for delivery to Nagai. The actor's previous letter, however, passed through the eyes of the censors before arriving at Nagai's address.

54. SCAP censorship documents translate the account "Manira no higeki" alternately as "Tragedy of Manila" and "Tragedy in Manila." In the English translation of the preface, the documents have "rape of Manila."

55. Braw, *Suppressed*, 99.

56. At this time, Nagai's *Kono ko o nokoshite* already sat comfortably at number one. See list in *Jiji tsūshin*, news bulletin no. 1023, April 9, 1949, app., 1.

57. Nagai, *Nagasaki no kane*, 174–75.

58. Nagai Takashi, *Genshi bakudan shisha gōdō sō chōji*, MS, delivered on November 23, 1945. Preserved at NTMM.

59. Nagai, *Nagasaki no kane*, 174.

60. This number, 114061, indicated the intended target, or mean point of impact (MPI). By this time, the Twentieth Air Force, of which the 509th was a part, no longer made a clear distinction between MPI and aiming point (AP). It was referred to as both in the reports. See Okuzumi Yoshishige, Kudō Yōzō, and Katsura Tetsuo, trans. and eds. *Beigun shiryō: Genbaku tōka hōkokusho—panpukin to Hiroshima, Nagasaki* [Tactical Mission Report (Mission No. Special/Flown July 20–August 14, 1945/Copy No. 12), Headquarters Twentieth Air Force APO 234] (Tokyo: Tōhō shuppan, 1993), 213, 47.

61. Theater Intelligence to Colonel Bratton, January 12, 1948, folder 000.73 Censorship News Articles in Japanese Press, box 8519, SCAP, as reprinted in Braw, *Suppressed*, 100. Emphasis in original.

62. Takahashi Shinji, *Zoku Nagasaki ni atte tetsugaku suru: Genbakushi kara heiwa sekinin e* (Tokyo: Hokuju shuppan, 2004), 103; Mashima, *Tsukurareta besuto seraa*. In Mashima's film, Nagai's publisher Shikiba Shunzō explains that his publishing company, Hibiya shuppan sha, had never before received paper from SCAP, also generally known as General Headquarters (GHQ), to print books, especially of *Nagasaki no kane*'s nature, but did occasionally receive paper to print pamphlets.

63. For "unrationed paper (senka)" for 30,000 copies of *Nagasaki no kane*, see PPB, CCD, Book Department, February 10, 1949, SCAP; document courtesy of Takahashi Shinji.

64. All copies of the books mentioned here with circulation numbers written on their covers by SCAP censors are preserved at the Gordon W. Prange Collection, University of Maryland Libraries.

65. Lisa Yoneyama, *Hiroshima Traces: Time, Space, and the Dialectics of Memory* (Berkeley: University of California Press, 1999), 12. Yoneyama notes that the "notion of using the atomic bombs against populated cities had made even U.S. officials wonder if they might be 'outdoing Hitler' in barbarity." See also John W. Dower, *War without Mercy: Race and Power in the Pacific War* (New York: Pantheon, 1986), 37–38.

66. General Willoughby to Staff re Censorship of Book on Bombing of Nagasaki, March 31, 1948, folder 000.73 Censorship of News Articles in Japanese Press 1948, box 8519, SCAP, as quoted in Braw, *Suppressed*, 99.

67. Dower, *Embracing Defeat*, 415.

68. "Manira no higeki," appendix to *Nagasaki no kane* (Tokyo: Hibiya shuppan sha, 1949), 193; appendix: 191–319. In English, the appendix is entitled "Japanese Atrocities in

Manilla [*sic*]," and in Japanese, "Manira no higeki" (lit., Tragedy of Manila). The letter discussed here was, oddly, reprinted in English with no Japanese translation. Of course, by asserting that the people of the Philippines are "our nationals," Thomas was reasserting the colonial legacy of the Western nations over Southeast Asia.

69. Shikiba Ryūsaburō, preface to Nagai, *Nagasaki no kane*, 2–3.

70. Several scholars have noted the ironic outcome. See, e.g., Dower, *Embracing Defeat*, 415; or, Robert Jay Lifton, *Death in Life* (New York: Random House, 1967), 329.

71. This translation is from RMS to TJH, February 10, 1949, SCAP.

72. Historian James J. Orr has written extensively about this point. In *The Victim as Hero*, he writes, "war victim consciousness was promoted by Allied psychological warfare agents and Occupation authorities to encourage alienation from the wartime state and its military." He continues that the "vision of the Japanese as innocent war victims reached its purest expression in the public dialogue over nuclear weapons" (7). Orr also writes that in antinuclear discourse, Japan bears the title *yuitsu no hibakukoku* (the only country to have suffered the atomic bomb), a term whose etymology is the same as the word for atomic-bombing victims, hibakusha; he continues that "Japan's unique experience of Hiroshima and Nagasaki gave the Japanese an exclusive and seductive claim to leadership of the world antinuclear weapon movement" (36).

73. Office of the Military Secretary, Psychological Warfare Branch to Military Secretary to the Commander-in-Chief, "Weekly Military Plan for Psychological Warfare," July 28, 1945, RG 208, Records of the Office of War Information, OWI Overseas Branch, Bureau of Ove[r]seas Intelligence, Central Files, Information File on Asia 1942–1946 C Japan 6.17.1 to 8.2.4 Factors of Political (Entry 370), box 403, National Archives.

74. Frank Capra, dir., *Know Your Enemy—Japan* (1945). For more discussion of the film, see, e.g. Dower, *War without Mercy*, 18–23.

75. Harry Truman, quoted in Gar Alperovitz, *The Decision to Use the Atomic Bomb and the Architecture of an American Myth* (New York: Alfred A. Knopf, 1995), 563.

76. CCD, RMS to TJH, February 10, 1949, SCAP; document courtesy of Takahashi Shinji. RMS argues that a "typically Japanese opinion is expressed in the sentence in top preface [by Shikiba], page 2, underlined in blue." The underlined sentence in the document reads, in English, "We must reflect seriously upon the Manila events just as we are impressed by the tragedy in Nagasaki." RMS bases his worries on this sentence, which clearly suggests the equation of Manila with Nagasaki. However, the original context and wording of the Japanese sentence actually encourages Japanese readers to reflect on Manila before they pass judgment on the United States for bombing Nagasaki. The preface does not equate the two tragedies per se, at least not as obviously as the SCAP version of the English translation does. The verb "reflect" (*hansei*) implies both regret and the need for reflection.

77. Capra, *Know Your Enemy—Japan*.

78. See Dower, *War without Mercy*, 163.

79. "Manira no higeki," in *Nagasaki no kane*, 194–96. Also see Mashima, *Tsukurareta besuto seraa*.

80. CCD, RMS to TJH, February 10, 1949, SCAP; document courtesy of Takahashi Shinji.

81. "Manira no higeki," in *Nagasaki no kane*, 195.

82. CCD, RMS to TJH, February 10, 1949, SCAP; document courtesy of Takahashi Shinji.

83. "Manira no higeki," in *Nagasaki no kane*, 196. Also see Mashima, *Tsukurareta besuto seraa*.

84. John Whittier Treat, *Writing Ground Zero: Japanese Literature and the Atomic Bomb* (Chicago: Chicago University Press, 1995), 95.

85. See ibid., 92–107.

86. Captain Irvin W. Rogers to Commanding Officer, CCD, Fukuoka, "Censorship of Publication," March 18, 1947, and letter from Delnore to American occupation censors in Fukuoka, March 1947, Victor E. Delnore Papers, Gordon W. Prange Collection, University of Maryland Libraries.

87. Major George P. Solovskoy to Commanding Officer, Kyushu Military Government Region, Hq. & Hq. Det., APO 929, Fukuoka, Kyushu, July 16, 1947, Victor E. Delnore Papers, Gordon W. Prange Collection, University of Maryland Libraries.

88. The comments of those surveyed can be found in the files pertaining to *Masako taorezu*, Gordon W. Prange Collection, University of Maryland Libraries.

89. Copy of Fujin taimuzu sha (1949) version of *Masako taorezu* preserved at the Gordon W. Prange Collection, University of Maryland Libraries. Braw, *Suppressed*, lists the final publication date as April 26, 1949 (92–93, 169n12).

90. Copies of Masako's books used by the censors are preserved at Gordon W. Prange Collection, University of Maryland Libraries.

91. Treat, *Writing Ground Zero*, 90.

92. "Tokushū: Nō moa Hiroshimasu," special issue, *Shūkan asahi*, August 7, 1949, 3.

93. Takahashi, *Zoku Nagasaki ni atte*, 251.

94. See, e.g., John W. Dower, "The Bombed: Hiroshimas and Nagasakis in Japanese Memory," in *Hiroshima in History and Memory*, ed. Michael J. Hogan (Cambridge University Press, 1996), 116–42, where Dower shows how the victimization of Hiroshima and Nagasaki have become icons of Japan's wartime experience as a nation.

95. Fujiyama had served during the war as part of a "comfort group" (*imondan*) that traveled around Southeast Asia providing entertainment to Japanese troops. His song "Nagasaki no kane" is still a popular karaoke song today.

96. Dower, *Embracing Defeat*, 198.

97. Nagai, *Itoshigo yo*, 206.

5. WALLS OF SILENCE

1. The term *hibakusha no kurai jiki* (the dark era of the hibakusha) is from a 1996 publication entitled *Nagasaki genbaku hibaku go jū nen shi*, published by the Nagasaki-shi genbaku hibaku taisaku ka; discussed in Yamada Hirotami, "Nagasaki no hibakusha," in *Nagasaki kara heiwagaku suru!*, ed. Takahashi Shinji and Funakoe Kōichi (Kyoto: Hōritsu bunka sha, 2009), 52.

2. Yoshikuni Igarashi, *Bodies of Memory: Narratives of War in Postwar Japanese Culture, 1945–1970* (Princeton, NJ: Princeton University Press, 2000), 13–14.

3. Committee for the Compilation of Materials on Damage Caused by the Atomic Bombs in Hiroshima and Nagasaki, *Hiroshima and Nagasaki: The Physical, Medical, and Social Effects of the Atomic Bombings*, trans. Eisei Ishikawa and David L. Swain (New York: Basic Books, 1981), 535–36.

4. Ibid.

5. Yamada, "Nagasaki no hibakusha," 52–53. For more on General Farrell, see Takemae Eiji, *Inside GHQ: The Allied Occupation of Japan and Its Legacy*, trans. Robert Ricketts and Sebastian Swann (London: Continuum, 2002), 428. General Farrell's statement was largely a response to an article by an Australian journalist named Wilfred Burchett, who had claimed that people were dying in Hiroshima from a "mysterious illness" brought on by radiation; Takemae, *Inside GHQ*, 389.

6. Committee for the Compilation of Materials, *Hiroshima and Nagasaki*, 564.

7. Ibid., 539, 559, 552. The name of the council, Nagasaki-shi genbaku shōgaisha chiryō taisaku kyōgikai, literally means Nagasaki City Atomic Bombing Disabled Persons Medical Treatment Provision Council.

8. Ibid., 542–43, 552, 556–57.

9. Kamata Sadao, "Nagasaki no ikari to inori: Hankaku shōgen 36 nen no kiseki kara," in *Nihon no genbaku bungaku*, ed. Kaku-sensō no kiki o uttaeru bungakusha no seimei chomeisha (Tokyo: Horupu shuppan, 1983), 15:413. This article originally appeared in the journal *Fukuin to sekai*, August 1981.

10. Committee for the Compilation of Materials, *Hiroshima and Nagasaki*, 605.

11. Kitamura Seibō, "Heiwa kinen zō ni tsuite," in *Nagasaki dansō* 37 (November 1955): 1–2.

12. Committee for the Compilation of Materials, *Hiroshima and Nagasaki*, 605.

13. Nagasaki shiyakusho sōmubu chōsa tōkeika, ed., *Nagasaki-shi sei roku jū go nen shi* (Nagasaki: Nagasaki shiyakusho sōmubu chōsa tōkeika, 1959), 3:1151.

14. Nagasaki hibaku kyōshi no kai, ed., *Chinmoku no kabe o yabutte* [Breaking down the walls of silence] (Tokyo: Rōdō shunhō sha, 1970), 17–18. My title for the present chapter and the idea of "walls of silence" come from this book.

15. *NN*, August 9, 2002. For more on the criticism of municipally funded statues in the city, see, e.g., *NS*, December 23, 2003.

16. Committee for the Compilation of Materials, *Hiroshima and Nagasaki*, 560.

17. For a more detailed look at the Nagasaki peace movement until 1959, see Nagasaki shiyakusho sōmubu chōsa tōkeika, *Nagasaki-shi sei roku jū go nen shi*, esp. 3:646–93.

18. Yamada, "Nagasaki no hibakusha," 58.

19. Committee for the Compilation of Materials, *Hiroshima and Nagasaki*, 544.

20. Naono Akiko, "Tsugunai naki kuni no hibakusha taisaku: Imada kanawanu hibakusha engo hō," in Takahashi and Funakoe, *Nagasaki kara heiwagaku suru!*, 65.

21. See, e.g., Yamada, "Nagasaki no hibakusha," 58–59.

22. Committee for the Compilation of Materials, *Hiroshima and Nagasaki*, 559; Yamada, "Nagasaki no hibakusha," 58.

23. Yamada, "Nagasaki no hibakusha," 58–59.

24. As quoted in Ishida Tadashi, *Zoku Han genbaku* (Tokyo: Miraisha, 1974), 49.

25. For an example, see *NS*, August 1, 1970.

26. Committee for the Compilation of Materials, *Hiroshima and Nagasaki*, 564–69; Hiroshima-shi, Nagasaki-shi, Genbaku higai shi henshū i'inkai, ed., *Hiroshima, Nagasaki no genbaku saigai* (Tokyo: Iwanami shoten, 1979), 455. This second reference is the original Japanese version of Committee for the Compilation of Materials, *Hiroshima and Nagasaki*. I cite it here because I have translated some terms differently from Ishikawa and Swain.

27. Hiroshima-shi et al., *Hiroshima, Nagasaki no genbaku saigai*, 455–56; Committee for the Compilation of Materials, *Hiroshima and Nagasaki*, 568.

28. Dominick LaCapra, *History and Memory after Auschwitz* (Ithaca, NY: Cornell University Press, 1998), 9.

29. For a different interpretation of the silence of many hibakusha, see Monica Braw, "Hiroshima and Nagasaki: The Voluntary Silence," in *Living with the Bomb: American and Japanese Cultural Conflicts in the Nuclear Age*, ed. Laura E. Hein and Mark Selden (Armonk, NY: M. E. Sharpe, 1997), 155–72.

30. For more on continuation of censorship in general, see, e.g., Takemae, *Inside GHQ*, 391–92.

31. Shimonoseki genbakuten jimukyoku, ed., *Genbaku to Tōge Sankichi no shi* (Shimonoseki: Chōshū shinbunsha, 2000), 49.

32. Takemae, *Inside GHQ*, 482. SCAP censorship was not always thorough and seemed sporadic at times. For example, the August 7, 1949, *Shūkan asahi* special issue on Hiroshima published three articles on the bomb that included a photo of a "shadow of death" on a concrete slab where a person was killed by the atomic bomb.

33. Kamata, "Nagasaki no ikari to inori," 415.

34. Social discrimination has lasted in certain forms to the present day.

35. Committee for the Compilation of Materials, *Hiroshima and Nagasaki*, 420.

36. See, e.g., *MS*, August 1, 1970.

37. Committee for the Compilation of Materials, *Hiroshima and Nagasaki*, 420. Many other factors besides discrimination affected the marriage rates of hibakusha; see esp. 420–27.

38. *MS*, August 1, 1970.

39. See Committee for the Compilation of Materials, *Hiroshima and Nagasaki*, esp. 214–33.

40. Unnamed hibakusha, quoted in *MS*, August 1, 1970.

41. Committee for the Compilation of Materials, *Hiroshima and Nagasaki*, 13–14.

42. In Japanese, "*Ki no omoi koto deshita.*"

43. Yamaguchi Senji, "Ano hi kara: Watashi no ikita hibi," in *Mō iya da, dai 3 shū: Wagami kogasarete mo nao*, ed. Nagasaki genbaku seinen otome no kai (Tokyo: Chōbun sha, 1985), 136–38.

44. See John Whittier Treat, *Writing Ground Zero: Japanese Literature and the Atomic Bomb* (Chicago: University of Chicago Press, 1995), 125. For more on Hara, see esp. 125–53.

45. Gotō Minako, as quoted in Treat, *Writing Ground Zero*, 29.

46. Kamata, "Nagasaki no ikari to inori," 411–16.

47. Tanaka Toshihiro, "Nagasaki no genbaku bunbaku: Shisōteki shinka e no jikan," in Takahashi and Funakoe, *Nagasaki kara heiwagaku suru!*, 77–78.

48. Kamata, "Nagasaki no ikari to inori," 411–16.

49. Kamata Sadao, "Genbaku taiken no keishō to kokumin kyōiku e no tenbō: Nagasaki no kussetsu shita taiken no naka kara," in Nagasaki hibaku kyōshi no kai, *Chinmoku no kabe o yabutte*, 192–93.

50. Akizuki Tatsuichirō, quoted in Takahashi Shinji, *Nagasaki ni atte tetsugaku suru: Kakujidai no shi to sei* (Tokyo: Hokuju shuppan, 1994), 203–4. Akizuki's work was originally published as *Nagasaki genbaku ki: Hibaku ishi no shōgen* (Kōbundō, 1966), 164.

51. For a good discussion of how Nagai's narrative of the bombing affected the ability of some Catholic hibakusha to confront their individual trauma well into the 1980s, see Jack Wintz, "Nagasaki: A Peace Church Rises from the Nuclear Ashes," *American Catholic*, n.d., accessed February 26, 2017, https://web.archive.org/web/20150709210645 /http://www.americancatholic.org/Features/WWII/feature0283.asp#top. Wintz points to a comment made by Pope John Paul II during his visit to Hiroshima in 1981 as the source of a change in perception of some Urakami Catholic hibakusha toward Nagai's interpretation of the bombing as Providence. The pope stated that "war is the work of human beings"—in other words, war is not the work of God as Nagai had suggested. Some felt that the Pope's statement lifted a burden from their shoulders and inspired them to become more active in the peace movement. Furthermore, that the pope made his comments while in Hiroshima reflected, in a way, how Hiroshima persisted as the center of historical discussions of the bombings and, more generally, of the Second World War in the global atomic narrative.

52. Akizuki, quoted in Kamata, "Nagasaki no ikari to inori," 415.

53. For "living witnesses," see Nagasaki hibaku kyōshi no kai, *Chinmoku no kabe o yabutte*, 2.

54. Yamada, "Nagasaki no hibakusha," 54–55.

55. Committee for the Compilation of Materials, *Hiroshima and Nagasaki*, 575–77.

56. Yamada, "Nagasaki no hibakusha," 55.

57. Committee for the Compilation of Materials, *Hiroshima and Nagasaki*, 577–78.

58. Yamada, "Nagasaki no hibakusha," 55.

59. Ibid., 56–57. The English translation for the Nihon Hidankyō is from Committee for the Compilation of Materials, *Hiroshima and Nagasaki*, 579.

60. Naono, "Tsugunai naki kuni no hibakusha taisaku," 65.

61. Yuki Tanaka and Peter Kuznick, "Japan, the Atomic Bomb, and 'Peaceful Uses of Nuclear Power,'" *Asia-Pacific Journal: Japan Focus* 9, issue 18, no. 1 (May 2, 2011). See especially Kuznick's contribution, "Japan's Nuclear History in Perspective: Eisenhower and Atoms for War and Peace." For more on the Atoms for Peace campaign, see also Ran Zwigenberg, *Hiroshima: The Origins of Global Memory Culture* (Cambridge: Cambridge University Press, 2014).

62. Years earlier, Nagai Takashi had also promoted discussion of the possibilities for peaceful uses of atomic energy in his books.

63. Taniguchi Sumiteru, "Ni jū go nen me no kaisō to shōgen," in *Nagasaki no shōgen: 1970*, ed. Nagasaki no shōgen kankō i'inkai (Nagasaki: Ayumi shuppan sha, 1970), 8–9. Peter Townsend wrote a book about Taniguchi titled *The Postman of Nagasaki* (HarperCollins, 1984).

64. Taniguchi, "Ni jū go nen me no kaisō to shōgen," 9; Taniguchi Sumiteru, lecture at the Department of Education, Nagasaki University, June 30, 2004.

65. Taniguchi, "Ni jū go nen me no kaisō to shōgen," 9.

66. Kamata, "Nagasaki no ikari to inori," 410. The original footage taken by the American military can be viewed, among other places, on this author's YouTube page, https://www.youtube.com/watch?v=d0mf7xer4Yk. The footage of Taniguchi begins at 18:30 and lasts for three minutes. For a study of the collection of film footage taken by American military personnel in the months after the bombings, of which the Taniguchi footage is a part, see Greg Mitchell, *Atomic Cover-Up: Two U.S. Soldiers, Hiroshima & Nagasaki, and the Greatest Movie Never Made* (New York: Sinclair Books, 2011).

67. *AS*, July 3, 1970.

68. Kamata, "Nagasaki no ikari to inori," 410.

69. Taniguchi, "Ni jū go nen me no kaisō to shōgen," 8.

70. Kamata, "Nagasaki no ikari to inori," 409.

71. Kamata, "Genbaku taiken no keishō," 192.

72. Kamata, "Nagasaki no ikari to inori," 415–16.

73. Ibid., 409.

74. Ibid., 409–10.

75. *NS*, July 30, 1970.

76. Interview with Yamada Kan, "Kioku no koshitsu: Yamada Kan shi ni kiku," *Josetsu* 19 (August 9, 1999), 66–67, entire interview, 51–70. The interview was conducted at Yamada's home by five scholars for the purpose of the publication. For a detailed discussion of Yamada's view of Nagai and his influence, see esp. 66–68. Yamada mentions a 1955 essay, a rare instance of a scholar addressing the "Nagai problem"; Kashiwazaki Saburō, "Chabangeki no keifu: Nagai Takashi no imi suru mono" *Chijin* 5 (October 1955). Kashiwazaki's article can also be found partly quoted in Nagasaki shiyakusho sōmubu chōsa tōkeika, *Nagasaki-shi sei roku jū go nen shi*, 3:703.

77. Yamada Kan, "Gizensha: Nagai Takashi e no kokuhatsu," *Ushio* (July 1972): 231–32. Also see Takahashi, *Nagasaki ni atte tetsugaku suru*, 194.

78. The official biography is Kataoka Yakichi, *Nagai Takashi no shōgai* (Tokyo: San Paolo, 1961).

79. Takahashi, *Nagasaki ni atte tetsugaku suru*, 194.

80. Yamada, "Kioku no koshitsu," 66–67.

81. For more on Nagasaki survivor poetry as a vehicle for social and memory activism, see Chad R. Diehl, "Lambs of God, Ravens of Death, Rafts of Corpses: Three Visions of Trauma in Nagasaki Survivor Poetry," *Japanese Studies* 37, no. 1 (2017): 117-138.

82. Yamada, "Kioku no koshitsu," 61.

83. The change in tense (*shita*) is in the original.

84. This is only part of the poem; see Ienaga Saburō, Odagiri Hideo, and Kuroyoshi Kazuo, eds., *Nihon no genbaku kiroku* (Tokyo: Nihon tosho sentā, 1991), 20:178.

85. Yamada "Kioku no koshitsu" 63.

86. Committee for the Compilation of Materials, *Hiroshima and Nagasaki*, 556–57.

87. James J. Orr, *The Victim as Hero: Ideologies of Peace and National Identity in Postwar Japan* (Honolulu: University of Hawai'i Press, 2001), 170.

88. See, e.g.,, Orr, *The Victim as Hero*, 37. Other scholars, too, have noted how 1954 marked a turning point in atomic memory when the cities became symbols in the antinuclear peace movement; see, e.g., Shi-Lin Loh, "Beyond Peace: Pluralizing Japan's Nuclear History," *Asia-Pacific Journal: Japan Focus* 10, issue 11, no. 6 (March 5, 2012).

89. For a recent study of Hiroshima within global frameworks of memory of the Second World War, see Zwigenberg, *Hiroshima: The Origins of Global Memory Culture*.

6. RUINS OF MEMORY

1. Pierre Nora, "Between Memory and History: Les Lieux de Mémoire," *Representations* 26 (Spring 1989): 7–24.

2. Jorge Otero-Pailos, "Mnemonic Value and Historic Preservation," in *Spatial Recall: Memory in Architecture and Landscape*, ed. Marc Treib (New York: Routledge, 2009), 241.

3. See, e.g., Jeffry M. Diefendorf, "Reconstructing Civic Authority in Post-War Germany," in *The Blitz and Its Legacy: Wartime Destruction to Post-War Reconstruction*, ed. Mark Clapson and Peter J. Larkham (Burlington: Ashgate, 2013), 123–36; Carola Hein, "Hiroshima: The Atomic Bomb and Kenzo Tange's Hiroshima Peace Center," in *Out of Ground Zero: Case Studies in Urban Reinvention*, ed. Joan Ockman (Munich: Prestel Verlag, 2002), 62–83; Marc Treib, ed., *Spatial Recall: Memory in Architecture and Landscape* (New York: Routledge, 2009).

4. Regarding Pierre Nora's discussion of sites of memory, Christina Schwenkel writes, "There is an implicit assumption here that cultures 'frozen' in past memory and engaged in ritual remembrance are unmodern and do not possess what Habermas . . . has called 'the historical consciousness of modernity' that advocates a forward-oriented rupture with the past"; Schwenkel, *The American War in Contemporary Vietnam: Transnational Remembrance and Representation* (Bloomington: Indiana University Press, 2009), 11.

5. Kamohara Haruo, "Nagasaki no yokogao: Nagasaki annai no kotoba," *Nagasaki dansō* 8 (April 1931): 69.

6. Nagano Hideki thinks that the reporters, Miyamoto and Oshikawa, were probably from Tokyo or Osaka; Nagano, "Genbaku wa 'Kami no setsuri' ka: Nagai Takashi no zenkei to kōkei," *Josetsu* 19 (August 9, 1999), 43.

7. The version of the article that is referenced here is from *NS*, September 15, 1945.

8. Op-Ed, "Kieru tsume ato: Urakami tenshudō tekkyo no shinsō," *Shūkan shinchō*, May 19, 1958, 28.

9. Takase Tsuyoshi, *Nagasaki: Kieta mō hitotsu no "Genbaku Dōmu"* (Tokyo: Heibon sha, 2009), 115. For discussion of the committee's submissions to the mayor, see also Nagasaki City Council Meeting Notes, February 17–18, 1958, "Kyū Urakami tenshudō no genbaku shiryō hozon ni kan suru ketsugian" [Resolution regarding the Preservation of the Old Urakami Cathedral as Atomic-Bombing Record], preserved at the Nagasaki shigikai jimukyoku, gijika [City Council Executive Office, Proceedings Division], Nagasaki.

10. *KH*, September 1, 1951.

11. *NS*, October 8, 1945.

12. Bishop Yamaguchi, as quoted in Op-Ed, "Kieru tsume ato," 29.

13. See, e.g., Motoshima Hitoshi, "Urakami no kirishitan no junnan: Kinkyōrei, yonban kuzure, genbaku," *Seibo no kishi* (October 2000).

14. Nagai Takashi, quoted in Kataoka Yakichi, *Nagai Takashi no shōgai* (Tokyo: San Paolo, 1961), 199.

15. Kataoka, *Nagai Takashi no shōgai*, 202.

16. The wooden church was completed in 1946. For details of the provisional church (*kari seidō*), including its construction, see, e.g., Kataoka, *Nagai Takashi no shōgai*, 202–3. Father Nakada led groups into the mountains to collect lumber for the new church (202). Allied occupation forces contributed materials (*shizai*); *NS*, November 15,1945.

17. *NS*, November 15, 1945. For the new church's completion in December 1946, see, e.g., Takase, *Nagasaki: Kieta mō hitotsu no "Genbaku Dōmu,"* 266, "*kanren nenpyō.*" Concerning the first public building erected after the bombing, see Kataoka, *Nagai Takashi no shōgai*, 203.

18. Nagai Takashi, *Hana saku oka*, in *Nagai Takashi zenshū*, ed. Nagai Tokusaburō (Tokyo: San Paolo, 2003), 1:190.

19. Nagai, prologue to *Hana saku oka*, 1:143.

20. Nagai Takashi, ed., *Urakami tenshudō: The Church of Urakami, Nagasaki, Japan* (Nagasaki: Urakami tenshudō, 1949); page numbers are cited in text. The bilingual booklet was printed in Tokyo. The "[at]" that I include in the quote was penned in with pink ink, probably by Nagai.

21. Francis-Xavier Nakada, untitled document, n.d., Shiryō folder, NTMM. The page includes before and after photographs of the Urakami Cathedral.

22. Kataoka, *Nagai Takashi no shōgai*, 203.

23. *KH*, September 1, 1951.

24. *KH*, December 15, 1948. The number of Catholics in the Nagasaki diocese at this time was 60,624; see *KH*, December 15, 1948. By 1952, the Nagasaki diocese had risen to 69,740. It is interesting to note that in the 1950s, clergymen of the Nagasaki diocese were still actively engaged in work to "enlighten" (*kyōka*) the "hiding Christians" (*senpuku Kirishitan*); see *KH*, August 1, 1953.

25. *KH*, April 1, 1953.

26. *KH*, March 1, 1956. Yamaguchi left on May 5, 1955, and returned on February 9, 1956. During his time in the United States, the Villanova University School of Law, a Catholic school founded in 1953, bestowed on Yamaguchi an honorary law degree.

27. The original phrase in Japanese for "as if peeking in a zoo" is *Maru de dōbutsuen de mo nozoku yō na abekku no kyōsei mo nagareta.*

28. Bishop Yamaguchi, as quoted in Op-Ed, "*Kieru tsume ato,*" 29.

29. Kataoka Yakichi, quoted in Yamashita Heihachirō, "Chū ni mayou genbaku tenshudō: Saiken o habamu 'heiwa kinen' no yokoyari," *Shūkan sankei*, March 16, 1958, 47.

30. Yamashita, "Chū ni mayou genbaku tenshudō," 47.

31. The debate over the fate of the ruins was sometimes phrased in religious terms by both sides. The ruins were also referred to as the "Crucifix of the Twentieth Century" (Nijū seiki no jūjika); see Op-Ed, "*Kieru tsume ato,*" 26.

32. Ibid., 26–27.

33. Nagasaki City Council Meeting Notes, February 17–18, 1958. Iwaguchi said the city names, Nagasaki and Hiroshima, in that order.

34. The phrase in Japanese for "anchor for the hearts of the believers" is *Shinja no shōrai no kokoro no yoridokoro.* Nagasaki City Council Meeting Notes, February 17–18, 1958.

35. Ibid.

36. Op-Ed, "*Kieru tsume ato,*" 27.

37. The group headed by Fukahori was the Nagasaki-ken dōin gakuto giseisha no kai (Nagasaki Prefectural Association of [Atomic-Bombing] Victims Who Were Mobilized Students [during the War]).

38. Op-Ed, "*Kieru tsume ato,*" 30, 31.

39. Ibid., 29, 31. For a more detailed account of the days between the February meeting and the final decision to allow the removal of the ruins, see Takase, *Nagasaki: Kieta mō hitotsu no "Genbaku Dōmu,"* esp. 148–52. Takase discusses Mayor Tagawa's and Wakiyama Hiroshi's visits to Bishop Yamaguchi.

40. Nagasaki City Council Meeting Notes, April 21, 1958.

41. Op-Ed, "Kieru tsume ato," 30–31.

42. Ibid., 31. The Op-Ed says that the "heartless echoes of hammers" could be heard from April 14, 1958, but the Catholics actually began tearing down the ruin walls on March 14. See, among others, Takase, *Nagasaki: Kieta mō hitotsu no "Genbaku Dōmu,"* 266.

43. Op-Ed, "Kieru tsume ato," 31. On the removal of the ruins as representative of the Catholics wanting to forget the tragedy that befell their community, see Kamata Sadao, "Nagasaki no ikari to inori: Hankaku shōgen 36 nen no kiseki kara," in *Nihon no genbaku bungaku*, ed. Kaku-sensō no kiki o uttaeru bungakusha no seimei chomeisha (Horupu shuppan, 1983), 15:415.

44. *KH*, March 1, 1958.

45. Takahara Itaru and Yokote Kazuhiko, *Nagasaki: Kyū Urakami tenshudō, 1945–1958; Ushinawareta hibaku isan*, trans. Brian Burke-Gaffney (Tokyo: Iwanami shoten, 2010), 88.

46. Nagasaki City Council Meeting Notes, September 28, 1956.

47. Ibid.

48. For these and other rumors, see Op-Ed, "Kieru tsume ato," 27.

49. Takase Tsuyoshi considers Tagawa's visit to St. Paul, Minnesota, particularly telling of the desires of politicians from both cities to forget the violence of the war for the sake of improved political relations. The proposal of St. Paul officials to become Nagasaki's sister-city, Takase claims, was tantamount to a request to Nagasaki residents to "forget the event of the past that is the atomic bombing" because "we are no longer concerned with Pearl Harbor"; Takase, *Nagasaki: Kieta mō hitotsu no "Genbaku Dōmu,"* 126.

50. Takase argues that the choice of the anniversary of Pearl Harbor as the date of ratification for the sister-city treaty with Nagasaki suggested that St. Paul officials saw the atomic bombing as punishment for the Hawaii attack; ibid., 124–25.

51. Nagasaki City Council Meeting Notes, September 28, 1956.

52. Ibid., February 17–18, 1958.

53. Joseph L. Van Hecken, *The Catholic Church in Japan since 1859* (Tokyo: Herder Agency, 1963), 106. Yamaguchi Aijirō became archbishop of the Nagasaki Archdiocese. To this day, the only other archdioceses in Japan are Tokyo (since 1891) and Osaka (since 1969).

54. See, e.g., Kamata, "Nagasaki no ikari to inori," 415–16.

55. See, e.g., *NN*, August 8, 2002.

56. Odagiri Hideo, " 'Kaku no jidai' to kono kirokushū sei," in *Nihon no genbaku kiroku*, ed. Ienaga Saburō, Odagiri Hideo, and Kuroyoshi Kazuo (Tokyo: Nihon tosho sentā, 1991), 20:264. When UNESCO proposed making Hiroshima's Atomic Dome a World Heritage Site in 1996, it used similar arguments that the memory activists in Nagasaki had used in their pleas to preserve the Urakami Cathedral ruins, namely, as atomic ruins, the dome serves as an important medium of memory to convey the history of the tragedy; see Matthew Charles, "Imaginative Mislocation: Hiroshima's Genbaku Dome, Ground Zero of the Twentieth Century," *Radical Philosophy* 162 (July–August 2010): 18–30, esp. 19.

57. A national publication in 1951 presented Nagasaki in much the same way. *Iwanami shashin bunko 38: Nagasaki* [Iwanami photograph collection 38: Nagasaki] (Tokyo: Iwanami shoten, 1951) presents sixty-four pages of photographs, about four per page, representing the urban identity of Nagasaki based on its international past, exemplified by its historical relationship with foreign cultures. Among the hundreds of photographs, paintings, and maps, the city's Christian history figures largely, and, furthermore, the seven photographs

that somehow relate to the atomic bombing are of the Urakami district, including several of the ruins of the cathedral. Indeed, the one page (41) dedicated to the bombing is titled "Genbaku no chi, Urakami" (Place of the atomic bomb, Urakami).

58. *Nagasaki e no shōtai*, ed. Kamura Kunio (Nagasaki: Nagasaki bunken sha, 1959).

59. See, e.g., the guidebook *Hiroshima*, ed. Chūgoku shashin insatsu sha (Hiroshima: Chūgoku shashin insatsu sha, 1955).

CONCLUSION

1. Motoshima Hitoshi, "Hiroshima yo, ogoru nakare," *Heiwa kyōiku kenkyū* 24 (March 1997): 9–12.

2. Ibid.

3. Kamata Sadao, who at the time was the head of the Nagasaki heiwa kenkyūjo (Nagasaki Peace Research Institute), also contributed a short analysis (less than one page) of a survey (Ibid., 41).

4. The museum is located directly behind NHK (Japan Broadcasting Corporation), the government television station, near Nagasaki Train Station, and does not receive business donations or government funding of any kind. It became a nonprofit organization in 2003, and it is operated entirely by volunteers. For more on the museum, see Takahashi Shinji and Funakoe Kōichi, eds., *Nagasaki kara heiwagaku suru!* (Kyoto: Hōritsu bunka sha, 2009), 121.

5. For a recent example, see esp. Takahashi and Funakoe, *Nagasaki kara heiwagaku suru!*

6. Motoshima Hitoshi, as quoted and discussed in Norma Field, *In the Realm of a Dying Emperor: A Portrait of Japan at Century's End* (New York: Pantheon Books, 1991), 178–79.

7. Ibid., 247.

8. Nagasaki City Hall compiled a collection of these letters and published them as *Nagasaki shichō e no 7,300 tsū no tegami* (Komichi shobō, 1989).

9. See, e.g., *MS* and *NS*, January 19, 1990.

10. See, e.g., Motoshima, "Hiroshima yo, ogoru nakare," 9.

11. Wakiyama Hiroshi, quoted in "Japan: Tale of Two Cities," *Time*, May 18, 1962.

12. Nagasaki City official site, accessed May 2, 2011, http://www1.city.nagasaki.nagasaki .jp/toukei_data.

13. The translation given here is the official name in English.

14. Mitsubishi Heavy Industries official site, accessed May 2, 2011, http://www.mhi.co .jp/en/nsmw/products/index.html.

15. Ibid., http://www.mhi.co.jp/en/products/detail/vertical_launching_system_mk4 .html.

16. "Proceedings of the Eighty-Sixth Conference on Education Research," Nagasaki University, August 30, 2010, accessed May 2, 2011, http://www.nagasaki-u.ac.jp/ja/about /guidance/conference/education/2010/index.html.

17. RECNA official site, accessed September 24, 2015, http://www.recna.nagasaki-u.ac .jp/recna/about.

18. For Article 41, see Kōsei shō hoken iryōkyoku kikaku ka, *Genbaku hibakusha kankei hōrei tsūchi shū* (Tokyo: Gyōsei, 1996), 725; see also the official site of the Nagasaki National Peace Memorial Hall for the Atomic Bomb Victims, accessed May 2, 2011, http://www .peace-nagasaki.go.jp/about/index.html. On the cost of the Nagasaki museum, see, e.g., Kyōdo tsūshin, news release, July 6, 2003, accessed May 2, 2011, http://www.47news.jp /CN/200307/CN2003070601000184.html.

19. Official site of the Nagasaki National Peace Memorial Hall for the Atomic Bomb Victims, accessed May 2, 2011, http://www.peace-nagasaki.go.jp/information/i_07.html.

20. Ibid., accessed September 24, 2015.

21. Official "Nagasaki–NY 2015" Facebook page, accessed September 24, 2015, https://www.facebook.com/Nagasaki-NY-2015-297811337035310. The 2014 event in New York City is recorded in the photographs section of the webpage.

22. See, e.g. Yamaguchi Hibiki, "'Heiwa e no chikai,' kōbo hōshiki hajimaru," *Nagasaki—Hiroshima tsūshin* 210 (October 15, 2016), 12.

23. See, e.g., Okada Shōhei, "'Heiwa e no chikai' jinsen, rainen ichigatsu ni shinsakai kaishi," *AS*, October 12, 2016, accessed November 29, 2016, http://www.asahi.com/articles/ASJBC56LVJBCTOLB00T.html. See also Yamano Kentarō, "'Heiwa e no chikai' jinsen, kōbo de shi no suisen toriyame," *AS*, January 18, 2017, accessed February 8, 2017, http://www.asahi.com/articles/ASK1K3SMKK1KTOLB004.html. For more on the selection process of the new system, see the official Nagasaki City webpage, accessed February 8, 2017, http://www.city.nagasaki.lg.jp/heiwa/3020000/3020300/p029325.html.

Index

Agawa Hiroyuki, 117
air-raid trenches, 17–19, 22, 150
Akahata (Red flag), 101, 127
Akizuki Tatsuichirō, 127, 130–31, 151
Akutagawa Ryūnosuke, 148
Allied occupation, 16, 30, 41–47, 58–61, 66,
    77, 95, 117, 121, 137, 152, 160, 171, 200n32;
    British Commonwealth forces of, 43; Civil
    Censorship Detachment (CCD), 99–100,
    115, 127; Civil Information and Education
    Section (CI&E), 95, 104; Civil Intelligence
    Section (CIS), 105, 108; demilitarization
    and democratization during, 42, 46–47,
    55–57, 95–96, 98; Economic and Scientific
    Section (ESS), 103, 105; and freedom of
    religion, 73, 89, 104; G-2 (Intelligence
    Division), 105, 112; Information Dissemi-
    nation Branch (IDB), 95; Press, Pictorial
    and Broadcast Division (PPB), 99, 104;
    Public Health and Welfare Section (PHW),
    103, 105; publishing industry during,
    95–101; "reorientation program," 95;
    reverse course, 101. *See also* censorship;
    Nagasaki Military Government Team
    (NMGT); Press Code
Ambrose, Mary, 83
American culture, 42, 55–57, 181n56
Angelus bells, 54, 68, 148
antinuclear and peace movement, 1, 3, 5, 6, 8,
    33, 88–89, 118, 120–27, 132–43, 145, 151,
    164–65, 171, 174. *See also* memory activists;
    entries for individual names of groups
Asahi gurafu (Asahi graph), 117, 128
Asahi shinbun (newspaper and company), 16,
    20, 123, 135, 178n15
"ashes of death," 16, 132. *See also* radiation
Atom Bowl (football game), 48–51
Atomic Bomb Casualty Commission (ABCC),
    7, 60–61
atomic bombing: damage, 15–21; deaths, 17; as
    retribution, 93; target of, 15, 107, 197n60
atomic-bombing illness (*genbaku shō*), 119–20,
    125, 128–29
Atomic Bombing Museum (Nagasaki), 36, 170,
    173

atomic-bomb literature, 7–8, 109, 114–17,
    130–31, 137, 139, 178n22. *See also entries for
    individual titles*
Atomic Dome (aka Peace Dome), 3, 36, 137,
    145, 148–49, 164, 167, 169, 205n56
atomic energy, 96–97, 102; peaceful uses of, 77,
    90, 97, 134, 202n62. *See also* Atoms for Peace
    campaign
atomic sickness (*genshi byō*), 86
Atomic Soldiers, 49, 185n32
Atoms for Peace campaign, 134

Bankston, John D., 47–49
banzai, 40, 69, 171
Baptist missionaries in Manila, 113
beauty pageants, 36, 42, 56, 57, 186n54. *See also*
    Miss Nagasaki
beer, 46, 48
Berlin, 147, 157
Bertelli, Angelo, 49–51
Bible, 66, 70, 78, 103, 188n16
black rain, 16–17
Blair Hospital, 121
Buddhism, 35, 71, 173
Buenos Aires, 38
bundan, 114

cancer, 16, 48, 60, 65, 129, 140. *See also* leukemia
capitalism, 87, 90–91
Capra, Frank, 112–13
censorship, 46, 60, 62–63, 77, 93, 95–102, 109,
    114–18, 127–28, 141, 194n4, 200n32;
    wartime, 98. See also *Nagasaki no kane* (The
    bell of Nagasaki); Press Code
Chiaki Minoru, 80, 190n51, 197n53
Chicago, 83, 156, 160, 162
Chicago Bears, 50
Chinatown, 40, 173
Chinmoku no kabe o yabutte (Breaking down
    the walls of silence), 132, 138
Christian image of ground zero, 8–11, 65–67,
    75, 112–13, 127, 130–32, 137, 140, 143, 149,
    164, 178n12, 205–6n57. *See also* "Hiroshima
    Rages, Nagasaki Prays"; Nagai Takashi;
    Urakami Cathedral: ruins of

Manhattan Project, 16, 19, 121
Manila appendix, 97, 106–13, 117–18, 197n54,
197–98n68
Manira no higeki (Tragedy of Manila). *See*
Manila appendix
Marshall, Bruce, 84, 191–92n76, 192n77
martyrdom, 2–3, 5, 9, 37, 38, 67, 73, 83, 104,
112, 130, 152, 156, 171
Maruki Toshi and Iri, 178–79n23
Masako taorezu (Masako shall not perish),
62–63, 93, 115–16
Masuda Kaneshichi, 37–38
McSwanson, Clement S., 54–55
medical treatment, 3, 60–61, 78, 85, 120–25,
129. *See also* Hibakusha Relief Law; *entries for
individual hospitals*
Meiji period, 167
memory, 1, 3–7, 11–12, 15, 25, 26–30, 36–37,
40, 65–67, 91, 98, 118, 120, 132–43, 145–52,
155, 159, 162, 164–67, 169, 171, 176,
178n22
memory activists, 3, 4, 14, 118, 120, 127,
130–43, 146–48, 150, 158–59, 164–66,
175–76, 202n81, 205n56. *See also entries for
individual names of groups*
The Mikado, 30
Milam, David C., 47–49
military, Japan, Imperial Army of, 32, 69, 72,
170. *See also* Self-Defense Forces
military, United States: Office for Occupied
Areas in the Department of the Army, 95;
Second Division Marines, 43, 46–51; Sixth
Army, 43, 46; Eighth Army, 43, 46–47. *See
also* Allied occupation; atomic bombing;
Office of War Information (OWI);
psychological warfare
Miss Atom Bomb. *See* Miss Nagasaki
Miss Hiroshima, 36–37
Miss International, 36–37, 187n63
Miss Nagasaki, 56–59, 186n53, 186n54, 187n63
Mitsubishi, 16, 21, 22, 39, 44, 47, 173
Miyamoto Musashi (book), 80, 107
Miyamoto Musashi (person), 190n51
Monument for Those Children, 86
Moriyama Midori. *See* Nagai Midori
Mother Mary, 81, 156, 183n87
Motoshima Hitoshi, 9, 169–72
municipal vision of reconstruction, 1–2, 7,
14–15, 21, 28–31, 42, 62–63, 66, 76–77, 162.
See also urban identity: of Nagasaki
mushroom cloud, 16–17, 183, 191n69; as
"beacon of peace," 154; as symbol of trauma,
172

Nagai boom, 81–82, 87, 92, 102
Nagai Kayano, 20–21, 72, 78, 81, 85, 93
Nagai Makoto, 20–21, 72, 78, 81, 85, 93
Nagai Midori, 68, 90, 99, 193n111
Nagai *sakura*, 86
Nagai Takashi, 7, 18–21, 29, 37–38, 63, 72,
101–2, 121, 151–52, 171, 191n66; awards,
86–87, 92; best sellers, 66, 67, 77, 81, 84,
87–88, 92, 97, 101, 107, 108, 130; as challenge
to representations of Nagasaki atomic experience, 117, 119, 130–32, 137–40, 151;
criticism of, 86–92, 130–31, 137–40; dislike
of communism, 90, 96–97, 101–2, 193n105,
195n18; eulogy of November 1945, 72–75,
77, 89–90, 103–4, 107, 113, 130, 188n3;
leadership among Urakami Catholics, 65–76,
79, 180n28; paying taxes, 84–85, 192–93n90;
representative of nation's victimization by
atomic bombings, 92–93; royalties from writings, 76, 84–85, 191–92n76, 192–93n90;
writings of, 63, 76–86, 96–97, 109, 114, 118,
131, 151, 191–92n76; view of death, 69–70;
view of atomic bombing, 2–3, 6, 66, 72–75,
89, 96–97, 114, 118; view of war, 73, 103,
107–8, 111, 115, 118. *See also* Providence;
sacrificial lamb; walls of silence; *entries for
individual titles of books*
Nagaoka Some, 74
Nagasaki Association of Atomic Bombing
Educators, 131–32
Nagasaki Atomic Bomb Casualty Council, 121,
124
Nagasaki Atomic Bombing Association of
Young Men and Women, 133, 135, 158
Nagasaki Atomic Bombing Young Men's
Association, 133
Nagasaki Atomic Bombing Young Women's
Association, 133
Nagasaki Citizens Hospital, 121
Nagasaki City Construction Office, 23, 34
Nagasaki City Council, 34, 86, 149, 157–59, 172
Nagasaki City Facilities Department, 23
Nagasaki City Tourism Association, 150
Nagasaki City Tourism Office, 156
Nagasaki Council of Atomic Bombing Victims
(Nagasaki hisaikyō), 125, 133–34
Nagasaki Cultural Association, 23, 150
Nagasaki Federation of War Victims, 132–33
Nagasaki Military Government Team (NMGT),
29, 43, 55, 56, 62, 115. *See also* Victor E.
Delnore
Nagasaki minyū (newspaper and company), 13,
27–28, 81

Studies of the Weatherhead East Asian Institute

Columbia University

SELECTED TITLES

(Complete list at: http://weai.columbia.edu/publications/studies-weai/)

Darwin, Dharma, and the Divine: Evolutionary Theory and Religion in Modern Japan, by G. Clinton Godart. University of Hawai'i Press, 2017.

The Social Life of Inkstones: Artisans and Scholars in Early Qing China, by Dorothy Ko. University of Washington Press, 2017.

Dictators and their Secret Police: Coercive Institutions and State Violence, by Sheena Chestnut Greitens. Cambridge University Press, 2016.

The Cultural Revolution on Trial: Mao and the Gang of Four, by Alexander C. Cook. Cambridge University Press, 2016.

Inheritance of Loss: China, Japan, and the Political Economy of Redemption After Empire, by Yukiko Koga. University of Chicago Press, 2016.

Homecomings: The Belated Return of Japan's Lost Soldiers, by Yoshikuni Igarashi. Columbia University Press, 2016.

Samurai to Soldier: Remaking Military Service in Nineteenth-Century Japan, by D. Colin Jaundrill. Cornell University Press, 2016.

The Red Guard Generation and Political Activism in China, by Guobin Yang. Columbia University Press, 2016.

Accidental Activists: Victim Movements and Government Accountability in Japan and South Korea, by Celeste L. Arrington. Cornell University Press, 2016.

Negotiating Rural Land Ownership in Southwest China: State, Village, Family, by Yi Wu. University of Hawai'i Press, 2016.

Ming China and Vietnam: Negotiating Borders in Early Modern Asia, by Kathlene Baldanza. Cambridge University Press, 2016.

Ethnic Conflict and Protest in Tibet and Xinjiang: Unrest in China's West, coedited by Ben Hillman and Gray Tuttle. Columbia University Press, 2016.

One Hundred Million Philosophers: Science of Thought and the Culture of Democracy in Postwar Japan, by Adam Bronson. University of Hawai'i Press, 2016.

Conflict and Commerce in Maritime East Asia: The Zheng Family and the Shaping of the Modern World, c. 1620-1720, by Xing Hang. Cambridge University Press, 2016.

Chinese Law in Imperial Eyes: Sovereignty, Justice, and Transcultural Politics, by Li Chen. Columbia University Press, 2016.

Imperial Genus: The Formation and Limits of the Human in Modern Korea and Japan, by Travis Workman. University of California Press, 2015.

Yasukuni Shrine: History, Memory, and Japan's Unending Postwar, by Akiko Takenaka. University of Hawai'i Press, 2015

The Age of Irreverence: A New History of Laughter in China, by Christopher Rea. University of California Press, 2015

The Knowledge of Nature and the Nature of Knowledge in Early Modern Japan, by Federico Marcon. University of Chicago Press, 2015

The Fascist Effect: Japan and Italy, 1915-1952, by Reto Hofmann. Cornell University Press, 2015

The International Minimum: Creativity and Contradiction in Japan's Global Engagement, 1933-1964, by Jessamyn R. Abel. University of Hawai'i Press, 2015

Empires of Coal: Fueling China's Entry into the Modern World Order, 1860-1920, by Shellen Xiao Wu. Stanford University Press, 2015

Casualties of History: Wounded Japanese Servicemen and the Second World War, by Lee K. Pennington. Cornell University Press, 2015

City of Virtues: Nanjing in an Age of Utopian Visions, by Chuck Wooldridge. University of Washington Press, 2015

The Proletarian Wave: Literature and Leftist Culture in Colonial Korea, 1910-1945, by Sunyoung Park. Harvard University Asia Center, 2015.

Neither Donkey Nor Horse: Medicine in the Struggle Over China's Modernity, by Sean Hsiang-lin Lei. University of Chicago Press, 2014.

When the Future Disappears: The Modernist Imagination in Late Colonial Korea, by Janet Poole. Columbia University Press, 2014.

Bad Water: Nature, Pollution, & Politics in Japan, 1870-1950, by Robert Stolz. Duke University Press, 2014.

Rise of a Japanese Chinatown: Yokohama, 1894-1972, by Eric C. Han. Harvard University Asia Center, 2014.

Beyond the Metropolis: Second Cities and Modern Life in Interwar Japan, by Louise Young. University of California Press, 2013.

The Nature of the Beasts: Empire and Exhibition at the Tokyo Imperial Zoo, by Ian J. Miller. University of California Press, 2013.